Nearer my God to Thee

Airborne Chaplains in the Second World War

Linda Parker

Helion & Company Limited

Helion & Company Limited
Unit 8 Amherst Business Centre
Budbrooke Road
Warwick
CV34 5WE
England
Tel. 01926 499 619
Email: info@helion.co.uk
Website: www.helion.co.uk
Twitter: @helionbooks

Published by Helion & Company 2019
Designed and typeset by Mary Woolley (mary@battlefield-design.co.uk)
Cover designed by Paul Hewitt, Battlefield Design (www.battlefield-design.co.uk)

ISBN 978-1-912866-12-0

British Library Cataloguing-in-Publication Data.
A catalogue record for this book is available from the British Library.

For details of other military history titles published by Helion & Company Limited
contact the above address or visit our website: http://www.helion.co.uk.

We always welcome receiving book proposals from prospective authors.

Contents

List of Illustrations

In Plate Section

Acknowledgements

I would like to acknowledge the help and encouragement of the following people and institutions.

My thanks to the Revd Paul Abram, CVO, for allowing me to quote from his typescript history of the airborne chaplains, *Lower Than the Angels*, and from his superb collection of letters from and accounts by airborne chaplains. This collection formed my thoughts and ideas and provided much material for the book, and I am aware that it is the Revd Abram's hard work in the 1970s that has helped my research immensely.

Due to the passing of 50 years it has proved very difficult to contact the families of the chaplains who provided information for the Revd Abram's collection for permission to quote letters. I would be glad of any information from readers to rectify this.

I would like to acknowledge the help given to me by informal discussions and conversations with serving Army chaplains which have helped me place the role of the Second World War airborne chaplains in the context of modern military chaplaincy.

I would like to thank Mr David Blake, curator of the Museum of Army Chaplaincy, for his unfailing encouragement and enthusiasm in this project and for providing ready access to the archives of the Museum of Army Chaplaincy.

My thanks to the staff at the Parachute Regiment and Airborne Forces Museum at Duxford and the Museum of Army Flying at Middle Wallop, and for permission to use the images on Paradata. Thanks are also due to Mike Vockins, Neil Barber and James Hagerty for useful help and advice.

Duncan Rogers and the staff at Helion have once again guided me expertly through the publication process; my thanks to them all.

Lastly many thanks, as always, to my husband who has been a tower of strength making the writing of this book possible.

Introduction

In February 1919 the Chaplains Department of the British Army received the prefix 'Royal', given to it in recognition of the work it had done in the Great War, described by the king as "splendid work".[1] It became the Royal Army Chaplains Department (RAChD), and on 23 February 2019 the Department gathered for a special service at the Guards Chapel, Wellington Barracks to, mark the centenary of this memorable event. Paul Mason (Roman Catholic Bishop of the Forces) gave an address at the service. He talked about the sacrifice role of the Army chaplain throughout the Department's history, including remarks about G.A. Studdert and Kennedy and his fellow chaplains in the Great War. He ended his sermon praying for the souls of the chaplains departed this life and with his hopes for the present-day chaplains: "Pray for all those currently in service, that they will centre their lives on prayer, receive the gift of hope to inspire a positive ministry and work to engage professionally in today's Army in the service of God, Queen and country."

The Great War had been a steep learning curve for the chaplains. Almost four-and-a-half thousand chaplains were recruited in the First World War, with 179 losing their lives on active service. Of those, three received the Victoria Cross, 67 the Distinguished Service Order and 449 the Military Cross. It is generally accepted that during the war, chaplains had found a role that went beyond both the purely material and purely spiritual, and which involved them in a variety of roles, from base camps to field dressing units.

By the Second World War, the role of the Army chaplain had developed greatly since the Great War and their place in combat positions rather than behind the lines was not questioned. General Montgomery famously said: "I would sooner think of going into battle without my artillery as without my chaplains."[2] There is no doubt that by 1944, Army chaplains had a very real function and were held in high regard in the eyes of military commanders.

In this study of the chaplains who went to battle by plane and parachute or glider, the story of these brave men, of whom little has been written, will be provided, but an analysis of their role will also place them in the context of the last 100 years of Army

---

1   Army order no.93, Feb1919.
2   N.Hamilton, *Monty the Field Marshal*, 1944-1976 (Sceptre:1897), p.44.

chaplaincy, comparing and contrasting their experiences with chaplains who served before and after them. In the process of examining their actions in battle, I would like to think their thoughts and actions can be assessed in the light of modern studies and controversies in Army chaplaincy.

The airborne chaplains of the Second World War can be said to have practised the ministry of presence to its utmost extent, as they did exactly the same arduous training as their flock, and went into battle - through parachuting and landing in gliders - in exactly the same way as the men. Having learned quickly that they would not gain the respect of their men unless they jumped, the first parachute padres saw action in North Africa, both with the battalions who parachuted in advance of the main force to take airfields and with the battalions who were used as infantry in the long struggle to reach Tunis in the winter of 1942/43. Glider chaplains became involved in the invasion of Sicily, taking a full part in the disastrous glider landings which led, despite much loss of life, to capturing a vital road bridge, the Ponte Grande, in Operation Ladbroke and cost the life of Fr Hourigan, a Roman Catholic chaplain. Parachute troops were then involved in the capture of another vital bridge at Primosole in Operation Fustian, and were again accompanied by their battalion padres. Padre Ronald Lunt operated with the the SAS during the invasion of Sicily, while Padre Fraser McLusky was with the SAS in France.

When the 1st Airborne Division returned to Britain in late 1944, the 2nd Independent Parachute Brigade remained behind and saw service in the struggle to advance in Italy, the invasion of southern France and coping with incipient civil war in Greece. The newly formed 6th Airborne Division was in action with its chaplains in attendance at D-Day in Normandy and for several months after, until eventually relieved. Three chaplains were killed and one taken prisoner. During June and July 1944, Padre Fraser Maclusky served with the 1st SAS behind enemy lines in France. The 15 chaplains that the 1st Airborne Division took with them into Arnhem were in all areas of the battle and the shrinking perimeter, with Fr Bernard Egan being wounded and taken prisoner at the famous 'bridge too far'. Two were killed and nine taken prisoner, spending the rest of the war ministering to POWs. At the Rhine Crossing in March 1945, the Chaplains Department experienced two fatalities during and shortly after the drop, and the chaplains' were with their airborne battalions all the way to eventual victory in Europe in May. Shortly after, the 1st Airborne Division was sent to Denmark and Norway to supervise the surrender of German troops and the re-establishment of civil law and order.

The airborne padres, like all chaplains, had to perform a multiplicity of tasks. They were present at training, and performed religious services in camp and before operations. In camp they often had to deal with problems, such as family issues that could result in men going AWOL or have an effect on their efficiency as a soldier. They were there as men jumped and landed in gliders, providing both moral and spiritual help in supporting dangerous and tense situations. Once landed, they brought in wounded, often under fire, assisted the medical staff, cleared battlefields of the dead, continued to be the confidantes of both commanders and privates, and when conditions permitted took a variety of religious services in many different situations and venues.

Several aspects of the uniqueness of the airborne chaplains' job have caused controversy, both at the time and consequently. Some questions this account will tackle include:

- Was their position in the plane or glider worth losing a place for a soldier?
- To what extent did they take over military roles when the situation demanded it?
- Were airborne chaplains ever armed, in contravention of regulations?
- To what extent did they become a 'sounding board' for senior officers?
- Did they have a good effect on the morale of the soldiers?
- What lessons can today's chaplains draw from the experiences of airborne chaplains in the Second World War?
- And to what extent have ideas of the role of Army chaplains changed in the 21st century?

Nearer My God to Thee seeks to attempt to answer some of these questions, in addition to paying tribute to the brave airborne men of the RAChD by making the gripping and moving story of their exploits in the service of the wartime airborne divisions known to a wider audience.

1

Recruitment and training of airborne chaplains

On 5 September 1941 the Revd Robert Talbot Watkins, a Methodist chaplain who had been serving with the 2nd Battalion, the Essex Regiment, arrived at the gate of Hardwick Hall near Chesterfield, Derbyshire, a Tudor manor house built by Bess of Hardwick, which had become the headquarters for the selection and training of the newly formed airborne forces, who then progressed to training at the Central Landing School at Manchester's Ringway Airport.

An embryonic start to British airborne capability had been started by Major J.F. Rock in May 1940, and, impressed by the achievements of the German airborne forces in the *blitzkrieg* attack on Western Europe, and particularily by the capture of the fort at Eben-Emael in Belgium, Churchill had sent a letter on 22 June 1940 which was to speed up the development of the airborne experiment. Writing to General Sir Hastings Ismay, his chief staff officer, he demanded:

> We ought to have a corps of at least 5,000 parachute troops, including a proportion of Australians, New Zealanders and Canadians, together with some trustworthy people from Norway and France. I see more difficulty in selecting and employing Danes, Dutch and Belgians. I hear something is being done already to form such a corps but only I believe on a very small scale. Advantage must be taken of the summer to train three forces, who can, none the less, play their part meanwhile as shock troops in home defences. Pray let me have a note from the War Office on the subject.[1]

The Central Landing school was opened on 21 June 1940. Soon, men of No 2 Commando arrived to begin parachute training, making their first descents on 21 July. They were renamed 11 Special Air Service. By the end of 1940, over 2,000 jumps had taken place and 500 officers and men had qualified as parachutists. The unit was

---

1   TNA CAB120/262, Churchill to War Office, 22 June 1940.

redesignated on 15 September 1941 to become the 1st Parachute Battalion, and the future 1st Parachute Brigade thus began to form.

As there was now a Brigade Headquarters, the Army chaplaincy service became involved and a request for the normal establishment of three chaplains was received. At this stage no one considered that the chaplains appointed should become parachutists.

It was at this juncture that Revd Watkins was posted to the brigade. When he had been commissioned in May 1942 he had been the youngest Methodist chaplain, and when posted to the brigade after some time in a regular infantry unit, had imagined that he was being sent to a unit in a backwater because of his inexperience. HQ of the North Midlands area did not know why he had been sent to them, but eventually he was given his posting to 1st(P) Brigade. At the gate to Hardwick Hall he discovered that 'p' meant parachute. His first reaction was to want to return immediately to Nottingham: "If my transport had not by that time departed I might have departed with it."[2] On the same day the Revd Bernard Egan, a Roman Catholic priest, arrived in similar circumstances. Egan was described in a newspaper article in 1944: "Father Egan, who is nearly 40, was a peace time games master at Beaumont College. He is descried as exceptionally fit physically and though naturally a quiet man has a fine adventurous spirit."[3] They were to be the first of the band of Army chaplains who accompanied the airborne forces in all the campaigns of the war, bringing religious sustenance and practical help to all ranks.

Egan and Watkins were posted as 'penguins', that is, non-flying staff, with no expectation that they would participate in jump training. At first they watched the men undergoing their ground training on commando-style courses, and visited the men doing jump training at Ringway. They soon realised that such was the nature of airborne training and warfare, that there was an impenetrable barrier between themselves and the men they were supposed to be ministering to. After having watched the initial training of the men on the parachute course, they appreciated that they would not belong and have a good relationship with their men unless they participated fully in training and learned to jump: "[T]hey were on the outside of an invisible fence and their ministry to the men was limited."[4] Egan considered that it was important to set an example to the men with whom he would be going into combat and that "he had no right to judge them or discuss their dangerous duties if he had not emptied the same cup to the last drop".[5] Watkins shared his thoughts on the

2   Museum of Army Chaplaincy Archives, Revd R.T. Watkins, *World War Two Memoirs 1939-1945* (unpublished).
3   *Birmingham Mail,* 1 April 1944, p.1.
4   Museum of Army Chaplaincy Archives, papers deposited by Revd P.R.C. Abram CVO. Typescript, *Lower Than the Angels* (1975).
5   Biography of Egan on Paradata website, https://www.paradata.org.uk/people/rev-bernard-egan.

topic in an interview with the *Methodist Recorder*.[6] If padres were not allowed to jump, he felt, they would be "placed in an intolerable position for a true padre. In his every day relations with them [the men] he would be a stranger in the midst of men bound together by a unique experience from which he, the padre was shut out." If padres were allowed to jump, he felt "a door had been opened to [the] interest and sympathy of the men".

The Royal Army Medical Corps were well advanced in their parachute training and also planning their role and dispositions in battle. The padres believed that unless they got a move on and became part of the airborne contingent, they would be left out of the vital operational planning. The two men started the physical ground training part of the course, but had to wait for permission from the senior chaplain to start jump training, which was at first denied. They decided to go ahead with the jump training solely on the authority and support of the brigadier, Richard Gale, and continued by participating in parachute training at Ringway. Later, what Watkins described as a "monumental rocket for disobedience [and] lack of discipline" was received from the Chaplain General.[7] Fr Egan and Padre Watkins eventually passed out on 3 January1942. Egan claimed that although they were on the same course, 'E' came before 'W', making him the first parachuting padre. Brigadier Gale described the first two airborne padres: "Two such utterly different characters – but both men dedicated to their mission and the airborne men with which they worked. Watkins, bright, quick and intelligent, brought almost a school boy enthusiasm to the job. Egan, pensive but warm, made an appeal as a man as well as a padre to protestants and catholics alike."[8]

Watkins explained his thoughts when he and Egan started the jump training:

> The nervous and emotional stress is the same for all, chaplains included … the tenseness of the experience arises from the fact that finally each man stands alone … yet one is not quite alone for the knowledge that the next man looks as green as you feel acts as a spur. Therein lies the sense of comradeship which is so characteristic of all parachutists. [9]

At first the RAF officers and other members of their course did not understand why they were there, and were rather scornful. Watkins remembered "the look of utter disbelief on the faces of its members on our arrival and their scarce-concealed derision".[10] In order to make the point that they were to minister to the men in all

6   Museum of Army Chaplaincy Archives, an article from the *Methodist Recorder* based on an interview with Watkins (undated).
7   Museum of Army Chaplaincy Archives, Watkins, *World War Two Memoirs 1939-1945*.
8   Museum of Army Chaplaincy Archives, a letter from General Richard Gale to Paul Abram, 22 Jan 1971.
9   Museum of Army Chaplaincy Archives, an article from the *Methodist Recorder* based on an interview with Watkins (undated).
10   Watkins, *World War Two Memoirs 1939-1945*.

circumstance, Egan and Watkins decided to wear their dog collars at all times, even though this was not the most comfortable dress for parachuting.

Meanwhile, on 29 October 1941, Major General F.A.M. 'Boy' Browning was ordered to raise an airborne division of parachute and glider troops. First three and then four battalions of the 1st Airborne Brigade began to be raised. In December 1941 a senior chaplain, the Revd J.J.A. Hodgins, was appointed to the newly formed 1st Airborne Division. During a secret interview in which Hodgins was not sure what he was being interviewed for, Browning quizzed him among other things on his attitude to the religious education of soldiers in their training, which was to lead to the formation of the Padre's Hour. The Padre's Hour was an initiative started by Browning in the Airborne Division, but which quickly spread to the rest of the Army. Men gathered informally, were allowed to smoke, and discussed aspects of religion and faith of their choice, which often consisted of the men questioning the padre intensively on matters of religion that they did not believe in, did not understand or wanted to engage with more deeply. Hodgins was also responsible for negotiating permission for the airborne chaplains to wear the famous red beret.

The first two chaplains were joining men who had been rigorously selected. The initial battalions of the parachute regiment were drawn from existing commando units who had been selected for their physical fitness and initiative. In order to become a parachutist, however, officers also had to show tactical ability and imagination, and troops were to display a good level of independence and reliability. When volunteers were required from other units, men had to prove a commando-level fitness. The failure rate was high, as much as 50 percent.[11]

A tragic accident in training showed the usefulness of their training. Just after Watkins had completed his parachutist training, he received a call to say that four men training at Ringway had dropped to their deaths. Watkins was able to join the Commanding Officer and medical officer in leading sticks that afternoon to raise the morale of the next men scheduled to jump. Watkins was the last to jump, and as he picked himself up after a hard landing, the CO, Colonel Ernest Dunn, was waving his walking stick at him and shouting, "Hurry up Padre you're late."[12]

Watkins and Egan decided to put aside religious and denominational differences to furnish a small hut for use as a joint chapel at Hardwick Hall. The altar was made with wood from the bar of a local pub, and the chapel hut served as a base for the chaplains' pastoral work as well as services. However, they did not spend much time there in daytime hours as they were with the men working and training. The Revd Paul Abram put it well in his account of the airbone chaplains: "The chaplain will only be welcome by a soldier in his free time if he had first met him during working hours." This attitude facilitated the padres to spend time with the soldiers in the barracks and

---

11   John Greenacre, *Churchill's Spearhead: The Development of Britain's Airborne Forces During the Second World War* (Barnsley: Pen & Sword, 2010), p.94.
12   Watkins, *World War Two Memoirs 1939-1945*.

the NAAFI: "Above all it made the men realise that the chaplains cared for them to the extent that he was prepared to stand in their shoes."[13]

Padre E.N. 'Joe' Downing was recruited early in 1942, while serving with the 51st Medium Regiment, Royal Artillery. He had been evacuated from France via Le Havre in 1940. He recalled having a letter asking for chaplains to volunteer for the parachute brigade: "Their age must be in the vicinity of thirty years. They must be fit and willing to undergo the necessary training." He was disinclined to volunteer, being happy where he had been stationed, but he realised that when he had been reading the letter, "a distant little voice had been whispering 'that's you'."[14]

Downing was the first to be accepted from this request for volunteers from chaplains of other units. As parachuting was then still a 'hush hush' activity, he was not told of his destination, just to report to the Assistant Chaplain General, Southern Command. He was told he would be picked up by the senior chaplain of the Airborne Division, who would be wearing "a wonderful new head gear – a red beret". He was also told, more worryingly in his opinion, that he would be expected to deliver a period of religious instruction every week to all airborne troops in his unit: "This was the first I had heard of Padre's Hour and I think I felt more scared by this than of dangling on a parachute."[15] The first part of the course was at Hardwick Hall, where what he called "synthetic" training took place with apparatus such as 'the tower', in which men were winched down about 50ft in order to experience dropping through space, and the less popular 'dummy hole', which involved dropping from a raised platform through a hole with the same dimensions as that of an aircraft.

Downing described in detail his experiences when he moved on to Ringway, including the method of departure from a Whitley bomber:

> Descent was through a hole amidships on the floor. You sat on the floor, five fore and five aft of the hole which was about 18 inches deep, 3 feet across at the top, tapering downward to about 2 ft 6 in. To jump you had to shuffle along on your bottom, throw your legs into the hole, place your hands on the edge, and with your arms thrust yourself forward and upward, so that you could drop through the hole at the position of attention. [16]

Failure to maintain this upright position resulted in injuries to the head and face, which were famously known as 'ringing the bell' and were "punishable by 'drinks all round' that evening".[17]

13   Abram, *Lower Than the Angels*, typescript, p.6.
14   E.N. 'Joe' Downing, *Padre with the Paras* (privately published, undated), p. 20.
15   Museum of Army Chaplaincy Archives, an account by Joe Downing.
16   *Ibid.*
17   Downing, *Padre with the Paras*, p.24.

At Ringway he was surprised to learn that officers and other ranks did jump training together, but understood the benefits: "I soon realised that this arrangement was a stroke of genius for it created a wonderful bond between us all, even more wonderful than that which I had known with the gunners."[18] Downing's training continued at Ringway under the supervision of RAF instructors, described by him as "magnificent men". His opinion that his ability to sink a pint was an important part of his ministry came in useful, when at Ringway he took part in a drinking competition between sergeants and officers. He made his first balloon jump, appropriately, on Ascension Day. Padre E.C. Phillips enjoyed his training, telling a group of Rotarians in a speech in August 1945: "I have never felt so fit in my life after the first two weeks training." However, then came the balloon jump training:

> Well imprinted in my memory is the arrival at the ground in the bus for our first jump. Others had arrived before us and the first sight which greeted us was that of someone dropping like a stone with his parachute only partly open. We all went several shades of green and it did not make us very keen on going up. Imagine you are sitting on the hole in the basket 800 feet up, waiting to jump and wishing you were anywhere else in the world. It is a memory that will never fade.[19]

Murdo Macdonald described his initial training as "gruelling in the extreme". He gave details of the tasks:

> We were made to run distances ranging between two and ten miles. There were assault courses which could only be described as cruel. We had to scale walls at least 12 feet high. We had to wade through moats, the water up to our armpits, holding our rifle above our heads. We had to crawl on our bellies under coils of barbed wire with live bullets zinging over our heads.[20]

Even so, he later asserted: "I enjoyed both the ground and jumping training immensely."[21]

Many of the airborne padres also had vivid memories of their training. Padre David Nimmo described how training started with the physical training course lasting about two-and-a-half weeks at Hardwick Hall, a course designed to make anyone liable to crack do so before he went any further, before, that is, he became a source of danger to others. At the end of this course they were subjected to 10 tests and had to pass seven

18   *Ibid.*
19   *West Sussex County News*, 31 August 1945.
20   M. E. Macdonald. *The Man From Harris* (Stornaway: The Stornaway Gazette, undated), p. 81.
21   Museum of Army Chaplain Archives, a letter from Revd Murdo Macdonald to Paul Abram, 8 June 1969.

of them, including the forced march. Nimmo greatly enjoyed the camaraderie and sense of belonging within his group:

> I found myself a member of a squad which included a medical officer, several NCOs and a majority of private soldiers. We were all just members of the same squad, everyone was put through the same mill, with no favours shown. For example, despite not being expected to carry arms, the airborne chaplains in training had to carry the same equipment as everyone including a rifle.[22]

John Gwinnett arrived at Ringway at the end of 1942 and was to join the 9th Parachute Battalion. He described the training as hard, but said that exercises were made as interesting and rewarding as possible. He particularly remembered a 10-day exercise in South Wales where he made a very hard landing near the cliffs at Manorbier. It was the first time he had dropped with the communion set which had been designed to fit into a pocket in the padre's smock.[23]

An example of the lengths that airborne padres were willing to go to keep up with their group of trainees was reported in the *Hartlepool Daily Mail* in May 1944. The king and queen visited the training school "somewhere in England" and were told of how the Revd H. Jenkins had been part of a training jump: "He left the aircraft at the given signal but part of his parachute harness became entangled with the rip line." Jenkins was left dangling in mid-air under the fuselage while the rest of the stick left the plane, and eventually was pulled back into the plane. Jenkins then directed the plane back to the dropping zone, on the grounds that he had not made his jump, where he made a "perfect jump".[24]

Fraser McLuskey, upon joining the Royal Army Chaplain's Department, was sent to the chaplains' training centre at Tidworth, which catered for all denominations except Roman Catholics. He Joined a group of 29 other chaplains in training. The commandant was Frank Woods, and Tidworth Parish Church was the base of their worship:

> We had arrived wondering how on earth a minister of religion fitted into the fighting machine, and in these two weeks the answer was given. We learned of the opportunities the army offers the padre and the place it gives him in its trust and affection. We learned some of the pitfalls to avoid. We heard a little of how the various branches of the serviced work … We heard some good advice on the subject of religion and the ordinary soldier.[25]

22 Museum of Army Chaplain Archives, an account by the Revd David Nimmo.
23 Museum of Army Chaplain Archives, notes sent by the Revd John Gwinnett to Brigadier John Smyth VC (undated).
24 *Hartlepool Daily Mail*, 22 May 1944.
25 J. Fraser McLuskey, *Parachute Padre* (London: SCM Press, 1951), p.20.

He discovered the practicalities of pay and allowance, equipment and transport, and mess etiquette: "We took turns at addressing the course as if it were a congregation of tommies and took turns in saying what we thought the reaction of those tommies would be."[26]

After training at Ringway, Joe Downing arrived at Bulford in Wiltshire and was attached to the 4th Battalion, which had been formed three months previously, and was glad that he was in at the start of building a new battalion and forming its traditions. Tony Deane, second in command, was very welcoming. Downing quickly obtained the nickname 'Holy Joe', but he pointed out that the 'Holy' was soon dropped and he became 'Joe' for the rest of his Army career. He found Padre's Hour difficult at first, as he felt the men were asking questions to catch him out, but when they came to know him they asked questions which prompted discussions on church parade and welfare problems. He sometimes used the poems of First World War Army chaplain Geoffrey Studdert Kennedy in his Padre's Hours: "Woodbine Willie [Studdert Kennedy's alias] could make a point so strongly and poignantly that I often fell back on him. I wished and wish that I could be anything like that wonderful man."[27] Downing was pleased to be invited to participate in periodic commanding officers' conferences and other ranks, where he discussed matters of importance to the morale of the battalion. It was felt that the padre's presence was necessary as quite a few problems, such as absence without leave, might be due to personal troubles and the padre might be useful in sorting out such issues. Downing also remembered how the divisional commander, 'Boy 'Browning, wanted his padres to be ready and willing to visit the homes of any of the men in any part of the country where they might help sort out problems affecting the soldier's morale or wellbeing.

Padre Roy Price, chaplain to the 1st Battalion, who was at Bulford camp just before the invasion of North Africa, recalled his role in ameliorating a problem with morale. Having made a jump from a Dakota for the first time, there were several casualties, including at least one fatality. That night he was asked to attended a meeting of about 20 parachutists who were concerned that they were being used as guinea pigs, and later recalled: "Discussion continued for about an hour and proved therapeutic." Price offered to go back to the CO and arrange a confidence jump, with unanimous approval from the men: "This little experience made me realise that a chaplain could not have dealt with this situation if he had not also been a parachutist."[28] Downing had a similar experience at Bulford when, at the end of 1942, there was a problem of large-scale refusal to jump among two batches of newly trained men, to the extent that some 40 percent of one intake and 30 percent of another were refusing. With the brigade commander convinced that mutiny was in the air, Downing considered that, "The padre was clearly one of those who must do some hard thinking about

---

26   *Ibid*, p.23.
27   Downing, *Padre with the Paras*, p.23.
28   Museum of Army Chaplaincy Archives, an account by the Revd Roy Price.

it." He explained to the CO that, in his opinion, the training at Ringway had been superb, and the men had faith in their instructors and jumped with confidence, but when posted to a battalion, "jumping had to be done in one's own confidence alone … things were very different". He suggested that before a man's wings were awarded, after which refusal was very serious, three more jumps should be made with the battalion, so that "if a man's confidence were not equal to the task, he would find a door still open to quit without dishonour". The rules for jumping were modified, and, Downing commented, "The modifications were a great deal less harsh, and a good deal wiser than I had suggested."[29]

Padre J.O. Johnston remained with his battalion when it converted to the Parachute Brigade and became the 7th Parachute Battalion. He was an international rugby player and rather large to comply with regulation size for parachute troops, but insisted on completing his training. In this he had help from adjutant Captain Penmay, who, in a good example of padre/officer friendship, promised to push Downing out of the aircraft as he had a fear of refusing to jump. Paul Abram described how this was resolved: "As a very pale chaplain swung his legs into the hole Penmay made an inane remark about not catching his braces as he went out in case he found himself back in again. Johnston roared with laughter and at the word 'go' went out still laughing. This incident forged a special bond between them and they became close friends."[30]

Padre John Hall joined the 12th Battalion in 1943. He had volunteered for a combatant role in September 1939 but was refused because of his status as a theological student. He decided to join as a chaplain once he had served his first year as a curate. He wanted to join the Navy as he thought he would see more action than being an Army chaplain, but there were no vacancies. He was helped by John Gwinnett to obtain a place in the 6th Airborne Division, and in September 1943 went for training to Hardwick Hall. Because there were not many officers in his intake, he ended up as platoon leader. He remembered: "It was somewhat embarrassing having led the platoon in an attack and reached the objective to be compelled to admit to the umpire I did not know to fire the Very pistol to signal success."[31] The day he joined the 12th Battalion, the Devons, he played rugby and swore in the game, thus breaking the ice. Medical Officer (MO) J. Binning felt that he had a "fine command of language "and that, quoting Mark Twain, "some of his words were not Sunday Words".[32]

Hall was also the padre to the division's Signal Unit and the 195th Air Landing Field Ambulance. He found the only place for a communion service at Bulford was a room in the NAAFI, which he had to clean out before each service. The voluntary services were in a church hut, half a mile from the Devons' lines and subsequently ill

29   Museum of Army Chaplaincy Archives, an account by the Revd Joe Downing.
30   Museum of Army Chaplaincy Archives, papers deposited by Revd P.R.C. Abram CVO. Typescript, *Lower Than the Angels* (1975), p.58.
31   Museum of Army Chaplaincy Archives, an account by the Revd John Hall.
32   Museum of Army Chaplaincy Archives, an account by MO John Binning.

attended. There was full church parade in Bulford Garrison church once a month, which Hall succeeded in making more popular by persuading the CO to forgo the preliminary inspection so long as the men made the effort to turn out smartly. After this, he remembered, "there was very little grumbling and most men seemed happy about it as long as the hymns were well known and the sermon short". He found the Padre's Hours useful in dealing with the resentment of church parade, with a great deal of time spent in helping soldiers with welfare problems. Many of the chaplains, including Hall, made home visits for soldiers who were AWOL to investigate the circumstances.

Another aspect to the training of the chaplains was the opportunity to have medical training. From 1944 onward, all chaplains went on a 14-day first aid course, but also had spells in the Tidworth Hospital operating theatre to get used to the sight and smell of blood and operations. Hall commented: "As the chaplain lived in action at the RAP [Regimental Aid Post] it was considered essential that in the initial stages of an operation behind enemy lines he should be able to assist the MO."[33]

When a chaplain's battalion went on exercise, he went with them and took part in route marches, field firing and range days. There were many reasons for this, not the least to make sure that he was not an encumbrance when they went to war. It also made sure he was part of the team, gaining the friendship and respect of officers and men:

> A man with a problem might not dream of going near a chaplain in barracks, but it was a different matter when they had just shared a route march. Then again the man who felt out of his depth or needed assurance, especially later when they were in action, could not help being inspired by the unarmed chaplain appearing with his cheery smile … war is a vile business and the chaplain is a key man in ensuring the soldiers retain their humanity, but to do this he must be with them.[34]

On 27 February 1942, airborne troops of the 2nd Parachute Battalion led by Major John Frost took part in Operation Biting, also known as the Bruneval raid. The purpose of the raid was to capture the German Wurzburg radar machine. The raid was a success and seemed proof that airborne warfare was effective, at least on small-scale raids. Padre Watkins wrote to and visited the families of the two men killed on the raid and the six reported missing.

Egan and Watkins were breaking new ground, working in previously uncharted territory for Army chaplains in an environment and circumstances that were knew to them and their flock. Egan and Watkins set the standard for what was to be expected

---

33   Museum of Army Chaplaincy Archives, an account by the Revd John Hall.
34   Museum of Army Chaplaincy Archives, papers deposited by the Revd P.R.C. Abram CVO. Typescript, *Lower Than the Angels* (1975), p.65.

from airborne padres. Watkins admitted that he was never free of self-doubt and feelings of inadequacy. Their main achievement was to make it possible for airborne troops to experience a Christian ministry in new and unknown military circumstances

Senior chaplain Hodgins now needed to build up a team of chaplains, and when the RAChD moved to Tidworth he was able to interview prospective candidates from the Airborne Division.

In April 1943 a permanent chapel was set up at Hardwick Hall, dedicated to St George. The chapel, according to a newspaper report, was to be "A memorial of Britain's airborne forces in every theatre of war and the repository of a roll of honour containing the names of all airborne troops killed in the war, whether parachutists, glider borne troops or glider pilots." The report continued: "It will act as a link between the experienced airborne units now in action in different parts of the world and the steady stream of eager young volunteers constantly flowing through the depot." The report concluded by commenting on the camp in general: "The welfare and social arrangements in the camp are excellent. The troops have cinema shows with up to date films practically every night and ENSA [Entertainments National Service Association] concerts are much appreciated."[35]

Padre Roy Price, who was sent home from the North African campaign as he had suffered several attacks of cerebral malaria, was appointed chaplain at Hardwick Hall. Perhaps because of his medical condition, Price did not accompany the men on all their manoeuvres, but "tried to show a genuine interest in all their military achievements". He aimed to get to know the trainee parachutists well, and was able, because of his own airborne experiences in North Africa, to empathise with their problems and concerns: "Frequently they discussed their problems and difficulties, inviting my confidence … truthfully I can say that to the best of my knowledge, relationships between the padre and all other ranks were of the highest 'espirit de corps' - the morale of the troops was 'par excellence', despite intense, novel and intensive exercise and practice."[36] His experience was particularly useful when dealing with casualties in training and being a listening ear as they recounted their experiences.

The Glider Pilot Regiment had been formed in February 1942, the Air Ministry having decreed that glider pilots would be part of the Army and that glider pilots would be officers or NCOs. Lieutenant Colonel George Chatterton, then second in command, made it very clear the calibre of man that would be allowed to enter the Glider Pilot Regiment (GPR) in an address to a new intake: "A soldier who will pilot an aircraft and then fight a battle, a task indeed … only the best will be tolerated." [37] The GPR consisted of two wings, and glider pilot training consisted of initial flight training in powered light aircraft and Hotspur training gliders at an

35 *Yorkshire Post and Leeds Intelligencer*, 27 April 1943.
36 Museum of Army Chaplaincy Archives, an account by Revd Roy Price.
37 Address by Lt Col George Chatterton, quoted in M. Peters, *Glider Pilots in Sicily* (Barnsley: Pen and Sword, 2012), p.20.

elementary flying training school (EFTS), and then a move to one of the new glider pilot schools at Haddenham, Weston on the Green, Stole Orchard, Kidlington and Shobdon, where they grappled with flying and landing larger unpowered aircraft such as Horsas and Hamilcars.

The Revd W. Chignell was posted as camp padre at Hardwick Hall in December 1943, replacing Price. He wrote home, "I don't think this means I will be attached to the airborne division as I am over age for that." He was, however, given a red beret to wear as the CO considered that "the men would think absolutely nothing of me" if he did not wear one. He settled down well and, despite not jumping, seemed to have the confidence of the men, running Padre's Hours and being available for chats: "I have several Padre's Hours each week and lots of men coming to see me and generally speaking I am kept very busy." Chignell described how challenging the Padre's Hours were for the padre: "They ask all sorts of questions and it is often very difficult to imagine what might be going on in their minds."[38] He took part in ground training - what he called "battle school" - and accompanied men on their initiative or 'escape' exercises. He was also kept well occupied in the pastoral care of his flock, helping to sort our family problems. On 9 February 1944, he held a large parade service in the cinema/gym for about 700 troops, with a dance band playing the hymns.[39]

Chignell's busy routine at Hardwick, however, was soon to be disrupted. A phone call from the RAChD in London offered him a posting as chaplain to the GPR, emphasising that this was voluntary, as were all postings to the regiment. Having obtained 24 hours to think it over, Chigwell asked advice in the mess. "Don't go near that lot of flying coffins," he was advised by one colleague, but Chigwell was ready to take on a new role and travelled to Blakehill Farm RAF station in Wiltshire, the HQ of No 2 wing of the GPR, in order to start a new phase in his ministry to airborne troops. His new flock also included the nearby stations at Down Ampney and Broadwell.

The Royal Army Chaplain's Department was involved in the ministry to airborne troops, both parachute and glider, from their inception. Watkins and Egan set the precedent for the involvement of the padres in all aspects of training, and won the respect that was to be given to most airborne padres. The relationships built up in training and the pastoral care given to men in training and base camps was to be vital to the way men and padres worked together in battle. The padres were to prove themselves worthy of the place they took in parachute sticks or gliders by their courage, compassion and leadership.

Before the first airborne troops left for action in North Africa, John Hodgins obtained the first version of the airborne padres' Holy Communion set, which could be carried in pouches attached to the webbing belt. Hodgins also wrote the Airborne

38   Mike Vockins, *Chig: Sky Pilot To The Glider Pilots Of Arnhem* (Solihull: Helion and Company, 2017), p.103.
39   *Ibid.*

Forces Collect, which was uniquely for all men who wore the red beret. The Collect takes its inspiration from the *Old Testament* book of Malachi, Chapter 4, Verse 2:

> May the defence of the Most High be above and beneath, around us and within us, in our going out and in our coming in, in our rising up and in our going down, through all our days and all out nights, until the dawn when the son of righteousness shall arise with healing in his wings for the peoples of this world, through Jesus Christ our Lord. Amen.

This simple prayer was to be the inspiration for the airborne forces in the dark days of the war and in eventual victory.

2

The 1st Airborne Division in North Africa, November 1942 to May 1943

The concept of airborne troops had been expanded considerably by June 1942, when an Air Directorate was created at the War Office under the leadership of Brigadier Richard Gale. The 2nd Parachute Brigade was formed in July, and on 1 August the Parachute Regiment followed, to act as an umbrella for the parachute battalions. In November the 3rd and 4th Parachute Battalions were formed. The parachute brigades trained intensively during the summer of 1942. The 1st Parachute Brigade was ready and on a war footing, and was detached from the division for service with the First Army.

On 8 November the Allies launched their attack on North Africa, Operation Torch. Here was the opportunity for the airborne forces to contribute in far larger numbers for the first time, and to be used in the role for which they had been designed, that of landing ahead of the ground forces and cooperating with them, leading the way. As we have seen, senior chaplain Hodgins had been building up a team of chaplains, four of whom accompanied the airborne forces: Padre Roy Price (Anglican) with the 1st Battalion, Padre Revd Murdo Macdonald (Church of Scotland) with the 2nd Battalion, Padre Alistair Menzies (Anglican) with the 3rd Battalion and Padre Bernard Egan (Roman Catholic). Apart from Egan, these chaplains had only joined their units within the last few weeks, and in company with many of the men, this was to be their first experience of action. The chaplains were to be heavily involved in the action, initially at drops at Souk Al araba and Depienne.

Due to a lack of Dakota aeroplanes, of which only 33 could be mustered, only B and C Companies of the3rd Battalion left Britain by air, leaving behind a disappointed cadre of the remainder of the battalion, including their chaplain, Menzies. The remainder of the battalion and the 1st and 2nd Battalions had to travel by sea, arriving in Algiers on 13 November. Price, padre to the 1st Battalion, made the most of this opportunity to get to know his men and organised a service on board. Meanwhile, Lieutenant General Kenneth Anderson, having landed with the First Army 500 miles west of Tunis, was marching towards the city, which was regarded by the Allies and Axis powers alike as the key to holding North Africa. He was hoping to reach Tunis in seven days. The terrain was mountainous, the roads few and there was one single-track railway line. The prospect of a swift breakthrough, at the beginning of winter weather, was optimistic. Robert Watkins, one of the first two airborne padres, commented: "A single breakthrough to the Tunisian coastal plan would have been a miracle, but if the miracle was not achieved it was not for want of trying."[1]

B and C Companies of the 3rd Battalion, 360 strong, having been assembled and briefed at Maison Blanche airfield, took off at first light on 12 November to capture Bone airfield, midway between Algiers and Tunis. A majority of the men were unfamiliar with the Dakota aircraft and had not had a practice jump. The pilots of the Dakotas had, as Hilary St George Saunders pointed out in his account of the British airborne forces, accumulated thousands of hours in their civilian flying careers, but had no experience of flying over enemy territory or facing anti-aircraft fire.[2] They landed unopposed but experienced a hard landings as the air was more rarefied, and suffered 13 casualties: one dead and 12 injured. One officer was knocked unconscious during landing and remained so for the next four days, on occasion being heard to murmur, "I'll have a little more of the turbot, waiter!"[3] The fatal casualty was caused when one man accidentally shot himself with his Sten gun. There had been rumours that Germans paratroopers had got there first: a German parachute unit did actually arrive over Bone slightly after the landing, but decided not to contest possession of the airfield.

Together with No 6 Commando, the task force held the airfield for a week, coming under attack from *Focke-Wulf* and *Messerschmitt* aircraft during that time. They were then taken back to join the rest of the battalion, which had disembarked at Algiers on 14 November.

On 16 November, the 1st Battalion was dropped at Souk el Araba, well ahead of the main force and 90 miles west of Tunis, with instructions to seize the road junction at Beja and persuade the French troops garrisoned there to support the Allies. This was the first opportunity that an airborne padre had to drop with his troops in action. Padre Roy Price was disappointed initially not to be included in the drop, and complained bitterly to Brigadier Edwin Flavell, CO of 1st Parachute Brigade. The commander of the operation, Lieutenant Colonel James Hill, set off and flew with the first aircraft, with the rest flying in line astern, but bad weather forced a return to base. When the operation took off again, Price had made sure he was included. With his batman, he was positioned at the front end of a stick in one of the aircraft, much to the annoyance of Private Moyes, who then became 13th in the stick and was in fact injured in the

---

1   Museum of Army Chaplaincy Archives, Revd R. Watkins, *World War Two Memoirs 1939-1945.*

2   Hilary St George Saunders, *The Red Beret* (London: Michael Joseph), p.66.

3   *Major General Julian Thompson, Ready for Anything: The Parachute Regiment at War (London: Fontana, 1990), p.55.*

drop.[4] Price had chosen his batman on the criteria of who would be of most use to the battalion when they landed.[5] Price explained that operationally the unarmed chaplain was supposed to have an armed batman: "At that time I had no batman so I asked for a volunteer. I chose a corporal who would be most useful to the battalion on arrival."[6]

Hill and his battalion dropped at Souk unopposed, but there was one fatality and five injured. The fatality had got his parachute tangled up and was throttled. Price took the funeral, which was watched by 3,000 people, including the French colonial troops who were guarding the town but had welcomed the parachutists. Alec Pearson, second in command, shook hands with everyone at the funeral, as was the French custom.

The battalion moved to Beja, but Hill wanted to impress on the French that he had a large number of men, and paraded them in and out of the town several times in different headgear (including helmets and red berets). Some Italian troops who escaped from Beja took exaggerated accounts of the size of the force back to the Germans in Tunis [7]. At Beja, the battalion sent out patrols to find enemy, while Price based himself with the surgical teams of the 16th Parachute Field Ambulance. On 19 and 20 November, German *Stuka* attacks caused many casualties among civilians and the troops. Price was the anaesthetist in theatre, a role that many Great War chaplains had performed. Medical Officer Lieutenant Charles Robb, in command of the surgical team, carried out over 150 operations despite suffering from a fractured kneecap. Continuing his work, he carried out another 22 operations the next day, even giving a pint of blood to save a wounded soldier.[8] Price went to see the wounded at Souk el Khemis and was attacked by *Stukas* again.

Price went to find the priest in Beja and discovered that the church had been bombed. Amidst the rubble was a statue of the Virgin Mary, whose crown had slipped. Price climbed up to set it right.[9] On Sunday, 21 November Price celebrated Holy Communion at the lower hospital in Beja and was moved by the large number of communicants. He had lost his Holy Communion set in the bombing, so used an aluminium plate and cup which he utilised for the rest of his time in North Africa. He used ration biscuits and local wine, provided by the local priest, as the elements for the service.

On 23 November Lieutenant Colonel Hill attacked an Italian tank laager, and he and his adjutant were wounded. Price was present when they were brought in and helped the surgical team led by Lieutenant Robb. Price remembered: "When we took him in I could scarcely hope for his survival. The CO had four bullet wounds in him,

4   Museum of Army Chaplaincy Archives, papers deposited by Revd P.R.C. Abram CVO. Typescript, *Lower Than the Angels* (1975), p.12.
5   Museum of Army Chaplaincy Archives, an account by Revd Roy Price.
6   *Ibid.*
7   Saunders, *Red Beret*, p.84.
8   Obituary of Charles Robb, *Daily Telegraph*, 16 August 2001.
9   Abram, *Lower Than the Angels*, p.13.

one in the lung and another a quarter of an inch from his heart."[10] Hill did survive, actually being able to visit Price six weeks later when the padre was in hospital with malaria, but Price had buried two soldiers who died in this raid, and felt the loss as he had known them both personally.

Price was involved in two incidents in this period of patrol activity. In the first, an RAF Spitfire flying in support of the patrols was shot down and Price ran to the aid of the pilot, not realising he was running through a minefield. Finding the pilot was dead, Price returned more carefully, skirting the area, the men having by now informed him the land was mined. In the second incident, Price took a burial party to a farm to bury the bodies of some American soldiers who were in a considerable state of decomposition: "By the time the funeral was over they were all in a state of nausea."[11] Fortified by some wine from the farmer's wife, and also provided with some *Eau de Cologne*, they departed, only to realise they would have to pass a German patrol. They drove on slowly, waving their Red Cross flag: "To their astonishment the Germans gave them a salute which they returned."[12] Their activities had been seen and respected by their foes.

The 1st Battalion was withdrawn to rest in an area south of Mateur, and Price caught up with the provision of services and correspondence concerning his duties, which included censoring and writing letters to families of his men. The whole brigade was based there until after Christmas.

Meanwhile the 2nd Battalion, based in Algiers, had been getting to know their chaplain, Padre M.E. Macdonald, who soon established a reputation for forthright sermons. Lieutenant Colonel John Frost, C O of 2nd Battalion, remembered:

> Murdo Ewan Macdonald, who was with the 2nd, became a famous preacher. I would like it known that his preaching, which was pretty fiery, made a distinct impact on the battalion before they went into action. There were many temptations in Algeria at the time and I feel he did much to help the men to withstand them.[13]

On 29 November, at about 3:00 p.m., Frost and the 2nd Battalion dropped at Depienne, 30 miles to the south-west of Tunis, 50 miles behind enemy lines, with the aim of destroying airfields there and at Oudna. Bad weather had prevented reconnaissance and the drop was disorganised, with the airfield and landing grounds waterlogged. One man was killed by a candling parachute (one which failed to open properly) and was buried by Macdonald where he fell.

10   Museum of Army Chaplaincy Archives, an account by the Revd Roy Price.
11   *Ibid.*
12   *Ibid.*
13   Museum of Army Chaplaincy Archives, letter from John Frost to Abram, 4 March, year unknown.

The battalion set of for Oudna just after midnight on 30 November. The route was along a road for a mile and then by tracks over the hills, and they were within 12 miles of Tunis by morning. In bitter weather, when the battalion was ordered to rest everyone was wet through and cold. It was impossible sleep because of the cold, as the men had no blankets, only a shirt, jumper and camouflage canvas jacket. The going was so hard that that even the mules found it difficult and bent at the knees. Nevertheless, the airborne troops attacked Oudna airfield unopposed on the afternoon of 30 November, but an hour later the Germans counterattacked with five tanks, supported by *Messerschmitts* and *Stuka* dive-bombers. Frost gave orders for the battalion to withdraw to Prise d'Eau. Macdonald helped load the wounded on mule carts and guided the mules, then assisted at the RAP, which was manned by No 2 Section of 16th Parachute Field Ambulance under Lieutenant J.C. McGavin.

In the early hours of 1 December, Frost received a radio message that the armoured thrust to link up with them had been held up and that he was to rejoin the Allied forces. He realised his position would soon become untenable as he was approximately 40 miles from the nearest Allied-held points at Medjez El Bab and Tebourba and was surrounded by Axis forces.[14] The enemy were beginning to arrive in strength, with armoured cars patrolling the roads, and the battalion came under attack from artillery and aircraft. Frost therefore began to withdraw the battalion westwards. The 150 casualties made the first part of the march, but when it became dark it was decided that the companies should move independently and that the wounded would prevent them keeping up the pace which was necessary to allow them to slip through enemy lines. At this stage Frost had asked Macdonald to assume some combat duties. Writing to Paul Abram in 1971, Macdonald remembered: "I had moved over to combat duties before I came to grief in North Africa."[15]

Lieutenant McGavin of the surgical team was isolated with the casualties at a farm house, and Frost asked Macdonald to give McGavin a map reference so that he could rejoin the battalion. However, McGavin told him he was too involved with wounded to rejoin, and Macdonald returned to the unit, but was wounded twice, first in the left arm by a bullet and then in the right arm by fragments of a mortar bomb. What was left of the battalion then began the process of fighting their way back to the Allies, leaving the wounded with Lieutenant Playfair and his platoon to protect them. The remnants of the battalion arrived back at Medjez El Bab on the evening of 3 December. Of the 500 men who had jumped, just 140 made it back together to Medjez El Bab, with another 80 turning up in small parties over the next few days.

Meanwhile, the wounded spent a night in very cold conditions. Macdonald recalled: "All through the long miserable night I listened to the incessant clicking of teeth and the moans of the badly wounded and dying." Although seriously wounded and in pain

14   *Ibid*, p.66.
15   Museum of Army Chaplaincy Archives, letter from Revd M.E. Macdonald to Abram, 6 July 1971.

himself, Macdonald was able to minister to the dying. At 7:00 a.m. the next morning, German soldiers form the *Afrika Korps* turned up, and very efficiently took the British survivors prisoner, giving them chocolate mixed with hot water. Macdonald, being wounded in both arms, could not hold a cup but he remembered the German soldiers helping him drink the chocolate,

The prisoners, meanwhile, were taken by truck to Tunis, and on the way Macdonald recognised a friend, Lieutenant Ken Morrison, lying dead near the road. He asked permission for the truck to be stopped so that he could pay his respects to his friend, and the German officer not only stopped but arranged for a grave to be dug quickly so that Macdonald could bury his friend: "They dug a grave and very gently lowered Ken into it. I took up my position at the head of the grave. Two soldiers had to shore me up as I had lost a lot of blood and I had no food for these days."[16] Macdonald recited from the *Book of Revelations*: "And I saw a new heaven and a new earth: for the first heaven and first earth had passed away and there was no more sea."[17]

In Tunis, Macdonald's wounds were operated on and he was among those flown to Italy because of their injuries, accompanied by the MO James McGavin. During the flight, McGavin and Macdonald decided they would try to blow up the aeroplane when they landed. There were blankets and petrol cans at the rear of the plane, and when they landed at Naples, Macdonald pretended to be so sick that he was taken off the aircraft in some commotion. While the Germans were distracted, McGavin placed a time pencil bomb that had been hidden in Macdonald's sling among the blankets. As they walked away, the aircraft blew up. All, including the crew, had disembarked by the time of the explosion and there were no casualties. In a rage, the Germans lined them up against a haystack and were about to shoot them until stopped by an officer, who took them to *Luftwaffe* HQ. There they were stripped, examined and questioned, and Macdonald's wounds were dressed, which he found extremely painful and considered a "rather pointless exercise, as execution was still on the cards". The *Luftwaffe* officer then made a few telephone calls and announced, "execution cancelled, let's have some tea".[18] They were then taken to the railway station and placed in a guard's van, whereupon Macdonald was "gloriously sick".[19]

Upon arrival at Rome they were kept for a few days in the civilian prison, before surprisingly being treated to a tour of the sights of the ancient city! Macdonald was full of praise for McGavin, who looked after him during these events: "By this time I was fairly sick as my wounds had gone septic and Jim McGavin proved to be a kind of saviour. No praise is too high for him."[20] Lieutenant Colonel Frost heard a rumour

16   M.E. Macdonald, *Padre Mac: The Man From Harris* (Stornaway: The Stornaway Gazette, undated), p.91.
17   *Ibid*, p.92.
18   *Ibid*, p.95.
19   Museum of Army Chaplaincy Archives, letter form Revd M.E. Macdonald to Abram, 6 July 1971.
20   *Ibid.*

that the doctor and padre "were considered persons of great interest to the Germans" and that there were plans to exhibit them in Rome. In fact they were transported to Germany. Yet their adventures were not over, as McGavin broke both legs jumping off a train in an escape attempt and, according to Frost, Macdonald later "enjoyed a short spell of freedom by escaping through a lavatory window"[21] when being transferred between hospital and a camp in Germany. The padre was free for three days before being recaptured. Writing to Abram after the war, Frost commented further on this episode: "He was an object of particular interest to the German army authorities because they had not visualised 'jumping padres'. Their destruction of the enemy aircraft at Naples must rank as a most outstanding feat … I do feel it set a magnificent example of which airborne forces can be proud."[22] He continued: "Church and padres rather got in the way as far as we sinners were concerned, but as soon as we saw what they could do for us before, during and after the action, they at once became well beloved and trusted members whom we did not want to be without ever again."[23]

Meanwhile, the 1st Parachute Brigade had concentrated in Beja. The 3rd Battalion, which after their landing at Bone had endured many cancelled operations, travelled to rejoin the brigade. Their padre, probably Alistair Menzies, managed to hit a chicken on the head with a stone, and then purchased it from its annoyed owner. Unfortunately, when the chicken was served the giblets had not been removed by the cook, and it was inedible.[24] Weather prevented much action. After taking services on Christmas Day, Price reported sick and was sent to 95 General Hospital suffering from malaria and a raging fever. His first bout was severe and developed into an attack of cerebral malaria, a severe infection of the brain which can cause seizures, confusion and increasing tiredness, even leading to coma and death. He was to survive two further such attacks.

In his history of the Parachute Regiment, St George Saunders explained the reasons for the parachute battalions to be used as infantry of the line in the remainder of the Tunisian campaign rather than in their primary role of seizing key points to the rear and flank of the enemy, creating alarm and confusion, and facilitating the advance of a main force. The Allied advance had stalled in the appalling weather, forcing Lieutenant General Anderson to abandon his plans for the use of the parachute troops to pass through the Guards Brigade, exploiting the hoped-for capture of Longstop Hill. Instead of this scenario, the Allied force was hard-pressed to retain the position it had gained by Christmas 1942.

21   Robert Peating, *Without Tradtion: 2 Para 1941-1945* (Barnsley: Pen and Sword, 1994), p.89.
22   Frost's recollections contradict each other. In *Without Tradition* he reports that McGavin broke both legs, but his letter to Abram says he broke his arm.
23   Museum of Army Chaplaincy Archives, letter from John Frost to Abram, 4 March, year unknown.
24   Saunders, *Red Beret*, p.100.

On 2 January 1943, the 3rd Battalion moved for an attack on Green Hill, which had a commanding tactical position overlooking the Sedjenane-Mateur road. A Company was to join with the Buffs and B Company with the Royal West Kents. There was a long journey over mountainous terrain to reach the area, and on Sunday, 3 January, Menzies found no opportunity for even a small service. Lunch was made from compo (field) rations and Menzies joined some commando sergeants. The sergeant in charge was a "breezy blasphemous young fellow from Clydeside … his highly coloured conversation was amusing". When Menzies thanked him for letting him share the food, he remarked "there was someone else who fed a bloody sight more people with less food".[25]

This was the first action experienced by Menzies. The padre spent the evening before the action in trying to study the gospels, and on the evening of 4 January they moved off. He wrote in his diary: "Eventually came to a ridge occupied by a battalion of the Buffs, we took over the position. There were two 'wog' huts, one for CO etc. and the other for the signals officer Dixie Lapage, Fred Whitaker and myself and our batman."[26] In the morning they discovered that the hut was in a direct line of fire so they moved. After having spent most of the day in a slit trench, the 4-mile march to Green Hill, three of them across the hills, began in the afternoon. After a very cold night in a hut, casualties began to come in to the RAP and Menzies had his introduction to the reality of battle wounds. A Company had secured the western flank by mid-morning of 5 January 5. B Company attacked the enemy positions in the early hours of 6 January, but after fierce fighting was forced to withdraw because of lack of ammunition. The attack was driven back by the German troops, Menzies describing how the battalion was forced back to its starting lines. He experienced the wounded coming into the aid station, mainly with shrapnel wounds: "The wounds looked like raspberry jam on the men's arms and legs." The first experience had perhaps unsettled him, as he reported he "felt disinclined to eat". He did, however, give out the rum ration to HQ Company, and luckily there was "plenty to go around and we all felt better!".[27]

On 8 January the battalion was transported back to Souk el Khemis and Menzies had the chance of a heart-to-heart with Major David Dobbie, who told him of the fate of Bill Blewitt in the recent attack. Blewitt had attacked sounding a hunting horn, but after capturing a machine-gun post was shot dead. He learned that the Germans had gone into the attack chanting and that the paratroopers had replied in kind, with a Private Jones singing 'Men of Harlech'. Menzies heard that there were 30 men killed or missing.

25   Diary of Rev A.C.V. Menzies, North Africa, 1943. Paradata https://www.paradata.org.uk/media/155.
26   *Ibid.*
27   *Ibid.*

On Sunday, 10 January, they were moved by train, so Menzies had no opportunity to organise a service. On the train he shared some whisky with the commanding officers and some second lieutenants. They arrived at Bou Farik at dusk on 11 January, and then travelled on to a large farm about eight miles outside St Charles. The British airborne forces were now concentrated in the Algiers area, where they could enjoy some well-deserved relaxation. Menzies reported in his diary on 11 January that he had slept for the first time in a while in pyjamas. The two chaplains were kept busy. Fr Egan covered the Roman Catholics in every unit, while Menzies had to look after all the Protestants as Macdonald was a POW and Price was ill with malaria. The chaplains of the brigade were issued with motorcycles, although Fr Egan often used a bicycle, and they visited company locations for Sunday services and Padre's Hours.

Menzies' diary for the next two weeks sheds light on the work and activities of the chaplains at rest and at base camps in all its variety. On 13 January Menzies accompanied a lorry to take men to the dentist at the 94th General Hospital at Algiers. While in Algiers he visited men from the 2nd and 3rd Battalion who were in hospital, and on the way home visited some Royal Army Medical Corps (RAMC) friends. Censoring letters took up much time, as did travelling to different units to arrange services. He also managed to arrange for 30 American paratroopers to attend a church parade service. He did, however, have time to socialise with his fellow clergy, including a lunch appointment with a Reformed Church minister in Algiers and dinner one evening with Fr Egan. He also spent time writing letters home to his family and letters "for or about the troops".[28]

On 18 January he reported "a heartening parade service" for HQ and A and B Companies in the farmyard, followed by "an even better one for sappers and RMC in the evening at Bou Farik after which four stayed for Holy Communion". The rest of the day was spent catching up on reading, including Evelyn Underhill's *Christian Sacraments* and Rupert Brooke poems. There was some relaxation on 19 January, with a swim, a glass of wine and attendance at a boxing match. However, attendance at a nurses' dance on the 22nd was curtailed by being called back to base because the brigade was on the move as an operation was imminent. On February 23 he took a Padre's Hour and talked on "The Implications of Faith", before "a day of great activity" on the 24th when the 1st and 3rd Battalions were returned to the front and embarked there on the *Queen Emma*. As the First Army were not able to move on, and were having difficulty sustaining their position, the 1st Parachute Brigade now had to fight as infantry in a ground role.

On 2 and 3 February the 1st Battalion, with the Grenadier Guards and French Foreign Legion, attacked Green hill at Djebel Mansour.

28   Diary of Rev A.C.V. Menzies, 15 January.

Thomas Davies described his experiences at Djebel Mansour:

> I recall the prominent hills and mountains of North Africa as if it was yesterday. The locals called them Djebels. One such mountain was Djebel Mansour and it stands out in my mind like a molten burning fire. It was here that the bitterest fighting was experienced … It was in the hands of the German Fallschirmjäger, elite paratroopers who were well dug in when the battalion attacked. After many hours of attack and counter attack we eventually forced our way up the mountain, in the process scrambling up different paths under murderous fire.[29]

After a very steep climb the 1st Battalion swept into the enemy position with the bayonet. The Foreign Legion, a thousand yards away, reported that cries of "Waho Mohamed" could be heard above the rattle of small-arms fire.

It was at Djebel Mansour that Price returned to action. He waited at the RAP to help with casualties, and when the battle was at its height visited the battalion HQ. In his account he said, "Went with battalion to Djebel Mansour, the scene of a very fierce struggle." A Vickers machine gun had just arrived and it was vital that it should reach the top of the Djebel as soon as possible. Price volunteered to take it. He roped the gun to a mule and set off across the dry water course of a wadi, recalling coming under heavy fire:

> The way led through an open Wadi with a dry stream bed. It was quite some distance before there could be any cover. I drew fire on myself, fortunately ineffective. The mountain side was very precipitous and I was glad to grab the mule's tail and be helped up the steepest part. At one point my glasses were snatched from me. They had to be searched for with some difficulty as I dare not release the mule.[30]

The arrival of the Vickers was hailed with delight, but it had no packing for the cooler so was useless. Very disappointed, Price recalled: "I would have done anything that could have helped in the desperate situation." He spent the rest of the day on the mountain, crawling from position to position to visit groups of men: "Losses were heavy but nonetheless everyone was in good heart."[31] Price then made his way back down the mountain, escorting some wounded. On the way down they were attacked by *Stukas*. Price and his party threw themselves into a dry river valley, under the cover of a wooden bridge. Miraculously, no-one was hurt. Price returned to pick up more wounded with the help of an Italian motor tricycle carrying a stretcher. He continued

---

29   Roger Payne, *PARA, Voices of the British Airborne Forces in the Second World War* (Stroud: Amberley Publishing, 2014), p.85.
30   Museum of Army Chaplaincy Archives, an account by Revd Roy Price.
31   *Ibid.*

these trips with motorcycle until the last day of the battle. During 4 February the Djebel Mansour position became untenable. Under Brigadier Flavell's orders, Price found a rest area where what was left of the battalion could assemble. After this action Price reported only small patrol activity for the battalion. Price succumbed to malaria again in May and was invalided home. The Divisional Medical Officer told senior chaplain Geoffrey Harper that unless Price was sent home he could not be responsible for his life. Upon recovery, Price was made chaplain of Hardwick camp.

Bernard Egan was also very much involved in this battle. He joined 16th Parachute Field Ambulance and assisted in the evacuation of casualties. It took 10 hours for the stretcher bearers to carry the wounded down from Djebel Mansour, so the Field Ambulance moved closer to the1st Battalion. After the attack on Djebel Mansour, a draft of 12 officers and 164 other ranks reinforced the1st Parachute Brigade, including Padre Robert Watkins. He was attached to HQ but also took an interest in 1st Battalion because Price was in hospital again. It was Brigadier Flavell's policy to move the chaplains around the battalions, but while this worked in England, it was not convenient under battle conditions.

For two weeks all three battalions were in a relatively quiet and static position known as 'Happy Valley', and Watkins used the time to get to know the men. Even in this quiet sector it was inadvisable for large gatherings of men to assemble, being limited at most to 10 men. Fr Egan would say Mass for a few men gathered together or Menzies would hold prayers for a handful. Watkins would talk to the men in their positions and hold the occasional Holy Communion service. He developed a 10-minute service which he called 'family prayers', during which prayers were said for loved ones and friends, well-known Bible passages were read and the service finished with a short talk. This informal approach was welcomed by the men.

The care of the 1st Battalion now fell to Watkins, but he based himself at Brigade HQ as he needed transport to visit the different units. He managed to commandeer a horse, which was the best way of travelling around the uneven terrain to the scattered units, and although unused to riding he soon could be seen trotting around the area and became "a cause for merriment". However, the horse was killed by a sniper's bullet on one of Watkins' journeys.

The 1st Parachute Brigade was attacked on 26 February by General Jürgen von Armin's crack troops of the Fifth *Panzer* Army. The asault fell mainly on the 3rd Battalion, which was the strongest of the three battalions and held an excellent defensive position. They inflicted severe casualties on the enemy. Menzies, who was helping with the wounded, reported in his diary: "Tried to bring Giles Bromley Martin in but heavy machine[-gun] fire. He died." On the morning of the 27th he attended B Company to bury British and German soldiers.

Lieutenant Colonel Geoffrey Pine-Coffin said of Menzies' actions:

> It was an occasion when the safest thing was to stay put and hope that the enemy
> would finally appear to your front. Menzies did not seem to consider what was
> the safest thing but moved about from company to company and undoubtedly

contributed to the success of the day. He introduced a sense of normality in a mad scene and this in addition to the comfort he gave to the sick and dying.[32]

On the 28th, Menzies was able to take a short service and reported meeting Watkins for the first time: "We had a long pow-pow."

Robert Watkins helped a French farmer and his family, whose farm was in no man's land, to evacuate their belongings on two donkeys. Menzies took them away in an ambulance with some other refugees and eventually arranged for French officials to look after them.

The battle continued in the Tamara area. On 8 March there was a German attack which required defensive measure from all three battalions. Price was with the 1st Battalion and was trying to visit companies without being targeted by snipers. He found himself burying dead, but with water filling the graves as soon as they were dug. The enemy was determined to break through in this northern sector of the line, so the advanced dressing station of the Parachute Field Ambulance remained far forward. By doing so they were an encouragement to the fighting men.[33] Watkins positioned himself with the Ambulance and observed: "I am sure no field ambulance was ever intended to be as far forward as this one."

Menzies' diary for 8 March gives a sense of his role during the battle:

> Soon after 0600 hours Germans launched big attack along hill East of the Tamara station. 1st Battalion heavily engaged but took 150 prisoners. I watched the battle from our hillside in the morning. Hurri [Hurricane] bombers attacked Germans and Churchill tanks moved up and down the road to the station. C Coy went up the hill opposite their position to beat back the Germans attacking the 2nd Battalion. At C Coy I organised a party for grave digging, as we did this MEs again attacked the Valley. Shells burst only yards away as we clutched at the earth under the bushes. I buried Taffy Evans. He had led a counterattack sucking his pipe, his men shouting 'Whoa Mohamed.'[34]

On 13 March Menzies reported going with Major Smith to the old A Company positions and being asked to draw sketches of Commando Hill and the Sedjenane road. In his post-war account, Geoffrey Pine-Coffin explained this request:

> When a battle is over it is always difficult to find out just what did happen from people's descriptions of the action so I had this idea of having someone to make a panoramic sketch of the area. Teddy Smith my 2/i/c said he thought the padre

---

32 Museum of Army Chaplaincy Archives, letter from General Pine-Coffin to Paul Abram, 12 November 1967.
33 Saunders, *Red Beret*, p.113.
34 Diary of Rev A.C.V. Menzies, 15 January.

was pretty good at sketching. So that is how he found himself doing just that. He must have found it a bit odd.[35]

On 15 March Menzies reported: "Most miserable night ever. Blankets and tunic wet through. Feet encased in wet boots. Double Rum ration for HQ Coy."

Watkins was with the 16th Parachute Field Ambulance, and like the other chaplains found visiting the men difficult as the enemy who occupied Djebel Bel Harch commanded the whole area. The padres started writing to the families of the bereaved: "The sight of the chaplain, sitting in a trench or medical tent and writing to relatives, often under fire, was commonplace."[36] Roy Price reported that these letters often started a considerable and lengthy correspondence. Price made a point of sending a sprig of heather or other plant, taken from near the soldier's grave. He described writing to the families of those killed:

> This was nor formality. One was genuinely grieved for the losses which one had to report. These letters often started lengthy correspondence, as was natural everyone wanted every scrap of information about the deaths of their loved one. I always made a point of enclosing a flower or sprig, usually of heather, found growing near their graves. Usually it was heather. It became obvious that this small gesture was tremendously appreciated. I also recall the poignancy of a letter from the parents of a soldier killed, begging me to look after his brother who was also with the Battalion. I knew that he too was now among the dead and wondered how I should write this second letter. The next of kin at home became very real to me even though I had not met them.[37]

Bernard Egan had been with the 2nd Battalion throughout the battle. The war diary of the 2nd Battalion shows almost daily contact with the enemy in February and March.[38] Egan was physically and emotionally tired, not least because his batman, Private J. Scrutton, had been killed. In 1944 the *Hartlepool Daily Mail* reported about Egan: "The first Roman Catholic to jump with an airborne unit has been awarded the MC for gallantry and devotion to duty. He is Father Bernard Egan, a Jesuit and chaplain to the forces, who has been attached to a parachute battalion from February 1943." The newspaper went on to quote part of the citation: "During the heavy fighting in the northern sector of Tunisia in March 1943 he was often at the forefront of the battle, comforting the wounded and encouraging all ranks under heavy fire."[39] Egan, in a letter in 1971, summed up this action very modestly: "Djebel Mansour

35   Museum of Army Chaplaincy Archives, an account by General R.G. Pine-Coffin.
36   Museum of Army Chaplaincy Archives, Abram, *Lower Than the Angels*, p.25.
37   Museum of Army Chaplaincy Archives, an account by the Revd Roy Price.
38   Peating, *Without Tradition*, p.90.
39   The *Hartlepool Daily Mail*, April 1944.

originally started as a small operation for the 1st Battalion but turned into a major battle. Having gone up with the brigade Medical Officer after breakfast ... we found the battle in progress and I stayed to the end."[40]

The 1st and 3rd Battalions were now withdrawn, but had to return to the battle quite swiftly to cover the retreat of the 2nd Battalion from Cork Hill, which they had been holding determinedly with mounting casualties.

With the battalions withdrawn from the Tamara Valley for a few days' rest and refitting, after the red mud of the valley had been washed off, the priority of the chaplain was to hold services. Fr Egan said Mass for the Roman Catholics and Watkins arranged a service for everyone else. Watkins was ministering to the Protestants, who found that although few of them were regular worshipers at home, and would ignore a chaplain in England, appreciated the services overseas, especially after battle. Watkins discovered that if a man was afraid in action he would swear rather than pray, and any chaplain who attempted to pray at such a time was either ignored or sworn at: "When men were quiet and had time to think then they wanted to pray."[41] Watkins considered that when the men were at rest from one action and gearing up for another, their morale and psychological defences could be lowered by thoughts of their loved ones at home, and that the chaplain's job was to help them rebuild their defences: "Theologically, we may say that that is not good enough, that there must be recognition of a man's total inadequacy and need. Perhaps so, but that is the chaplain's burden for his own prayers. With his people he can sometimes only meet people at the point of their need."[42]

The Battalion HQ sent word round that there was to be a service. Padre Price remembered:

> They came in all sorts of dress to the workings at the head of the mine where they sat on the ground or on pieces of machinery. The pattern of the service was 'family prayers' which Watkins used frequently. Lt Col Frost read the lesson, Joshua Chap 1, v 1–9 and Watkins talked on the theme of 'Be strong and of good courage and be not afraid, neither be thou dismayed: for the Lord thy God is with thee wither so ever thou goest.'[43]

The hymns had to be well known as there were no books and no music. Watkins commented: "That was all there was to it, but the service still lives in the memories of the men who were there." He explained: "This was the only approach I knew."[43] During

---

40   Museum of Army Chaplaincy Archives, letter from the Revd Bernard Egan to Paul Abram.
41   Museum of Army Chaplaincy Archives, Abram, *Lower Than the Angels*, p.27.
42   Watkins, *World War Two Memoirs 1939-1945*.
43   Watkins, *World War Two Memoirs 1939-1945*.

this brief period of rest, Watkins lost his Holy Communion set, but the men made a paten out of a circular tobacco tin and a chalice with a stem fixed to an aluminium cup.

On 27 March, the entire brigade participated in a general Allied offensive aimed at taking control of the area around Tamera. The 1st and 2nd Battalions launched an attack at 11:00 p.m. the same day, taking numerous prisoners and securing their objectives, and then repulsed a German counterattack, albeit with heavy losses. Further heavy and often confusing fighting continued, with several companies of 3rd Battalion having to be attached to 2nd Battalion to reinforce it. The 1st Battalion also seized its own objectives, and by the end of 29 March the brigade had secured all of its objectives and taken prisoner 770 German and Italian troops. On 15 March the brigade took up positions covering the left flank of 46th Division, and for the next two weeks it remained in the area, conducting numerous patrols but encountering little opposition.

The 1st Brigade advanced as far as Sedjenane and remained there from 1-14 April. These two weeks were very busy for the chaplains, writing to relatives, censoring letters and editing the *Union Jack* newspaper. Sunday services were taken with all units on 4 and 11 April. Menzies organised a series of debates and gave a talk entitled 'What are we fighting for?'.

On 15 March the brigade was relieved by the 39th US Regimental Combat Team and moved to the rear. It then travelled to Algiers on 18 April. Brigadier Flavell left for England to take up a new command, and was replaced by Brigadier Gerald Lathbury. Shortly afterwards the brigade rejoined 1st Airborne Division and began training for the airborne landings that would take place during Operation Husky, the Allied invasion of Sicily.

The brigade had been involved in hard fighting from November 1942 until April 1943, mostly in the infantry role. Before this experience they had been an unknown quantity, but during the North African campaign the airborne troops had proven their worth. They were also very much respected by the enemy, who dubbed them the 'Red Devils'. This reputation was not gained cheaply: in five months of fighting, 83 officers an 1,600 other ranks had been killed, wounded or were missing out of a total strength of over 2,000 men. Hilary St George Saunders, in his history of the Parachute Regiment, gave the following opinion of their actions: "They proved themselves again and again, to be troops of the highest order. Implacable in attack, steady in defence, they earned the sobriquet bestowed by them on the enemy [red devils], not once but many times."[44]

In August 1943 Watkins arranged for the War Graves Commission to tidy up the battlefield as some bodies were still unburied. The 1st Parachute Brigade wanted to revisit the battlefield before departing for Italy, and Watkins was worried about the effect on morale of seeing areas which still bore the marks of the desperate battles. Watkins did a tour of the area and got the graves unit to sort out the unburied or

44 Saunders, *Red Beret*, p.120.

partially buried bodies. The Royal Engineers of the 1st Parachute Regiment made oak crosses which were set up on every grave.

A concrete obelisk, 11ft high and with a path and three steps leading to it, was also set up on the site of the Parachute Field Ambulance in the Tamara valley. The plaque on the memorial read: "In memory of the officers and men of the 1st Parachute Brigade of the British army who gave their lives for king and country Nov 1942–April 1943." On a smaller plaque the following battle honours were inscribed:

> Bone, Souk el Araba, Depienne, Beja
> Mdjez el Bab
> Djebel Mansour, Bou Arada
> Tamara Valley

Realising that not many of the men directly involved or their families would see the memorial, Watkins arranged for photographs be put in the national press and also made 6,000 postcards. This meant a lot to the airborne forces, as the Revd Paul Abram explained:

> It might appear that Airborne forces should be composed of men capable of suppressing their feelings, that it should be a military machine rather than a human organisation. Nothing could be further from the truth. From the beginning to the present day the individual and his concerns have been regarded as vital.[45]

A letter from General Harold Alexander, commander of 18th Army Group (comprising Anderson's First Army and the Eighth Army), dated 19 April 1943 was kept by Watkins as part of his wartime diary:

> Now that it has been possible to relieve the Parachute Brigade, who have for so long a time played a most valuable role in the North, I should like to express my thanks to and admiration for, every officer, NCO and man for the conspicuously successful part they have taken on the recent fighting. They have proved their mastery over the enemy, who have a wholesome respect for this famous Brigade which is best described in their own words for them –'The Red Devils'.[46]

The airborne padres of the Parachute Regiment had undergone their baptism of fire and first experience of battle in North Africa, and had proven equal to the task, jumping with their battalions and enduring the appalling weather conditions in some of the grimmest and most uncomfortable country in the world. For much of their time

---

45   Museum of Army Chaplaincy Archives, Abram, *Lower Than the Angels*, p.31.
46   Watkins, *World War Two Memoirs 1939-1945*.

in North Africa those padres and their battalions were experiencing the use of the Parachute Regiment as front-line infantry.

Soon they would experience landing by glider and parachute in the vanguard of the Allied invasion of Sicily.

3

Operation Ladbroke and Operation Fustian, Sicily, July 1943

At the beginning of July 1943, General Montgomery sent a personal message to his men of the Eighth Army: "The time has now come to carry the war into Italy and into the continent of Europe … Therefore, with faith in God and with enthusiasm for our cause and for the day of battle let us enter into this contest with stout hearts and a determination to conquer."[1] In this way the British contribution to Operation Husky was launched, and after the setbacks and eventual triumph of the war in North Africa the next stage of the war was to begin. The operation was to involve the first troops returning successfully to Europe since Dunkirk more than three years ago.

A few days before Operation Husky, Major General George Hopkinson, commander of 1st Airborne Division, invited Padre Geoffrey Harper, the senior chaplain, to accompany him to time the 'nautical sunset' at one of the bases set up in infertile scrubland near to the coast that the Airborne Division had been moved to in June. Harper felt that this was an excuse for Hopkinson to talk to him about the forthcoming operation of the 1st Air Landing Brigade. Hopkinson was aware of the difficulties of landing an entire brigade by glider, but it was Hopkinson who had persuaded Montgomery that a glider landing should be attempted, in darkness, with undertrained air crews and using unfamiliar American gliders. According to Harper, Hopkinson revealed himself in that conversation to be a religious man who was very aware that the fate of the airborne troops was dependent on his orders and decisions.[2] Hopkinson used Harper as a sounding board for his feelings before the invasion, and they discussed on several occasions his feelings of guilt if he made the wrong decision. Harper considered that they had a good relationship: "I came to know Hoppy very

---

1 Letter from General Montgomery to Eighth Army, dated July 1943; facsimile produced by ParaData https://paradata.org.uk.
2 Museum of Army Chaplaincy Archives, papers deposited by Revd P.R.C. Abram CVO, Typescript, *Lower Than the Angels* (1975), p.33.

well in his capacity as Brigade Commander and I think we hit it off."[3] This was not an isolated case of commander/chaplain cooperation.

The role of the recently formed 1st Airborne Division was to be crucial to the planning of the operation. The 1st Air Landing Brigade and 1st Parachute Brigade, who had established their battle credentials in the Tunisian campaign, were to be given a decisive role. Their objective was to capture and hold two vital bridges which would be essential to the progress of the main landing force en route to the stronghold port of Messina. These were the Ponte Grande and Primosole bridges. The capture of Messina would hinder the escape of Axis troops to the Italian mainland. In these operations the gliders would play an essential part for the first time.

In May 1943 the 1st Airborne Division was at Mascara in Algeria, 60 miles south of Oran, enduring high temperatures and sand storms. They were in training for an operation which was to be one of the most decisive of the war. In this period of preparation, the airborne chaplains were able to maintain Sunday services, usually at 6:30 a.m. before the heat of the day. The Padre's Hour was a regular part of the routine. Padre Robert Watkins recorded: "I have got the Padre's Hour going again and it is immensely popular. One lot is asking for it twice a week instead of once." Even though the Sunday services were more of parade nature, Watkins found that, "Even now the response is great and the men are keen to listen. It certainly keeps me on my toes. If I trot out an address that is not up to standard I soon hear about it." He found that in the relative peace of training, family issues with the men now raised their head and Watkins was kept busy, although the distance from home did not help: "It is difficult to tackle them out here."[4] Padre J. Rowell, with the 1st Border Regiment, managed to keep Padre's Hours going and hold regular services.

The 1st Airborne Division had known as far back as February of plans to deploy them in operations in June and July. It was realised that there would be difficulties in training a sufficient number of glider pilots in time, and so, according to the later report on the operation: "It was decided that approximately 50 crew would receive a concentrated programme of training with squadrons of 38 Wing during March and April, while approximately 60 crews who had carried out little flying in recent months should proceed to North Africa in the first convoy and receive concentrated training in North Africa with USAAF aircraft."[5] However, the delay caused by the need to assemble the Waco gliders meant that there was a hold-up of several weeks in starting training, beginning with conversion to the new glider, resulting in "a last minute operational rush" to complete night flying training.[6] A message was sent back to England requesting that night flying training be completed there, but apparently

3   Museum of Army Chaplaincy Archives, an account by Revd Geoffrey Harper.
4   Museum of Army Chaplaincy Archives, an account by Revd R. Watkins.
5   TNA CAB 106/687 – report on the operations of the 1st Airborne Brigade in the invasion of Sicily, p.9.
6   *Ibid.*

this was not possible, as the next batch of glider pilots arrived in June without night landing training. As there was then no time to complete such training, they could only be used as second pilots.

Doubts had been expressed about the role of 1st Air Landing Brigade. Major General Hopkinson, commander of the 1st Airborne Division, had pressed hard for the inclusion of a glider-borne force. Lieutenant Colonel George Chatterton, the British glider pilots commander, had attempted to warn Hopkinson and Montgomery of the dangers of such an operation, but was threatened with dismissal. At the end of the conversation he decided to comply: "I finally made up my mind that I must stand by the men, despite the fact that I considered the plan to be mad."[7]

He recalled in later years that the popular 'Hoppy' Hopkinson had "sold" an airborne landing to Montgomery, who knew even less then Hopkinson of the required conditions for success. However, Hopkinson seemed determined that the time had come for the deployment of airborne troops by glider and was not to be deterred by opinions such as those of Group Captain T.B. Cooper, who advised Montgomery that a complicated glider landing at night with inexperienced aircrew was not practical, but to no avail. Cooper had argued that the British glider pilots were not experienced with Wacos or with night towing.

Victor Miller, a glider pilot who had arrived by sea, described the flying training experienced by the pilots as they grew accustomed to their Waco gliders: "The Waco was an entirely new machine to us. Opinion varied, but on the whole we were satisfied with its appearance ... training flying was, however, considerably restricted by the small number of gliders and towing aircraft available." However, in June he commented:

> We had mastered the technique of flying her under all circumstances, although I must say that we never did, in my opinion, undergo sufficient operational training including mass landings by day or night ... not once did we carry [out] a night landing exercise with more than two gliders. This undoubtedly contributed to the failure of the Sicilian landings, which were carried out at night.[8]

Padre 'Joe' Downing arrived at Oran with the 4th Battalion on 23 April. The captain of the ship they were on liked to broadcast over the tannoy that they were approaching port and broadcast a short prayer of thanksgiving for a safe journey, and if a padre was on board he was asked to do this. On this occasion Downing recalled the captain announced "'I am asking the padre to come to the microphone and say a prayer of thanks for a safe journey' ... I was sitting on the lavatory at the time and I made what

---

7   Conversation quoted by M. Peters, *Glider Pilots in Sicily* (Barnsley: Pen & Sword, 2012), p.52.
8   Victor Miller, *Nothing is Impossible: A Glider Pilot's Story of Sicily, Arnhem and the Rhine Crossing* (Barnsley: Pen & Sword, 2015), p.43.

speed I could, but before I emerged the voice came over again 'where's the bloody padre?' I have always regretted not having a microphone to reply 'on the Bl**** ***'."[9]

Between 19 June and July, the 1st Airborne Division moved to M'saken, a small village between Sousse and Kairouan, 1,200km away from their base at Mascara. The Kairouan area consisted of 18 airstrips set in a sparse and dusty area. The orders confirming Operation Ladbroke were given on 6 July 6 and the 1st Air Landing Brigade was to be given the prestigious but dangerous task of being the first Allied troops to land in Nazi-occupied Europe. On 8 July Montgomery visited the airborne troops and gave a morale-boosting speech. Watkins described Monty's tactics:

> He did a quick drive round; it appeared perfunctory, but those steely eyes missed nothing. Then he drove to the middle. "Break it up, boys. We don't want this, do we?" The troops broke ranks and crowded round his jeep. Monty spoke his informal, but carefully prepared piece. "Any questions?" Of course there were none, and off he went. Everyone thought this was wonderful; he was a great chap; he was one of us. This was Monty's standard act, a carefully prepared parade with bags of bull, laid on to his standards; he knew it would be good and needed no inspecting; he broke it up as an irrelevance, and spoke quite simply, but with every word prepared, and went off leaving every private Snooks convinced that here at last was a General who cared.[10]

On 9 July the 1st Parachute Brigade was briefed for Operation Fustian.

Senior chaplain Harper described the days spent preparing and training here: "Regular training of the glider borne troops was carried out route marching in full kit … in the heat of the desert." In a letter to Abram after the war he described a lighter incident: "Being a parachutist yourself you will appreciate that in that very hot climate, and particularly in the afternoon when the heat was at its greatest, many chaps having jumped just floated about 'up there'. I have often watched this and experienced everyone's amusement. Some went 'up' and only came down by spilling their chutes. You can imagine the fun of all this." Harper prepared his chaplains for the assault on Sicily by holding meetings in which they discussed their likely part, also discussing technical topics such as requirements for burial. On the final morning before the 1st Air Landing Brigade took off, Harper held a communion service for his chaplains.[11] Watkins noted in his diary that he took five unit services and three communion services spread over the few days before operations.

It was decided by the chaplains that whatever they would do for their own people they would do for men of other denominations. Padre D.F. Hourigan (Roman Catholic) spoke Italian and was requested by the commanding officer to go with the

---

9   E.N. Downing, *Padre with the Paras* (privately published).
10   Museum of Army Chaplaincy Archives, R. Watkins, *World War Two Memoiris 1939-1945*.
11   Museum of Army Chaplaincy Archives, letter from G. Harper to Paul Abram.

brigade's headquarters as an interpreter. Senior chaplain Harper agreed to this so long as Hourigan was allowed to wear his dog collar, a Red Cross armband and the chaplain's blue armband with 'chaplain' on it.

On the evening of 9 July, 2,000 men in Hadrian and Horsa gliders towed by Dakotas from the US 51st Wing took off in bad weather. The objective was to land near to and then capture by midnight the Ponte Grande, a bridge over both a river and canal just south of Syracuse, then during the night occupy Syracuse town which Eighth Army units would reach before 11:00 a.m. At 6:48 p.m. the 1st Landing Brigade, commanded by Brigadier Philip Hicks, started to take off. The brigade was in eight Airspeed Horsas and 135 Waco Hadrians.[12] The brigade consisted of the 1st Battalion, The Border Regiment; 2nd Battalion, South Staffordshire Regiment; 181st Air Landing Field Ambulance and 8th Field Company Royal Engineers. The Horsas were towed by seven Halifaxes and one Albemarle, and the Wacos by 109 C47 Dakotas and 27 Albemarles. The glider pilots were all from the Glider Pilot Regiment, supplemented by 24 USSAF glider pilots. Of the tug pilots, 109 were from the USAAF Troop Carrier Wing.

Eight Horsas carried A and C Companies of the 2nd Battalion, South Staffordshire Regiment, with sappers from the 9th Field Company. In the remaining gliders were the 1st Battalion of the Border Regiment, 181st Air Landing Field Ambulance and 9th Company, Royal Engineers. The Staffordshires were scheduled to land a the bridge and take it in a *coup de main* operation at 11:15 p.m., and the Borderers to capture Syracuse. The remainder of the brigade would land at a variety of landing zones (LZs) a few miles from the bridge and then gather at the bridge to defend it.

Victor Miller was clear about his role after the briefing: "We were to release at 1300 feet about half a mile offshore, glide in over the coast to one side of a jutting headland and set down in the field allotted to us." Miller described the tension; he was sweating profusely and the men of the gun crew, although enthusiastic, were, he suspected, under "severe mental strain": "This was the first airborne attempt on a large scale ever to be made by the British, and the degree of success could only be guessed."[13]

The American aircrews were inexperienced and only had a navigator in the lead aircraft of each section. They were not used to flak, and as their planes were unarmoured and unarmed they had been told to release their gliders 3,000 yards from the coastline to avoid heavy anti-aircraft fire. However, the weather conditions led them to underestimate the distance, and 73 of the 144 gliders landed in the sea, many drowned, and those who made it ashore had lost their supplies and weapons.[14] Mike Peters has described the scene: "A combination of inexperienced tug crews, enemy flak, searchlights, high winds and treacherous terrain had caused havoc among the

---

12 Peters, *Glider Pilots in Sicily*, p.132.
13 Victor Miller, *Nothing is impossible*, p.57.
14 Peters, *Glider Pilots in Sicily*, p.145.

glider formations, with many gliders ripped apart in the landing in the darkness and scattered miles from their planned LZs."[15]

Coming under fire on the approach, half the gliders were dropped short in the sea and the rest were widely scattered over some inhospitable country side. Padre John Rowell, chaplain to the 1st Border Regiment, described that having spotted the faint lights of Malta they could see the flak at Syracuse. When the glider he was in still seemed a long way off, the tug pilot signalled to cast off. It became clear that they would not reach the shore, so they prepared for ditching in the sea: "As soon as we hit the water, we were jumping out into the sea and then clinging onto the wings of the Waco." The glider was weighed down with a handcart and settled low in the water, but the wings and tail were above the surface. Everything that could weigh them down was jettisoned, even their boots:

> The men remained in good spirits, and some wanted to swim for the shore, but we must have been a good five miles from land. We felt that if the glider floated until dawn we had a good chance of being picked up. We joined in saying the Lord's Prayer and through the night kept up an endless conversation so that we should not fall asleep.[16]

Rowell's glider was picked up by HMS *Beaufort*, but the men on other gliders that had been dropped too early were not so lucky. Rowell's regiment suffered 250 casualties, mainly from drowning. Rowell had many letters to send to next of kin: "The work was not made any easier by the fact that so many men had been needlessly drowned."[17]

The 56 gliders that had landed on Sicily were widely scattered, most of them some way from their landing zones, but individual groups of men used their initiative and took aggressive action against the enemy wherever they found themselves. They gave the impression to the enemy that the whole airborne force had landed, thereby helping to ensure that the seaborne forces landed to less opposition.[18]

Harper had been given permission to go in Major General Hopkinson's glider but was not allowed at the last minute, and had to go on the towing Dakota. Harper helped the inexperienced pilot by lying down and looking out of the side door with the navigator, shouting instructions, but the glider was still dropped too early and landed in the sea. Harper recalled:

> I went to Sicily in the aircraft towing the General's glider. We flew on a map showing the coast of North Africa and the island of Sicily. When we approached Sicily and we could see it, the navigator remarked "well I guess we are nearly

15 *Ibid*, p.158.
16 Museum of Army Chaplaincy Archives, an account by Revd John Rowell.
17 *Ibid*.
18 G.G. Norton, *The Red Devils (Famous regiments)* (London: Leo Cooper, 1984), p.18.

there". He then went to the door in the side of the plane, opened it, lay down on his stomach with his map and shouted instructions to the pilot! I actually lay with him! When we got within the flak of Sicily the crew panicked and I suppose just cast off the glider. And down went the general.[19]

The glider landed in the sea and the men were luckily picked up by a destroyer. Hopkinson commanded the battle from Malta by radio link from Britain as the airborne powerful transmitters had gone into the sea.

The Revd Alan Buchanan, the chaplain to the 2nd Battalion, South Staffordshires, came down in Sicily but a long way from the LZ with a group of his men, and was captured by Italian troops. However, he managed to find an Italian soldier who spoke English, told him that they were surrounded by British troops and persuaded his captors to surrender. According to an account in the *The Cornishman* newspaper, "he had no idea where the nearest British party was and simply walked around with his flock of Italians following him until they encountered some of our troops".[20] A small fire fight ensued when they did find a British party, but Buchanan managed to run from one side to the other, pacifying both sides. He rejoined his unit, but not in time to reach the target, the Ponte Grande. A letter from Richard Duneman to Paul Abram after the war recalled him burying bodies from a Horsa that had exploded near Ponte Grande: "Alan gave a prayer over each body."[21]

In a letter to Paul Abram in 1972, Major General Roy Urquhart, who commanded the 231st Infantry Brigade Group in Sicily and went on to command the 1st Airborne Division at Arnhem, said of Buchanan: "I think you ought to make more of Buchanan in your story. To me he was one of the more outstanding padres. He did more than any other individual in the resuscitation of the South Staffordshires after their experiences in the Sicily operation. You will know that that unit lost many lives from drowning when they flew into Sicily."[22] Bob Boyce, who was a glider pilot during the war and later became ordained, remembered how Buchanan celebrated Holy Communion on the airstrip before the glider force set off for Sicily: "He invited everyone irrespective of denomination or even Christian affiliation to receive the sacrament. As one of the latter it is still a memorable moment, although it took me until 1953 before I was confirmed." After the Sicily landing, Boyce went to see Buchanan to seek advice on how to comfort the parents of a friend of his who was missing and whose body was never found. He said of Buchanan: "He was a very sensitive man and a first

---

19 Museum of Army Chaplaincy Archives, an account by Revd Geoffrey Harper.
20 *The Cornishman*, 5 October 1944, p.7.
21 Museum of Army Chaplaincy Archives, letter from Richard Duneman to Paul Abram, 27 October 1971.
22 Museum of Army Chaplaincy Archives, letter from General Roy Urquhart to Paul Abram, June 1972.

rate padre."[23] Harper also considered that Buchanan had performed well: "He was incredible and his men really loved him. I was told that in the awful muddle of the landing of the South Staffs the chaps were far more worried as to where their chaplain was than where they were."[24]

Fr David Hourigan landed in a Waco glider, Glider No 10, which made a hair-raising but lucky landing, just reaching landfall on a cliff after an approach low over the sea. The glider contained some of the brigade's HQ staff, with whom Hourigan was landing as interpreter, including the brigade's deputy commander, Colonel Osmond Jones. Close by was the coastal battery which was the brigade objective. They moved toward the battery during the night and, realising that no one had yet taken it, the seven senior officers and 10 soldiers took it in a daylight attack. It is not certain at which stage in the landing and moving inland Hourigan was taken prisoner, but he was killed deliberately by a grenade during the night in circumstances which amounted to murder. Apparently, because of his fluent Italian the Italians thought that he was an Italian who had joined the enemy. In an account of this incident which he wrote after the war, senior chaplain Harper revealed that he had contacted witnesses:

> Sometime after his death an R.C. [Roman Catholic] Officer – whose name escapes me, came to me and asked if I would write an account of what had happened as he wanted to get it through to the Vatican. David was a Roman Catholic Priest killed by Roman Catholics, and this very naturally riled the officer … I therefore got in contact with some of the men who were with David when he was killed.

He discovered that Hourigan, along with about four others, were allowed to see to the wounded after capture and then spent the night in a gun emplacement: "During the night one of the chaps was awakened by a bloke coming into this 'room' and this man apparently placed a grenade on David's chest and a few seconds later it blew David more or less to bits." Harper was told that this happened because Hourigan could speak such excellent Italian he was thought a fifth columnist who had landed with the British forces. In Harper's opinion, Hourigan was, "A most wonderful priest, devoted in every way. I am proud to have known him and hope some 'day' we will meet again."[25] A letter was written to the Father Provincial after Fr Hourigan's death by a Jewish chaplain who said that "Alone out of all the officers Fr Hourigan treated him with friendliness and many acts of cooperation and kindness which had left an indelible impression on his mind."[26]

23   Museum of Army Chaplaincy Archives, letter from Bob Boyce, 17 April 1999. Boyce was ordained in 1982 and took part in services at reunions of the Glider Pilots Association.
24   Museum of Army Chaplaincy Archives, an account by Revd Geoffrey Harper.
25   Museum of Army Chaplaincy Archives, an account by Revd Geoffrey Harper.
26   Salesian College Magazine 1943 p. 79 quoted by Tom Johnstone and James Hagerty in *The Cross on the Sword: Catholic Chaplains in the Forces* (London: Geoffrey Chapman, 1996)

Only one Horsa, No 15, with a platoon of Staffords infantry landed near the bridge. Its commander, Lieutenant Withers, divided his men into two groups, one of which swam across the river and took up position on the opposite bank. Thereafter the bridge was captured following a simultaneous assault from both sides. The Italian defenders from the 120th Coastal Infantry Regiment abandoned their pill boxes on the north bank. The attackers were reinforced by the occupants of other Horsas that had landed nearby, but at the point there were only 87 men at the bridge. At 6:30 a.m. Colonel A.G. Walch and some men from the 1st Borders, 2nd South Staffordshires and some glider pilots arrived, and Walch took command. Reinforcements arrived in groups all day, but lack of ammunition resulted in the whole force being withdrawn to a position east of the bridge. As mortar fire increased, the casualty rate grew considerably. When the last men holding the bridge ran out of ammunition, the bridge was retaken by enemy forces. However, they had managed to occupy it long enough to prevent it being destroyed, and 20 minutes later Eighth Army units arrived and were able to drive their tanks over the bridge and recapture it. Padre Rowell reported that Montgomery said in his message to 1st Landing Brigade: "Had it not been for the skill and gallantry of the air landing brigade the port of Syracuse would not have fallen until much later."[27]

Meanwhile, the 1st Parachute Brigade was also planning an operation in Sicily, and during June the 1st and 2nd Parachute Battalions had been moved from Mascara to Sousse.

The training scheme devised for the men at Sousse was rigorous, with reveille at 5:30 a.m. for an early run or forced march. After breakfast, admin and housekeeping chores were completed until lunchtime. To alleviate the boredom of inactivity in the heat of the day, the men often took to sea bathing in the afternoon. The conditions at the tented camps were difficult, with strong warm winds depositing a layer of sand over everything, including food. Water was rationed to a pint a day, and as a consequence strict regulations on washing and shaving were not enforced. Flies were also a constant problem. During this time, several exercises were carried out in preparation for the attack on the bridges.

The task of the 2nd Brigade was to attack a bridge south-west of Augusta and capture the town. The attack was planned for 10 July, and their padre, 'Joe' Downing, planned three short services with each unit before they went into action, as he recounted: "In the morning therefore I sped around my three charges, brigade HQ, the Sappers and the battalion, racing the 'Matchless' motor cycle which was then the chaplain's only transport. As I came finally to where the battalion was lined up and waiting I sailed along with cassock flying and, did a beautiful skid in the deep sand and sat down in it."[28] The skid ended dramatically at the feet of the commanding officer, Lieutenant Colonel J.A. Dene. However, the brigade's attack was stood down twice,

p.213.
27   Museum of Army Chaplaincy Archives, an account by Revd John Rowell.
28   E.N. Downing, *Padre with the Paras* (private publication, undated), p.37.

and was eventually cancelled as the Allied troops had made good progress on their way to Augusta and the operation was no longer necessary. Downing remembered the reaction of the men to this cancellation: "Never before or since, have I encountered such a stygian atmosphere of disappointment and gloom."

Operation Fustian – the taking of Primosole bridge

The job of the 1st Parachute Brigade was to attack the Ponte de Primosole to slow down enemy reinforcement of Catania. This action had been devised several months before in the early stages of the planning for Operation Husky. The 1st Parachute Brigade, commanded by Brigadier Gerald Lathbury, consisted of the the 1st, 2nd and 3rd Parachute Battalions, the 16th (Parachute) Field Ambulance, the 1st (Parachute) Squadron, Royal Engineers, and the 1st (Airlanding) Anti-Tank Battery, Royal Artillery. These units, some 1,856 men in all, were to be dropped to take the bridge, which was the only one over the River Simento. They were to land close to bridge, which two platoons of 1st Battalion with the 1st Field Squadron of the Royal Engineers were to take by *coup de main* and hold, while the 2nd and 3rd Battalions held the northern and southern approaches. The remainder of the 1st Battalion would then organise defences. The brigade was tasked with defending the bridge until the British XIII Corps arrived.

At the same time, No 3 Commando was to seize the Ponte Dei Malati bridge over the River Leonardo. The capture of these two bridges would open the way to Catania for the Allied troops. The paratroopers' heavier weapons comprised 10 6-pdr anti-tank guns (with 77 men) in 16 gliders towed by Handley Page Halifax aircraft and Albemarles of the British 295 and 296 Squadrons. The 21st Independent Parachute Company was to precede the force to mark the glider LZs and position Eureka-Rebecca radio beacons for the drop zones. There were only two chaplains with the brigade, as Roy Price had been invalided out with malaria and Alistair Menzies had been posted to the 4th Parachute Brigade. Watkins and Bernard Egan had to take services for all the units, and in the days before the operation Watkins took five unit services and three communions. The brigade major, Major D.R. Hunter, remembers Watkins saying: "There are no atheists in slit trenches."[29]

Watkins was to be attached to the field ambulance, which on landing was to quickly create the path of casualty clearance from the bridge to the ambulance casualty area. Watkins pointed out that this was the first time a field ambulance was to operate behind enemy lines, equipped for full surgical operations, as casualties could not be evacuated and had to be kept and treated. At 8:00 p.m. on 13 July, 133 aircraft carrying paratroopers and 19 tug /glider combinations took off. The 51st US Troop Carrier Wing would carry the British troops, with some 1,856 men in 105 of its Douglas C-47 transport aircraft. They were aided by 11 British Albemarles from the

---

29   Museum of Army Chaplaincy Archives, letter from D.R. Hunter, 8 February 1971.

RAF's 38th Wing. The gliders were transporting 77 men of the 1st (Airlanding) Anti-Tank Battery, R.A., with their anti-tank guns and 18 jeeps. Significantly, after the problems experienced in Operation Ladbroke, RAF planes were towing the gliders.

The planned flight time was 2½ to 3½ hours.

Watkins and Egan were with their sticks in the close confines of the aircraft. Some men slept, others quietly contemplated their tasks, while some laughed and joked and sang songs to relieve the tension. The side winds and thermals experienced over the Mediterranean meant quite a few were airsick, the smell of vomit adding to the claustrophobic atmosphere. On their approach the aircraft were fired on by Allied ships and Axis flak. Twenty-six aircraft returned to their bases without dropping their loads. Thirty-nine aircraft managed to drop their loads near the DZs and 48 dropped them from 880yds to 20 miles short. Four of the gliders landed on target and seven others were scattered more or less at random, so there were only 10 anti-tank guns available for action. Lieutenant Colonel Alastair Pearson, the 1st Battalion commander, had to resort to threatening the pilot of his plane with a revolver to get him to approach the Drop Zone. There seemed to be problem with the speed at which the aircraft was approaching. Pearson thought it was coming in too quickly:

> I thought we were going in too fast. We seemed to be going downhill as well. Out I went over the DZ, and I didn't think my chute had opened, because I was down on the deck as soon as I jumped. I had gone out no 10, my knees hurt but I was all right; my batman at number 11 was all right but the remainder of the stick suffered serious injuries or were killed.[30]

Knowing that their American pilots were inexperienced and had been unnerved by the friendly fire encountered on Operation Ladbroke a few day previously, the stick commanders decided to stand behind them until they were satisfied that they were over the right DZs. Watkins was to drop with stick two of the headquarters contingent of the 16th Field Ambulance, and was stick commander for his aircraft. The battalion had heard about the earlier incidents, and although he was in an RAF Albemarle, with RAF navigators, he decided to take no chances. On the night of the 13th, every officer who was in charge of a stick stood behind the pilot all the way until he was satisfied:

> I was stick commander for my plane. Although this was one of the few RAF Albemarles on the job I was taking no chances. Instead of going No 1, as I usually would, with a sergeant last, I reversed this. I stood unhooked in the cockpit for most of the journey.[31]

30 *Operation Fustian: Airborne assault on the bridges to Catania.* Warfare of History Network, posted 25 December 2018, https://warfarehistorynetwork.com/tag/operation-fustian/.
31 Watkins, *World War Two Memoirs 1939-1945.*

The aircraft experienced heavy friendly fire from the Royal Navy over the Sicilian coast. Watkins' aircraft took evasive action and he realised that they had crossed the coast at too high an altitude; he was alarmed to see Mt Etna immediately below him, and was able to look straight down the spout of the volcano. Placing his hand over the pilots's button that indicated jumping, Watkins persuaded the pilot to go out to sea and try again. On the second run in, the aircraft experienced flak from an Italian anti-aircraft gun situated at the mouth of the Simento River and one of the men was wounded in the leg through the floor of the Albemarle. However, the men from Watkins' stick came down in the right place, and on his return Watkins made his peace with the pilot by congratulating him on his skill at the second drop attempt.

Four DZs were planned: two north of the Primosole Bridge beside the Simento and and two to the south on the steep banks of the Gornulunga Canal which joined the Simento just above the bridge. A fifth LZ for one of the gliders was close to the southern edge of the bridge itself. However, of the aircraft that survived the run in, only 39 managed to drop their sticks in the correct place. Some landed as far away as the lower slopes of Mt Etna, 20 miles away.

Only 12 officers and 283 other ranks were left out of a total of 1,856 all ranks that had started the operation. Approximately 170 all ranks of the 2nd Parachute Battalion managed to rendezvous at 2:15 a.m., and when no more men appeared they set off to attack the bridge. By 5:00 a.m. they were in control of the high ground south of the bridge, then German parachutists who had machine guns and mortars intervened. Heavy fighting involving the German *Fallschirmjäger*, who had just arrived in the theatre, ensued, but men of the 1st Parachute Battalion managed to seize the bridge before the demolition charges could be activated and set up a defensive perimeter. Only four gliders had landed intact, but they brought three anti-tank guns to help defend the precarious hold on the bridge. A forward observation officer from 1st Airlanding Light Regiment managed to draw down fire from a British cruiser. During the day of 14 July, the attacks on the position at the bridge intensified, and at 5:00 p.m. Brigadier Lathbury made the decision to retreat, giving up the bridge.

Upon landing, after smearing himself with mosquito cream, Watkins set out to find the medical dressing station that had been set up in a farm 2,000yds south of the bridge. The anti-tank gunners had been flown in by Horsa gliders close by. Watkins described how one crash-landed and the heavy gun broke loose, killing or maiming the men in the glider. On the way to the field ambulance, Watkins and two medical orderlies came across a crashed Horsa. Just before he reached the glider, it was attacked by machine-gun fire from across the river and burst into flames. Watkins and the two orderlies were able to drag out two wounded men, but the rest were trapped and it would not be long before the ammunition exploded. Watkins was carrying morphia, and all he could do was go back to the burning glider, at great risk to his own life, and relieve the pain of the trapped men by injecting them with the morphia: "I left the orderlies to cope as best they could and went back into that glider alone."[32]

---

32   Watkins, *World War Two Memoirs 1939-1945*.

Watkins, having arrived at the farm, set out to find the battalion's medical officer, Captain M.H.K. Haggie, in order to arrange a route from the bridge to the field ambulance at the farm. He undertook the duties of a liaison officer with the brigade and proceeded to inform the brigadier of the situation at the Main Dressing Station (MDS).[33] Later, he concentrated on moving wounded to the farm where the 16th Parachute Field Ambulance was situated. In the afternoon he was helping carry in wounded on stretchers and whatever else could be used, and had the disconcerting experience of being followed by a sniper as he moved from cover to cover: "Later in the day I was followed as I moved from cover to cover by a sniper, he had several near misses and I did not enjoy it. It is one thing to be under fire; it is another to know that you personally are the target."[34] Lieutenant Colonel P.R. Wheatly RAMC stated in the summary of events in the 16th Field Ambulance diary: "Reverend Watkins reported from Brigade HQ that the situation was very grave and that the brigade intended to withdraw from the bridge at dusk."[35] When Brigadier Lathbury gave the order for the 1st and 3rd Battalions to withdraw to the 2nd Battalion's position on the high ground a mile from the bridge, the field ambulance was left dangerously exposed. Wheatly ordered groups of walking wounded, with surplus staff, to join the main force or to form laagers in a quiet place. Watkins, with the RSM, was in charge of a group of 14, who, having settled in a quiet gully, were surprised by a group of about 50 Italians, who appeared to be nonplussed by the presence of the British wounded. Watkins and his party were now prisoners, but gradually the Italian lost interest in them, leaving them to be guarded by an officer and just three men, while the rest positioned themselves at the head of the gully. Watkins and the RSM began to make plans to engineer the escape of their party. About midnight, heavy fire distracted the Italians and the British wounded took the opportunity to attack their guards with large stones. Watkins attacked the officer and felled him. He later described the officer as bearded and smelling heavily of cologne! He wrote in his diary: "My own share in this was not exactly RAChD style. I belted the officer and then to shut him up went for a couple of pressure points which would settle the lash of any man "[36] The following day the walking wounded, some of whom needed quite a lot of help, made their way back to the British lines at Lentini, joining forces with some parachutists who had been dropped wide of their targets.

Roman Catholic padre Bernard Egan had been in one of the sticks that had been dropped wide. His parachute had been holed with bullets as he descended and he stood no chance of getting to the bridge. He joined up with some men who had also dropped wide, and they spent four days and nights hiding in a dried-up water

33 N. Cherry, *Red Berets and Red Crosses: The Story of the Medical Services in the 1st Airborne Division in World War Two* (Renkum: R.N. Sigmond, 1999), p.58.
34 Watkins, *World War Two Memoirs 1939-1945.*
35 TNA WO177/701, War Diary 16 Parachute Field Ambulance.
36 Watkins, *World War Two Memoirs 1939-1945.*

course near a road which enemy vehicles were using constantly. Three Germans parked their truck near where Egan and the men lay, and relieved themselves into the gully. Luckily they missed them, and they were not discovered. Egan and the three men then managed to get back through British artillery fire to their own lines. Watkins considered that action deserved great credit as a lesser man might well have surrendered. Egan was later given the MC for his actions in Sicily and previously at Djebel Mansour in Tunisia. Egan later modestly summed up his action in Sicily: "Sicily, as far as I was concerned was useless. We were dropped in the wrong place and saw nothing of the action."[37]

After recapturing the Primosole bridge, the enemy force was reinforced by men from the 1st *Fallschirmjäger* Artillery Regiment. Early on 15 July, tanks and infantry from XIII Corps arrived, and the 1st Parachute Brigade and 50th Northumberland Division moved forward to attack the bridge again. During the day, after repeated assaults, the Durham Light Infantry managed to dig in on the southern end of the bridge. Meanwhile, the 1st Parachute Battalion managed to cross the Simento at a shallow point and established a position on the northern bank. The parachute brigade was transported back to Syracuse and sailed for Valetta on 17 July. During the operation they had suffered 141 fatalities, with 168 missing or wounded.

Watkins' appraisal of Lieutenant Colonel Pearson - the 28-year-old commander of the 1st Battalion of the Parachute Regiment - who was invalided home with malaria, illustrates the respect and confidence that could grow up between a commanding officer and his chaplain:

> Pearson was not a religious man in the ordinary way, but he knew that I was there to contribute to the well being and efficiency of his battalion. My Padre's Hours were wide-ranging; I had the *Manchester Guardian* weekly and the *Sunday Times* sent out to me, and I talked about the Beveridge Report [which was influential in founding the welfare state] and anything else that would set men thinking. Pearson sometimes dropped in and took part. He was all for Sunday services and in the field my family prayers. He slung welfare problems at me. It could be said that a canny pagan was using me and this is true. However it is not all the truth … out of that relationship of respect there came a situation when he and I were able to talk freely, unalike as we were. He came to trust me and my assessment of affairs and I trusted him. I could not have had a happier relationship with a commanding officer than I did with him.[38]

---

37 Museum of Army Chaplaincy Archives, letter from Revd B. Egan to Paul Abram, 11 November 1971.
38 Museum of Army Chaplaincy Archives, papers deposited by Revd P.R.C. Abram CVO. Typescript, *Lower Than the Angels* (1975), p.39.

The gratitude of chaplains to their commanding officers worked both ways, as a letter from Brigadier Edwin Flavell, CO of the 1st Parachute Brigade, sent to Abram shows: "No commander could have been better served by his chaplains and with this all units agreed and added more praise."[39]

The whole division now rested at Sousse and licked its wounds. Padre Buchanan met up with Revd Arnold Pare, who had just arrived from England, and together they travelled to Tripoli to visit the airborne wounded in hospital there. Watkins, armed with air mail letter forms and cigarettes, also set out to find them, a journey of 700 miles: "I toured all the hospitals in that area and found a lot of our folk and was able to assess their prospects. A known face from far away was welcome to them."[40] The padres had a great deal of visiting to do at Sousse, as many men were suffering from malaria and yellow jaundice. There was not much training and the men relaxed with sea bathing, while the padres organised a canteen in the olive groves. Dances were arranged, with nurses in attendance, and some light-hearted competitions and games, such as a donkey race for the commanding officers and a greasy pole challenge for the RSMs.

On 3 September the British Army landed in the toe of Italy for an advance to the Adriatic coast, followed by an American landing at Salerno. On 6 September Major General Hopkinson received orders that the 1st Parachute Division's battalions were to be ready to take part in a seaborne landing at Taranto, led by the 2nd and 3rd Brigades, with the 1st Brigade in reserve. On the way by ship, on 9 September, they heard that Italy had surrendered.

Padre John Rowell sailed to Italy with the Borderers with the Airlanding Brigade on HMS *Sirius* and enjoyed catching up with the ship's chaplain, Martyn Harvey, with whom he had been at school. On the way they saw the Italian fleet steaming to Alexandria to surrender. Rowell held a service on the journey which was attended, to his pleasure, by the glider pilots on board. They eventually landed at Taranto with no opposition.

The 6th Parachute Battalion had sailed on the minelayer HMS *Abdiel*, which was waiting to enter Taranto harbour at 11:00 p.m. on 9 September. The troops were ready to disembark, when at about midnight there was a large explosion. The *Abdeil* had hit a mine and the explosion detonated the mines on board, splitting the ship in two. It sank within two minutes.

On board was Fr Gerard Bankes, who had originally been told by the commander of the 127th Parachute Field Ambulance that he would have to wait until the second wave, but Bankes negotiated going with the first wave on condition he drove an ambulance. When HMS *Abdiel* exploded, Bankes was thrown into the air and came to lying on a gun turret on the opposite side of the ship. About 12ft from him, he saw

---

39   Museum of Army Chaplaincy Archives, letter from Brigadier E.W.C. Flavell to Paul Abram, 17 December 1971.
40   Watkins, *World War Two Memoirs 1939-1945.*

a jeep, a dead driver at its wheel, sliding down toward him, and all that prevented it from pinning him to the turret was a light guard rail. Fr Bankes desperately tried to move, but his legs were trapped. Fear gave him strength and he jerked his legs clear. Three times he tried to climb up the sloping steel deck, but his studded boots would not grip and he slid back, so he made his way along the side of the turret and eventually came to the side of the ship about 12ft above the water.

Bankes jumped into the sea and was surrounded by oil, which made his eyes smart as he gulped for air, moving away from patches of fire. He inflated his life jacket and started to swim for the side of a ship, where he was rescued and hauled aboard. Three months later he rejoined the2nd Parachute Brigade.

The 1st Airborne Division lost 58 dead in the incident, almost all from the 6th Battalion, and around 150 injured, while 48 of the ship's crew were also lost. There was an unconfirmed report that the ship's degaussing equipment, which would have helped protect it from mines, had been turned off to reduce noise and to allow troops to sleep better.

Members of the 1st Battalion, who came In the second wave, retrieved the bodies and arrange their burial. Watkins, Pare, Buchanan and Harper were involved in dealing with the mutilated and bloated corpses, and Harper, as senior chaplain, organised a military cemetery at Taranto.

As the 1st Airborne Division pushed forward, Padre 'Jock' Robertson found himself in what Harper described as "an Italian town perched high on a hill". On the way there, Robertson had buried a man by the side of the road. Later, some of the people of the town, hearing of this, came to him and insisted that the body be moved to be buried in the town. The townsfolk came with the town band and during a procession back into town they played 'God Save The King' and a slow march.

Robertson, who was given an enormous welcome by the people and the local clergy, recalled: "A right royal welcome on the steps of the cathedral." The delegation consisted of the all the local priests and the bishop.[41] Robertson, a Presbyterian padre, was offered the cathedral for a service, which he accepted. Harper recounted: "He was given ornate vestments to wear and then proceeded to take the service. The locals were surprised that this strange priest took the service with his back to the Altar and spent a long time in the pulpit."[42] Harper was told to reprimand Robertson severely for using a Roman Catholic church, but he commented: "I must say I sympathised with his action." Harper faced a similar dilemma when the divisional commander ordered him to take a service in the Roman Catholic church in Goia del Colle. But in the end Harper managed to arrange for a large cinema to be used and to convince the commander that this held more men.

The division advanced as far north as Foggia, Rowell being present with the Borderers. In October the 1st Airborne Division was recalled to Britain, travelling

---

41   Museum of Army Chaplaincy Archives, an account by Revd Geoffrey Harper.
42   *Ibid.*

home via Taranto and North Africa. They left behind Major General Hopkinson, who had been struyck in the head by machine-gun fire while observing the battle to take Castellaneta, near Taranto, on 9 September and died the next day.[43] Senior chaplain Harper was close by, and before he died the general was able to recognise and talk to him. It was then the chaplain's sad task to bury his general and friend in the cemetery at Taranto.

The chaplains accompanying the 1st Airborne Division in Sicily took part in the first use of an air landing force to take strategic targets behind enemy lines. They showed initiative and bravery, and suffered their first fatality in battle. They demonstrated their utilty both as a sounding board for commanders and for taking on leadership roles in the heat of battle.

43   Hopkinson was the only airborne general to be killed in the war.

4

The 6th Airborne Division in Normandy, Operation Overlord, 6 June to the end of August 1944

In the official history of the airborne forces in the Second World War, the author described their importance in planning for the Second Front, the invasion of Europe: "One thing soon became very clear. No successful invasion of Europe could take place without airborne forces able and ready to leap over Germany's vaunted west wall and thus bring its formidable forces to no account."[1] The 6th Airborne Division was formed in May 1943 and began to train for such a role. Glider training continued, and the ability to put ever larger formations in the air was developed.

In July 1943 the Revd J.J.A. Hodgins was transferred from his position as senior chaplain of the 1st Airborne Division to fill the same role with the newly formed 6th Airborne Division, and flew back to Britain to recruit chaplains to the division which was to be at the heart of operations on D-Day. Assisted by Padre John Gwinnett, chaplain to the 9th Battalion, Hodgins visited the chaplains school at Tidworth to find likely airborne chaplains. The recruiting drive attracted a young and vigorous team of prospective airborne chaplains, and no less than five of the 25 chaplains played in the division's rugby team (alas Hodgins, at 32, was too old). Brigadier James Hill also took an interest in the selection of chaplains for the 6th Airborne, and he and Gwinnett gave talks to the new intakes of chaplains. Gwinnett commented: "You can imagine what an impact James had … James was always a champion of the department and indeed to the church."[2]

At this stage in the development of the airborne divisions, all chaplains fully accepted the necessity of jumping, and in some cases were too keen. Padre Bill Briscoe, Roman Catholic chaplain to the 5th Parachute Brigade, was one of a selection of key people who had been forbidden to jump again before D-Day by Brigadier J.M. Poett. Shortly

---

1   *By Air to Battle, The Official Account of the British Airborne Divisions* (London: His Majesty's Stationery Office, 1945), p.7.
2   Museum of Army Chaplaincy Archives, letter from John Gwinnett to Paul Abram, 26 Novembe 1968.

before D-Day, Lieutenant Colonel Pine-Coffin, commanding the 7th Battalion, was at Netheravon, Wiltshire, inspecting a stick about to jump with a new kit bag. He went down the line of men, when an Irish voice said to him, "Not a word to the brigadier, Sir." Pine-Coffin was not surprised to see that it was Bill Briscoe sneaking in an unofficial jump.[3] A member of the 5th Parachute Brigade, Allan Brow, described Briscoe as "your typical Airborne 'Cadbury fruit and nutcase'", and added: "He was but [one of] a very long line of 'very special' padres the airborne had."[4]

One of the chaplains recruited into 6th Division was David Nimmo, a Church of Scotland minister who went for training at Hardwick Hall and Ringway. He recalled:

> It was a great day when we received our parachute wings ... but the one thing that really mattered to me as a chaplain was this - the airborne soldier looked upon his chaplain primarily as a member of the proud brotherhood to which he himself belonged, and accepted him and respected him as such. So the airborne padre was off to a "flying start". The men did not as it were, cross the street to avoid him when they saw him coming, they hailed him as a comrade, as one of themselves. This gave the chaplain a unique opportunity to do his job. He was much less hindered than parsons and priests usually are by common prejudices against men of the cloth [5]

Nimmo considered that:

> There was an excellent spirit among the chaplains of the 6th Airborne Division, for which much of the credit must go to our first senior chaplain, John Hodgins. So far as was possible he got us together every week to discuss and plan for our work in the division. There was no evidence of any denominationalism or nationalism. We worked with little regard for denominational distinction ... [the Padre's Hour] did much to help some of the men who came to unburden themselves of and talk over their private problems. Sometimes these were agonising and sometimes there was little light visible ... but it was often the beginning of finding out how to deal with it and we were always willing to lend an ear and help in any way we could.[6]

Paul Abram, in his work on the airborne padres, wrote that, "A man with a problem might not dream of going near a chaplain in barracks, but it was a different matter

---

3   Museum of Army Chaplaincy Archives, an account by General R.G. Pine-Coffin, November 1971.
4   Allan Brown, in Roger Payne, *PARA: Voices of the British Airborne Forces in the Second World War* (Stroud: Amberley Publishing, 2014), p.200.
5   Museum of Army Chaplaincy Archives, an account by the Revd David Nimmo, July 1971.
6   *Ibid.*

when they were just as tired on a route march."[7] He summed up the relationships formed: "War is a vile business and the chaplain is the key man in ensuring that soldiers retain their humanity, but to do this he must be with them."[8]

Revd Leslie Beckingham, a Baptist padre, had been appointed to the 6th Airborne Division in June 1943 and was training when the parachute of the man jumping in front of him did not open. Beckingham had to jump next. Later he had to break the news to the man's wife: "It was good to be able to tell her of the living Christ who could comfort and help as no other could."[9]

Beckingham, small and slight, showed the greatest determination in passing his selection tests, although he asserted that their terrors, especially those of the parachute course, were much reduced by the comradeship of the ordinary soldier. James Hill commented: "It always amazed me how such a small man, which physically he was, could obtain such a grip on the very tough Canadians whom we were lucky enough to have in the 3rd Parachute Brigade."[10] He was posted to the 8th Battalion and found that although he was concerned with his Baptist men, the strong ecumenical spirit which prevailed among airborne chaplains enabled him to cover the moral and spiritual needs of all the Protestants in the battalion.

Just before D-Day he learned that senior chaplain Revd G.A. Kay should drop with the 8th Battalion, and Beckingham was assigned to the 224th Parachute Field Ambulance. He had pestered 6th Airborne senior chaplain George Hales MC to be allowed to jump into Normandy, arguing that he had not been through the parachute course for nothing.[11] With the ambulance he worked with a few conscientious objectors who had volunteered to serve with the medical services: "Many of these were fine Christian lads with whom I found it a great privilege to serve and with whom fellowship was very real."[12] The function of the 224th Parachute Field Ambulance in Normandy was to treat and clear casualties of the 3rd Parachute Brigade in the area between the River Orne and River Dives. Beckingham considered carefully what his role as padre should be in these circumstances. He saw his task as "ministering to the wounded, giving moral strength to the sound and helping in any practical way possible to those in need". The padres had all been given instruction in first aid and had attended a week's course at Tidworth Military Hospital watching operations

7   Museum of Army Chaplaincy Archives, Airborne Chaplains papers deposited by Revd P.R.C. Abram CVO. Typescript, *Lower Than the Angels* (1975), p.62.
8   *Ibid.*
9   Pegasus Archive, account by A.L. Beckingham, courtesy of Hugo Mitchell, http://www.pegasusarchive.org/normandy/frames.htm.
10   Museum of Army Chaplaincy Archives, letter from Lieutenant Colonel James Hill to Paul Abram, 4 June 1971.
11   Museum of Army Chaplaincy Archives, letter from Revd John Gwinnett to Paul Abram, 26 November 1968.
12   Pegasus Archive, account by A.L. Beckingham, http://www.pegasusarchive.org/normandy/frames.htm.

being performed and becoming familiar with the help required by a surgeon in his work. In the days before D-Day, he was in a sealed camp at Down Ampney in Gloucestershire. He dismissed the idea that "men suddenly became spiritual", but he found that this was time when "there were many opportunities of talking to men seriously about God and life".[13]

Padre G.A. Harris, who was assigned to the Canadian Battalion, took a united service on the Sunday before D-Day, and in the evening organised a voluntary service which many attended. Major Darling, one of the surgeons of the field ambulance, gave a talk entitled 'Why I am a Christian', which, according to Beckingham, was very memorable.[14]Early in 1944, 'Boy' Browning of I Airborne Corps appointed Hales as senior chaplain to the 6th Airborne Division and Revd A.W. Harlow as senior chaplain to the 1st Airborne Division. Hales was 43 and had already served as a chaplain with distinction at the battle of El Alamein, where he won a Military Cross, and went on to accompany the Eighth Army in Sicily and Italy. As part of his training, Hales reported having made some "very unpleasant trips in Gliders".[15] Hales insisted, as his predecessor had done, that all his chaplains should receive medical training. He also continued the weekly chaplain meetings.

In the months leading up to D-Day, as well as concentrating on their role in future battles, the chaplains were busy with their pastoral and spiritual duties with the men. Commanding officers were mainly helpful and allowed regular Padre's Hours and services. Hales was surprised at the number of men who sought him out in his tent to talk about the future and their hopes and fears: "The most unlikely men wanted to talk about God ... most brave men are ready to go out hand in hand with God, although they would not put it like that and it is when they come to you just like that to talk and get some help that you feel that your job as chaplain is indeed worthwhile."[16] The padres were also involved in the moral welfare and morale of the men. When a man went absent without leave, it was often the padre's responsibility to help sort out the problem, and chaplains often travelled to talk to the wives and families of these men to iron out problems and difficulties.

Chaplains took part in the many and intensive training exercises, such as route marches, live firing and range exercises. They needed to make sure that they were as fit as the men they were to go to war with, and also continued to win the respect of the men as they shared their experiences to the full. John Gwinnett had accompanied his battalion on training exercise in Scotland. Under the leadership of Hales, the chaplains of the 6th Airborne Division were well prepared for D-Day.

Medical Officer John Binning with the 12th Battalion (the Devons) remembered an exercise in preparation for D-Day. On his way to the rendezvous point during the

13   *Ibid.*
14   *Ibid.*
15   Museum of Army Chaplaincy Archives, an account by Revd George Hales, July 1971.
16   *Ibid.*

exercise, he was tempted to call in on "a lovely old English Inn" but realised that he would get into trouble if he did. Battalion Headquarters began to gather at the RV (rendezvous point) and their padre, John Hall, was late in arriving. Binning recounted: "He had a most improbable story by way of an excuse. His jeep, he said, had broken down. This seemed quite possible, but that it should have broken down outside the most inviting hostelry was a piece of coincidence we all found difficult to believe."[17]

Padre John Gwinnett remembered rehearsing for D-Day with a model of the Merville battery at Hungerford. The postponement of D-Day due to bad weather allowed Gwinnett to take a parade service on the on the morning of 4 June. He organised a parade service for the 9th Battalion and half of the 1st Battalion at Broadwell in Gloucestershire, at which he dedicated a special flag made by the Women's Voluntary Service in Oxford. This flag was carried into battle by the men of the 9th Battalion.[18] Gwinnett took the following phrase as his text for the last service in England before their departure: 'Fear knocked at the door. Faith opened it and there was nothing there.' He described how those words kept recurring: "Mothers and fathers who had lost their sons or whose sons were missing were to write to me and tell me that their loved ones had incorporated those words into their last letters before emplaning. In the midst of the madness of war it was some comfort to know that these men whom I knew so well as individuals had listened and remembered."[19] Stuart Tootal, in his account of the 9th Battalion on D-Day, said of Gwinnett: "He was a paratrooper's vicar with an empathy for men and often overlooked their waywardness and the men loved him for it."[20] Private Ron Gregory described the atmosphere at Broadwell camp in the days before D-Day: "Life in transit was of unbelievable cramp, non-smokers smoking, non-drinkers drinking and non-believers believing."[21]

Both General Richard Gale, the 6th Airborne commander, and Brigadier Hill, of 3rd Parachute Brigade, had addressed the battalion. Gale had ended his talk by saying: "The Germans will think that no one but a BF [bloody fool] would go there, that is why I am going there." The brigadier had concluded by saying: "Gentleman, in spite of your excellent training do not be daunted if chaos reigns. It undoubtedly will, but we will prevail."[22] The Revd J.O. Jenkins took the 12th Battalion's service at their airfield at Keevil in Wiltshire. Major K.T. Darling noticed that Jenkins had a pile of pocket Bibles at his feet and the men were casually invited to take one: "At the

17   Museum of Army Chaplaincy Archives, John Binning, extract from unpublished typescript *Airborne No More*.
18   *Gloucester Journal*, 17 June 1944.
19   Museum of Army Chaplaincy Archives, John Gwinnett, notes sent to Brigadier John Smyth VC.
20   Stuart Tootal, The *Manner of Men: 9 PARA's Heroic D-Day Mission* (London: John Murray, 2013), p.139.
21   Barber, *The Day the Devils Dropped In*, p.39.
22   *Ibid*, p.40.

end of the service there was a mad scramble for the bibles and an onlooker might have thought they were chasing five pound notes."[23]

Lieutenant Colonel G.R. 'Dick' Stevens of the 12th Battalion of the 6th Airlanding Brigade was present at the pre-D-Day service conducted by John Hall in the transit camp of the main body of the 12th Devons: "It will remain in the memory of those who attended it; the robust singing of the hymns, especially Blake's hymn, and that the feeling throughout the service helped a lot."[24] Lieutenant Richard Todd, the well-known actor who served with the 6th Airborne in Normandy, remembered the service given by Revd George Parry before D-Day:

> As the shadows lengthened on Monday June 5, the stand-to order was given. The last ceremony that day was a drumhead service in a meadow near Fairford Airfield by our popular padre, Captain Parry, known to us all as Pissy Percy the Parachuting Parson. Parry was a wiry little Welshman with a nature as fiery as his red hair, and a heart and courage to match. Drawn-up in a semi-circle, 610 men faced inwards towards the padre who stood on an ammunition box. A more unlikely or piratical congregation could not be imagined, every man a bristle with weapons, his face and hands besmirched with black cream, his helmet on the ground before him, his rifle or Sten gun laid across it. Onward Christian Soldiers went well. Abide With Me was rather more ragged. It was not easy to sing that in such a setting and at such a moment.[25]

The airborne task in the first part of the invasion was to protect the flanks of the seaborne operation by seizing strategic points and communication centres and so stop German forces reaching the beachhead. The 6th Airborne Division was to land on the left flank. This included the double obstacle of the River Orne and the Caen Canal, and the higher ground that overlooked the beaches. It was imperative that this high ground which dominated the beaches and also the Merville battery was captured. Soon after midnight on 6 June, the pathfinders of the 22nd Independent Parachute Company began to descend, followed by the gliders carrying troops to attack the Orne and Caen canal bridges. Both bridges were captured intact. Padre Hales went in the same glider as General Gale, the division's commander, near to Pegasus bridge. He reported a smooth trip and an "incredibly lucky landing". Also in his glider was Chester Wilmot, the author and reporter, and Hales found himself carrying Wilmot's typewriter to the rendezvous. Upon arrival at the RV at Bas de Ranville, Hales joined the men in digging in, a trench which was to be his home

23   Museum of Army Chaplaincy Archives, letter from K.T. Darling to Paul Abram (undated).
24   Museum of Army Chaplaincy Archives, letter from Colonel G.R. Stevens to Paul Abram, 18 August 1971.
25   Account by Lieutenant Richard Todd, Pegasus Archive http://www.pegasusarchive.org/normandy/frames.htm.

for the next few days. He decided it was impracticable to keep burying dead at the cemetery at Ranville church, so obtained permission to use a patch of land for burial. A few days after D-Day the divisional engineers made a cross out of granite which was placed on the burial ground. There was a simple dedication service, to which a representative of each battalion came, and which Hales and Maurice McGowan, the RC padre, took together. The importance of the church at Ranville to the airborne troops was explained by General Gale:

> The church at Ranville came to mean a lot to us. It was a landmark standing clear of the villages, rising above the hubbub of battle. Somehow it seemed to stand for us. Though hit by shells it never fell. Coming over the bridges it greeted us. Coming down from Le Plein and from Amfreville it guided us. From La Mensil as one left the cover of the wood, it marked Ranville for us. Our comrades who were killed in the fighting nearby found their resting place in graves which the troops dug for their lost friends in the churchyard. But the churchyard was not big enough. So it was outside that we built another, our own, cemetery. The divisional commanders made a cross, a fine, simple cross. This we erected in our own piece of hallowed ground. We held a service there with chaplains of all denominations. And we dedicated ourselves to God and our cause. We prayed there for those who had gone and that we might have the strength to carry on where they had so valiantly left off.[26]

Padre David Nimmo remembered his take-off in a glider with his battalion, the 2nd Ox and Bucks. He described looking down on "the great fleet of ships, of all shapes and sizes steadily forging their way toward their objectives". As the glider approached the Landing Zone, they came under heavy fire from flak. He was impressed by the pilots of the plane that was towing them: "Our tow planes could not take evasive action without sending us to our destruction. They kept unwaveringly on their courses and did not seek to save themselves until they had released the gliders in the right area." Nimmo commented on the anti-glider poles placed by the Germans on likely landing grounds. In the event, his glider and others around him landed with few casualties, even though the gliders were irreparably damaged.[27] Their landing was unopposed and after rendezvousing the battalion moved towards Herouvillette. However, by morning they "had their hands full" taking Herouvillette, coming under a tank attack from the direction of Escouville, which they managed to fight off with difficulty.

Padre James McMurray-Taylor, chaplain to the Royal Ulster Rifles, took a non-denominational service before his battalion took off in the main glider life on the morning of 6 June. In his glider was Hugh Wheldon, who was awarded an MC on D-Day and later became Controller of the BBC.

---

26   R.N. Gale, *With the 6th Airborne in Normandy* (London: 1948), p.122.
27   Museum of Army Chaplaincy Archives, an account by the Revd David Nimmo.

Meanwhile, the 9th Parachute Battalion had dropped much of its men and equipment scattered at a distance from the Merville Battery, which it was their mission to destroy. Of the 750 men of the 9th Battalion that dropped, only 150 managed to get to the rendezvous. Many of them had drowned after being dropped in the flooded areas of the Dives valley. One of their number, John Speechley, described the sensation of landing in these circumstances:

> My heart's beating. I can't swim not with this bloody lot. I let go and went in and I sat on my arse. Looked up. I could see this green flickering; it was the moon shining up top. So I felt down; this was grass not mud and I realised I was in a flooded area. I stood up and I'd got the water up to my Adam's apple … Bloody Hell. I heard people in trouble. You could hear 'help bubble bubble' you know, one here, one there. It's just a case of survival now. I walked this way. I walked the other way. I waked another way and made a bit more headway and I got down to my ammunition pouches. I'm looking around and I went right around 360 degrees … I looked in one particular direction and it looked too straight. That's a railway line, it's got to be. So I made my way there … in the end I got almost to it and it turned out to be a road.[28]

Those who arrived at the RV at the battery were lacking in heavy weapons and equipment. Lieutenant Colonel Terence Otway, the CO, however, decided to press home the attack with the troops and equipment he had. They succeeded in capturing the battery and set about disabling the guns. Although the guns were of a lower calibre than expected, they would have still caused substantial damage if ranged on Sword Beach. At dawn the 75 survivors headed to Le Plein, but had to wait until the arrival of 1st Commando Brigade to capture the village later in the day.

John Gwinnett had dropped wide of the target and found himself floundering in the marshes that bordered the Dives. He was dismayed as he had desperately wanted to be with the men at the battery; the only time that he was more annoyed was when he lost his communion set two days later. It took him 15 hours to reach the brigade's headquarters near Le Plein, where he discovered that 20 casualties, wounded during the assault on the Merville battery, were lying in a house close to the battery at a stud farm, Haras de Retz, further along the Breville ridge. Although German troops were in the area, Gwinnett commandeered a captured 4cwt German truck to bring in the wounded. Private Alt drove the vehicle, and together they negotiated the badly cratered roads through mostly enemy-held territory.

Along the road to Breville they met some of the walking wounded who had left Haras de Retz to join the brigade: "We were near the Chateau St Come when we met the padre in a captured German vehicle with hundreds of holes in it. The padre asked about the more seriously wounded we had left earlier, before directing us the

28   Barber, *The Day The Devils Dropped In*, p.55.

shortest route to the Brigade HQ and the field hospital, before he set off to collect the wounded."[29] In spite of this he reached the aid post at 8:00 p.m. and eventually succeeded in clearing all the wounded that night back to the main dressing station in Ranville. At the house at Haras de Retz, one of the first people he saw was CSMI Bill Harold, who had jumped as part of the advance reconnaissance team. His final remark to the chaplain at Broadwell had been: "See you on the other side, padre, I'll have a cup of tea waiting for you." That was only 18 hours before, and now Gwinnett saw him coming towards him with a mess tin in his teeth, muttering, "Your tea padre". He had been shot through both arms and hands. "Unashamedly I recall that tears came into my eyes," Gwinnett recalled.[30]

Gwinnett and Alt returned for another trip to pick up the remaining wounded men. The journey was not straightforward, as recounted by Major Alan Parry of A Company:

> We nearly ran into an ambush en route and sheltered for half an hour in a chateau in which refugees had collected … A woman in the chateau hastily made us a red cross flag which we gave to a German orderly to hold. We placed him on the bonnet of the vehicle as a precaution. We hoped, by this to avoid getting shot at if we should encounter an ambush. As luck would have it we had no trouble and arrived at the MDS at 21.00.[31]

Late in the evening of 7 June, the 9th Battalion had dug in around a bungalow called Les Bois de Monts, and early on 8 June Terence Otway realised the importance of the position, for if the Germans held it they would have been able to shell the Orne and Caen Canal bridges. The task of the division was to secure the high ground around Breville, which the Germans still occupied. This meant the 51st Highland Division was unable to develop the bridgehead to the south and that the enemy dominated the division's left flank. During the heavy fighting of the next few days, Gwinnett several times attempted to bring in the wounded under fire. Otway was able to arrange a temporary truce, which enabled Gwinnett to lead a party into the area sitting on the front of a jeep waving a Red Cross flag, although the jeep was still fired on. The grisly task of bringing in bodies then began. Gwinnett supervised the evacuation of the wounded of the 9th Battalion to Le Mesnil and started to arrange the funerals of the dead of both sides which were lying behind the villa.

Ernie Rooke Matthew remembered Gwinnett burying his comrades:

---

29   Barber, *The Day The Devils Dropped In*, p.122.
30   Museum of Army Chaplaincy Archives, the Revd John Gwinnett, notes sent to Brigadier John Smyth VC.
31   Barber, *The Day The Devils Dropped In*, p.124.

Under the padre's leadership comrades who were killed were treated with the utmost respect … In the morning after 'Stand To' our dead comrades would be buried in a shallow grave dug in this plot. The padre gave every man a Christian burial, with some of the man's comrades breaking off from action to pay homage. These service were family services, not military, very simple, most sincere.[32]

On another occasion his casualty party was flagged down by a Canadian major wounded and trapped in a house. They had to batter a hole in the wall of the house to get him out, as the front entrance was covered by a German sniper. It was on one of these casualty runs that the jeep containing Gwinnett's Holy Communion set was captured, much to his grief. Later Gwinnett took a white flag and made an attempt to arrange a ceasefire:

He had it on a pole to start with and he took it out in front, out into the battlefields and waved it in front of the Germans. He was very brave. When we were collecting the wounded and dead we collected them all irrespective of whose side they were on. The Germans did stop shooting except for one fool who fired and that was when John Gwinnett, standing up there turned around and said in the most unparson like language 'you stupid bugger, can't you see my bloody dog collar.'[33]

John Gwinnett never forgot going out with Tom Nicol, the massive Presbyterian minister with the 5th Battalion, the Black Watch, to bring back a wounded man. On the way they were straddled with mortar bombs and Gwinnett felt the end of the stretcher go. When he looked around he saw his fellow chaplain standing with a look of amazement on his face, although otherwise unscathed. Nicol had lost his trousers from his kneecaps to his ankles in the explosion. The amusing part was that the wounded man beat them back to the Regimental Aid Post![34]

During the battle for the Chateau Chome wood, the Black Watch and the 9th Parachute Battalion were under pressure and morale was low. Stuart Tootal, in his book on the 9th Battalion, described how Gwinnett, at a critical moment in the combat, sensed his spiritual services were needed more by those who were still fighting: "In a successful attempt to rally morale he marched through the Bois des Monts gate and over to the right hand corner of the drive, where he proceeded to nail the battalion's flag to the tree."

After ferrying 20 wounded from Haras de Retz on the morning of D-Day, Gwinnett had gone to the to the Brigade HQ where he discovered that the Revd J.C.

32   *Ibid*, p.182.
33   Barber, *The Day The Devils Dropped In*, p.169.
34   Museum of Army Chaplaincy Archives, John Gwinnett, notes sent to Brigadier John Smyth VC.

McVeigh, a Roman Catholic padre, and George Harris, the Canadians' chaplain, were missing. Harris's fate was not known until 26 August, when, during the breakout from the Normandy beachhead, the 12th Devons took Honfleur, 20 miles east of the river Orne. A farmer told John Hall, the Devons' chaplain, that another man had descended on Harris's parachute. Colonel Bernd Horn gave an account of Harris's fatal descent in his book on Canadian paratroopers in Normandy:

Sometimes the exits from the aircraft were too fast. Corporal Tom O'Connell left the aircraft too quickly and his parachute got tangled up with another jumpers. "As we plunged toward the earth I heard the other fellow yell from below, 'Take it easy old man!'" Both men crashed to the earth. Around noon, a severely injured O'Connell had finally regained consciousness. Beside him was the corpse of Padre Captain George Harris. On the ground beside him he could see the two parachutes twisted together like a thick rope.[35] He had been killed on landing. Padre John Hall read the burial service over Harris's grave. George Alexander Harris was a British chaplain, an Anglican curate, from Solihull who was attached to the Royal Canadian Infantry Corps' parachute battalion. His grave is at Ranville and the inscription tells us that he had two elder brothers who had been killed in the First World War.

The Revd McVeigh had flown in with 3rd Brigade's Headquarters. After a second time around landing, McVeigh found the commander of the 224th Field Hospital, Lieutenant Colonel D.H. Thompson, and in a group of five tried to find out where they were, but without success, so decided to make for the coast. As they skirted Varaville, they came under fire and scattered. Returning to the scene of the ambush, McVeigh found Lance Corporal Chitty lying wounded. He and Chitty managed to avoid the enemy for two days, but were eventually captured. Brigadier James Hill remembered seeing quite a bit of John Gwinnett and occasionally Padre McVeigh, "who reputedly set about the Germans with his shillelagh after his capture on D-Day and they therefore refused to accept him as a padre and he was relegated to the worst of the prison camps in the Baltic".[36] McVeigh remained in captivity and was taken to a POW camp, where he remained for the duration of the war.

Alec Kay landed with the 8th Battalion, who were to take the bridges at Bures and Troarn. He was mortally wounded bringing in casualties. Kay was the son of Thomas and Fanny Kay, and husband of Janet Kay of Watermillock, Cumberland. He had an emergency commission into the Royal Army Chaplains Department in October 1940 and volunteered for airborne duties in 1943. He qualified as a military parachutist on course 91 and became chaplain to the 8th Parachute Battalion. He was killed on 7 June when a jeep he took out to collect the wounded came under machine-gun fire despite its Red Cross markings. Aged 34, he is buried at Ranville. The battalion

35   Bernd Hall, *Men of Steel*, quoted in WW2 Talk Forum, http://ww2talk.com/index.php?threads/padres-6th-airborne.53033/.

36   Museum of Army Chaplaincy Archives, letter from Lieutenant Colonel James Hill to Paul Abram, 4 June 1971.

was in the Bavent woods, their objective being to hold this most southerly point in the defensive line formed by the 3rd Parachute Brigade. In the first 24 hours of the operation the brigade had lost two of its four Protestant chaplains.

Captain Revd Leslie Beckingham of the 224th Parachute Field Ambulance landed with his batman and friend Private C.F. Phillips in a ditch near the River Dives. Phillips was, according to Beckingham, "a splendid Christian fellow who was always full of good humour". After saying a prayer, they joined the men who had landed nearby and arrived at Varaville as the Canadians had taken the village and Beckingham became separated from Philips. He was guided to the main dressing station at Le Mesnil by 11:00 a.m. and was present a little later when Alec Kay was brought in. Kay died almost immediately and John Gwinnett took the burial service for his brother chaplain. Beckingham now had to take over the 8th Battalion and the Canadian battalion. For the next two days, until they linked up with the seaborne troops, the two battalions were under continuous and heavy pressure from the enemy.

Batman Phillips turned up unharmed and was able to help Beckingham with identifying the dead, removing their personal possessions and then burying them under incessant mortar fire. With the 8th Battalion positioned in the forest of Bavant in isolated groups and morale low, Beckingham was able to move around the scattered troops dispensing chocolate, cigarettes and, most importantly, information as to the state of battle. At the main dressing station, he cheered up the wounded by his presence, cigarettes and sweets. After the first few days it became possible to take a brief service of prayer in the barn alongside the main dressing station. He described how "between June 6 and June 19 our 224 Field Ambulance performed 112 operations."[37]

The 7th Battalion had attended a service on 4 June taken by the Revd George Parry before emplaning for France. Parry was from Leytonstone, Essex, and had joined the 7th Light Infantry Parachute Battalion as its padre after serving as a chaplain for two years in West Africa and then completing his training course at Ringway, with Parachute Training Course no. 78, in August 1943. His report from that course said that he was "cheerful and enthusiastic and an asset to his stick".[38] Pine-Coffin wrote:

I will always remember how keen and enthusiastic he was about pretty well everything and how the other officers used to enjoy teasing him. At Bulford camp before the action some of the officer were ragging George. They were saying that he was small and puny, and that he could not wrestle with the officers anyway. George said that he could. He said that he could beat Nigel Taylor, Commanding Officer of A coy and a tremendous wrestling match started there

37   Pegasus Archive, account by A.L. Beckingham, http://www.pegasusarchive.org/normandy/frames.htm.
38   Biographical information on George Parry, Paradata, https://www.paradata.org.uk/people/george-e-m-parry.

and then. Each was determined not to be beaten … on and on they went until eventually I told them to stop because the furniture was getting damaged.[39]

An article in *The Times* in 2005 asserted that he was known as "Pissy Percy the Parachuting Parson" because of his love for beer.[40]

As they were about to take off, Parry took an impromptu communion service under the wing of a Stirling aircraft. This service apparently came about because Lieutenant Bill Bowers of A Company had a premonition that he was to die in action that day. Parry suggested that they prayed and took tghe communion service. A witness to that service, Ted Lough, later told Pine-Coffin that he would never forget it, with "just the three of them and a few others who were near and who saw what was happening, face blacked for action and held under the wing of the aircraft".[41] Bowers was killed in action that evening and is buried in Benouville church.

Upon landing, the battalion was scattered. Their task was to provide reinforcements for the glider attack on the Orne bridges. Pine-Coffin had only gathered 40 percent of his men at the bridge by 3:00 p.m. The war dairy for 6 June reported that the battalion dropped at 1:00 a.m. "but went into action with coys at half normal strength due to some plane loads being dropped in wrong places and one load not dropping at all".[42]

The 200 men of the 7th Battalion had to fight off enemy counterattacks until Lord Lovat with No 4 Commando appeared at 12.00 p.m. A report in the *Daily Record* described the incident: "While the fighting was going on and the men were valiantly holding the bridges they had captured, padre Parry moved among them encouraging those who were still fighting and giving what help he could."[43] He then went to help wounded from A Company who were at the RAP at Benouville. The RAP became cut off from A Company and from the main battalion, and soon after dawn more casualties were caused by a German Panther tank and a self-propelled gun. The RAP was overrun by German troops, who killed the wounded there, including Parry. According to Lieutenant Richard Todd, Parry "evidently fought like a tiger to defend them".[44] The newspaper report recounts that Parry immediately went to the aid of the helpless Britons lying on the dressing station floor. He is believed to have tried physical intervention and put himself between the Nazis and the wounded troops. The report then related how "a wave of fury and indignation" swept across the whole division, and the war correspondent filing the report wrote: "I was with the men of the battalion during many hours of D-Day watching their successful battle to hold

39   Museum of Army Chaplaincy Archives, account by Lieutenant Colonel R.G. Pine-Coffin.
40   *The Times*, 18 December 2015.
41   Museum of Army Chaplaincy Archives, letter from Edward (Ted) Lough to Paul Abram, 16 May 1972.
42   The National Archives, War Diary WO 171/1239.
43   The *Daily Record*, Thursday, 29 June 1944.
44   Account by Lieutenant Richard Todd, Pegasus Archive, http://www.pegasusarchive.org/normandy/frames.htm.

Fr Bernard Egan in North Africa. (Airborne Assault Museum, Duxford)

The Revd Robert T. Watkins with Lt J.L. Williams. (Airborne Assault Museum, Duxford)

Parachute training. (Peter Foote Collection)

Glider Landing, unknown location. (Peter Foote Collection)

Mike Lewis, late of Second Parachute Battalion at the 'Red River Valley' memorial, Tamara. (Airborne Assault Museum, Duxford)

Group of Airborne padres — Padres Buchanan, Timothy, Hales, Owen Jenkins and Gwinnett. (RAChD Museum, catalogue ref 2004.389)

The Revd Murdo Ewan Macdonald. (©
Stornoway Press)

The Revd John Gwinnett. (RAChD
Museum, catalogue ref 2007.2721)

The Revd George Parry. (© Dorset Archives,
ref: D-1345/1/3)

The Revd Fraser McLuskey. (© Glasgow
University)

Graves of six RAF airmen buried by Fraser McLuskey at Marigny-L'Eglise Communal Cemetery, Morvan. (Linda Parker)

Memorial to the American air crew buried by Revd Fraser McLuskey. (Nigel Parker)

Memorial to Revd Fraser McLuskey, cemetery in the woods, Ouroux, Morvan. (Linda Parker)

The cemetery in the woods, Ouroux. Graves of RAF airmen in foreground, graves of resistance fighters in background. (Nigel Parker)

No 17 Hartenstein. The Revd Chignell was based here before escaping in Operation Berlin. (H.J. Willink)

He that is Mighty hath done great things to me ; and Holy is His Name.

✝

PRAY FOR

DANIEL McGOWAN

ORDAINED PRIEST

JUNE 6th, 1937.

❖

May God bless all who have helped me to become His priest.

Printed in Germany

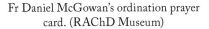
Fr Daniel McGowan's ordination prayer card. (RAChD Museum)

The Revd G. A. Pare. (Used without attribution in *The Torn Horizon*, by Chris Van Roekel)

Grave of Fr B.Benson, Oosterbeek Military Cemetery. (Linda Parker)

Grave of the Revd. H.J.Irwin, Oosterbeek Military Cemetery. (Linda Parker)

The posthumous funeral service of Fr Benson held on September 25 1945. Fr Dan McGowan leads the service. (H.J. Willink)

the bridge and I know how deeply they felt the loss of the men who had dropped with them."[45] Journalist Jenni Crane, when investigating the fate of George Parry, whose case she had found in a junk shop, interviewed two surviving veterans of the 6th Airborne Division. They confirmed that he had been popular and well-liked but felt that the report in the *Daily Record* had been exaggerating when it suggested that "there was no man in the battalion who that day did not fight to avenge the death of Padre Parry".[46] He was one of four officer casualties and 16 other ranks, as noted in the 7th Battalion's war diary. He is buried in Benouville cemetery near to his friend Bill Bowers.

The 12th and 13th Battalions had the task of seizing Le Bas de Ranville and the Ranvile–Le Mariquet area and holding them as a LZ for the 6th Air Landing Brigade. They too were widely scattered but managed to hold the area in spite of repeated attacks from tanks and infantry of the 125th Panzer Grenadier Regiment supported by self-propelled guns. The German reaction had been swift and the 12th Battalion bore the brunt of these attacks. Their chaplain was the Revd J.O. Jenkins, who served with them from July 1943 to June 1945. He landed carrying 60lb of medical supplies in addition to his own equipment. The bulk of this he carried up his parachute harness, so that the quick release box was under his chin. He carried with him a complete list of the battalion, with addresses of next of kin, which proved vital because the orderly room staff lost their copy. Jenkins realised that he was not officially supposed to be carrying this list, but it became invaluable in checking on the dead, missing and wounded. The battalion's doctor was wounded, and for a few days Jenkins was commanding the RAP until a replacement was found.

The 13th Battalion chaplain was the Revd Whitfield Foy (Methodist), who was their sole chaplain from August 1943 until 1947. Foy, very much included in the briefings for the operation, went with the officers to the model room and was told that the job of the 13th was to seize and hold the village of Ranville before moving on to Longueval. Foy's aeroplane took off from Brize Norton, but before setting of he read a psalm and "under the peaceful sky we said prayers". He remembered that "the light hearted cries of 'see you in France' were a little forced". Conditions in their Albemarle were cramped and stifling, a situation not helped by the failure of the interior light, which meant they had to prepare to jump in the dark. Foy realised during his descent that he had not been dropped in the right area, as he saw a railway line which had not appeared on the instructions for the drop. He landed east of the River Dives up to his neck in water just after 1:00 a.m. His batman had dropped nearby, and as they struggled out of the ditches Foy manage to accidently fire a round out of his batman's rifle which narrowly missed the batman. After crossing the Dives by a log bridge because the Canadians had blown the bridge, they met up with groups of men who had been dropped wide, including Captain Mike Kerr, who had landed

45   The *Daily Record*, Thursday, 29 June 1944.
46   *Church Times*, Friday, 23 December 2016, p.41.

right in the river. They then walked by a very circuitous route to Ranville, hoping that the battalion had congregated there. Foy recalled: "But as we finally trudged on to firm ground we had our reward, for there in the evening sky away to the North came streaming in a giant glider Armada. We whooped with joy, not least because we knew that Ranville must have been taken." Kerr's stragglers arrived at Battalion HQ by 1:00 p.m. Foy reported that "for five hours we were never in less than two feet of water very often in three and too often in five".

The story of the 13th Battalion's first few days in France was one of sitting tight in a position which was incessantly and heavily shelled and mortared by the enemy. The battalion dug in, facing constant bombardment. Foy remembered: "My own job in those early day was the burial of large numbers of the division." Today near the church at Ranville is the 6th Airborne Division cemetery for the Normandy campaign. Over 160 men had been buried there by 17 June. Foy added: "There is glory in war; there is amazing courage and patent self-sacrifice, there is common friendship of danger which forms unbreakable friendships but the horror of the burial ground remains, the torn flesh and the mangled bodies are realities."[47]

The Roman Catholic chaplain to the 5th Parachute Brigade, Fr Bill Briscoe, dropped with the 225th Parachute Field Ambulance. They established the main MDS at Le Chateau de Guernal in Le Bas de Ranville. Briscoe was seriously wounded when a shell struck the dressing station, having been in a barn adjacent to the chateau. He was given a coloured label, which indicated he was unlikely to survive and was therefore a low priority. He realised the significance of this, and in a moment of consciousness asked the orderly for a 'first priority' label, which meant he would have a blood transfusion. During the afternoon of 6 June a driver reported Germans approaching the barn. The medical officer, Lieutenant David Tibb, recounted how he heard a faint voice from Briscoe: "In a short silence I heard a faint voice at my feet. It was the padre, a much loved figure." Tibbs bent down to the gravely wounded padre, who said: "David, remove my gun. If the Germans find my pistol they'll shoot me."[48] Tibbs reflected that carrying a pistol was the fashion, and many padres and medical officers had them, but he quickly unstrapped the pistol and kicked it away under the straw. The expected attack did not materialise and shortly after Briscoe was evacuated to England, rejoining the regiment in time for the crossing of the Rhine in 1945.

The 1st and 2nd Battalions landed on LZs prepared for them by the 5th Parachute Brigade. On their approach they came under heavy flak fire, but the tow aircraft could not take evasive action until they had released the gliders. The chaplain of the light infantry battalion, the Revd David Nimmo, was impressed with the courage of the pilots: "They kept unwaveringly to their course and did not seek to save themselves

47   An account of the Revd Whitfield Foy, Paradata, https://www.paradata.org.uk/media/1073.
48   David Tibbs and Neil Barber, *Parachute Doctor: The Memoirs of Captain David Tibbs* (Devizes: Sabrestorm Publishing, 2012) p.51.

until they had released the gliders in the right area. I was deeply moved by their courage."[49] The battalions moved off to attack Herouvillette and Longueval. Nimmo's battalion captured Herouvillette easily, but came under attack from German tanks at Escoville.

The Royal Ulster Rifles, with their chaplain the Revd J. Murray Taylor, arrived in Normandy in the second glider lift on the evening of D-Day. He was in charge of his glider. Captain Hugh Wheldon, the future broadcaster, had experienced technical problems with his glider and had landed back in England, but joined Taylor's glider at the last moment. The battalion took Longueval but had to fight hard to retain it.

David Nimmo described how "when opportunity offered we buried our dead", at that stage in the Herouvillette village cemetery. He had soon organised a burial squad, at work identifying the dead, removing their personal effects, digging graves, interring and carefully recording all necessary facts. Being detailed for this task was not popular, but Nimmo used to persuade the men by saying to them, "If they themselves were killed, they would want someone to do the job and give them a Christian burial." He recalled one occasion burying a woman who had been killed by the German troops for aiding a paratrooper. There was no local Roman Catholic priest available, so Nimmo asked for a French prayer book and performed the service as best he could in French and according to Roman Catholic rites: "I couldn't help wondering what my Presbyterian colleagues back in Scotland would have thought, but I didn't care."[50] He went on to describe a burial service under fire:

> Occasionally men would have to be buried more or less where they had fallen. On one such occasion we were in the middle of a brief burial service when mortar bombs began to fall very close to us. We dropped to the ground and there was a brief pause. It was one of my helpers, a private soldier who took up the threads and resumed the Lord's prayer which we had been saying together. Such men were towers of strength.[51]

The 12th Battalion, the Devonshire Regiment, took over from the 12th Battalion, Parachute Regiment, near Le Bas de Ranville. Their chaplain, Revd John Hall, was a trained parachutist but had come in by sea, as General Gale had wanted a battalion of the division to land by sea in order to keep the division's G1098 tactical equipment intact. Hall was ordered to be the first off the landing craft in order to boost morale and to help the CO, Major Dobbie, to find the rendezvous point, eventually arriving with his battalion to relieve Pegasus Bridge. The casualties caused in the counterattacks at Pegasus often had to be buried where they fell, either in their own or a disused slit trench. MO John Binning described Hall's work at and around

---

49   Museum of Army Chaplaincy Archives, an account by the Revd David Nimmo.
50   *Ibid.*
51   *Ibid.*

the RAP: "Daily he went the rounds of the rifle companies in the forward platoons if the company commander approved. The Revd John Hall went to see the scattered members of his flock as often as he could … often creeping up to the forward platoons if the company commander approved, and I admired him for his tenacity of purpose and his courage."[52]

Binning remembered how on a Sunday evening when the battalion was in reserve below Breville, Hall held a service which included communion (happily he was a Presbyterian) and it made a lasting impression on him: "This communion service I relive at every occasion on which I hear the 23rd Psalm." Binning related the words of the psalm to their own position: "In the green fields and orchards beside the River Orne we were walking night and day in death's dark vale and the barking of the guns around Caen reminded one only too well of the presence of our foes."[53]

Hall remained with his battalion in the Breville/Ranville area for the next 10 weeks. Even in the 'rest' areas they were never more than 200yds away from the German forward positions, consequently only the Commanding Officer, Lieutenant Colonel Dick Stevens, and the padre, Hall, were allowed to wear their red berets. Services were conducted in slit trenches for about 12 men at a time, so to provide a short service for the battalion followed by communion took many hours to accomplish. Hall reported that about 90 men took Holy Communion. During July a cowshed became available for services. Hall considered that the chaplains provided a valuable service by providing "an ear for men to talk about home and also by providing a channel by which they could be put in the picture about what was going on". Hall continued to write to the next of kin of injured or killed men, which he found especially difficult when he knew some of the welfare problems of some families back at home. An abiding memory for him as the weeks wore on was the smell of corpses, many of them lying dead since D-Day. When such corpses were found it was part of his duties to identify the body, arrange for the burial and notify next of kin.[54]

The Air Landing Brigade's Roman Catholic chaplain, Fr. M. McGowan, came in with the 195th Air Landing Field Ambulance. He was wounded by an explosion and sustained several injuries, one of which left him deaf in his left ear, while assisting in the clearance of his glider under heavy fire. McGowan moved about the entire brigade, impervious to mortar bursts and small-arms fire. His method of transport was a small two-stroke motorbike which was especially adapted for airborne forces. With Fr McVeigh a prisoner and Fr Briscoe severely wounded, he was the only Roman Catholic chaplain with the division and the little motorbike had to work overtime to cover his enormous 'parish'.

52   Museum of Army Chaplaincy Archives, John Binning, extract from unpublished typescript *Airborne No More*.
53   *Ibid.*
54   Museum of Army Chaplaincy Archives, an account by the Revd John Hall.

George Hales, senior chaplain, went to Normandy by glider, landed with the division's HQ on the afternoon of 6 June and dug in at Le Bas de Ranville. The Revd G.A. Pare, the chaplain of No 1 Wing, the Glider Pilot Regiment, flew in a glider piloted by the CO of his unit, Lieutenant Colonel I.A. Murray. They took off from Harwell and made a perfect landing in the Ranville area. He then visited the other gliders and assisted the wounded. The order then came that glider pilots were to be withdrawn to England to prepare for the next airborne operation. Pare described the massive reinforcements he saw while making his way back to the coast. Apart from the wounded, the glider pilots were the first to get back to England.

On 12 June the 12th Parachute Battalion and a company of the 12th Devons finally ejected the enemy from Breville, by means of an evening attack planned by Richard Gale when the enemy was not expecting it. Padre J.O. Jenkins, their chaplain, followed the attack into Breville with the regimental aid post: "They had plenty to do, only 100 men of the 12th Battalion were capable of fighting after the battle."[55] Once Breville was taken, the division was occupied in a static role, but still engaged in minor attacks and aggressive patrolling.

Padre Hall, with the Devons, visited two companies a day, and made a point of wearing his dog collar and red beret when nearly everyone else was wearing their steel helmet. John Binning, the battalion's medical officer, admired the way Hall moved about the battalion when everyone else kept their heads down. Everyone felt that he would do his best to crawl up to the forward platoons. He worked well with Binning, whose call sign was 'starlight'. They became known as the 'brothers light'; 'star (light)' and 'lead kindly (light)'. Richard Sweetland wrote of Padre Hall:

> A man of God who instilled quiet confidence in all of us as he moved around amongst us in Normandy during 1944. He was the prime factor in moulding our battalion into a blend of comradeship, the like of which we never seem to encounter in civvy st these days. From CO downwards if we just say Lead kindly light, everyone knows we refer to Rev Hall. I think that sums up our tribute to this wonderful man.[56]

The battalion's second in command, Major P. Gleadell, wrote in his diary for 7 July:

> Came to a rest area, some orchard below Le Mesnil crossroads. For the first time opportunity was taken to hold company services with the congregations dispersed in slit trenches. I attended MM's [Maurice McGowan] and JH [John Hall] nipped around in his usual infectious way. The splendid work of these two

55   Museum of Army Chaplaincy Archives, an account by the Revd J.O. Jenkins.
56   Museum of Army Chaplaincy Archives, letter from Richard Sweetland to Paul Abram, 29 July 1971.

during the first tense month has deservedly earned for them the very highest regard of all ranks, irrespective of flock.[57]

A soldier, A.H. Cudmore, wrote of a communion service held in an orchard outside Ranville:

> I think back about padre Hall … When the word goes around that that Holy Communion will be held at so and so hours, not a very quiet place that orchard and I found myself a partaker. Frankly I was amazed to see a calm quiet padre taking a service – ignoring the bangs and topping it all with a surplice so snowy white that the T.V. whiteness of today seems grey. I say humbly that I was nearest God at that service than ever before and I must admit, ever since.

He recounted a mate who had gone to a funeral and reflected afterwards: "You know they gave me a gun and I am still scared stiff, but that padres bloke of ours just doesn't give a damn – He just carries on. Makes you think mate – It does."Cudmore concluded: "On army orders you salute an officer no matter what you think of him but I salute padre Hall because I respected him … I am pleased and proud to know him as our padre. He was a padre worth meeting."[58]

After the bitter fighting at Breville, Nimmo had to bury 300 men of both sides. He did his best to identify the German bodies as well as the British because he knew that somewhere there was a relative or friend who should be spared the agony of not knowing for sure. Men were not detailed for burial duties more than once, but during their first day at Breville, Nimmo had the assistance of a Jewish NCO who was so careful and thorough that he asked him to assist him in supervising part of the work. He agreed and the chaplain was deeply grateful for his help.

The division was still under enemy fire and casualties continued to be brought to the main dressing stations. On 16 June, Padre Leslie Beckingham was still working at the main dressing station of the 224th Parachute Field Ambulance, which had no opportunity to rest. At Le Mesnil in a forward and enclosed area it could not claim the protection of the red cross. The Field Ambulance came in for heavy fire from the 19th, but eventually during a lull in the shelling it was moved back from its exposed position.

As the Canadians could not replace George Harris, Beckingham became their chaplain, and lived with them in a brickworks at the RAP. The 8th Battalion had not got a replacement for Alec Kay, so Beckingham shared the care of them with Gwinnett until the Revd Ogilvy arrived on 9 July.

57   Museum of Army Chaplaincy Archives, extract from P. Gleadell's diary, quoted by Abram, *Lower Than the Angels*, p.73.
58   Museum of Army Chaplaincy Archives, letter from A.H.Cudmore to Paul Abram (undated).

During this time Padre Maurice McGowan, the only surviving RC chaplain, covered the Roman Catholics of the entire division, and visited all determinedly. He became known as the 'Daemon King' as he travelled around on his on his two-stroke motorbike. When visiting the 195th Air Landing Ambulance, he had to ride down 200 yards of open road, and often came under fire. J.C. Watts recounted how McGowan often indulged in some black humour upon his arrival:

> He gave for our delectation a dramatic impersonation of a case of 'battle exhaustion' twitching and stammering. This routine miming has an unfortunate effect on our ADMS [Assistant Director Medical Services] one morning when he was visiting us. Colonel MacEwan had very firm views on battle exhaustion, so when the padre entered giving his usual charade, the ADMS was quite horrified until our casual acceptance of theses pranks showed him that all was quite well with out padre's morale.[59]

During the second half of June, through July and the beginning of August, the 6th Airborne Division held the line, patrolling and suffering casualties. Padre Foy related how one evening in very bad weather, there was a devastating mortar attack on his position, an RAP in a brickworks: "Battalion Medics had a gruelling test and they responded magnificently. Stretchers were actually blown out of their hands by bomb blasts." Foy had to accompany Corporal Ware, who had been hit in the throat by a bomb splinter, to the main dressing station:

> Never shall I forget the drive down to Ranville. We crept through the inky darkness slowly because every jolt was dangerous to the wounded man. I felt personally responsible for every bump in the road … When we finally arrived at the MDS he was still alive … two days later I was grieved to hear that he had died … On the next journey on that frightful night I took a man whose legs and thighs had been smashed to smithereens. For two miles I heard his agonised screams – and all one could do was drive on at a walking pace.[60]

On 7 August the order to advance came at last and the division moved towards Le Havre. The town of Putot- en-Auge was captured during a night attack by the 7th, 12th and 13th Parachute Battalions as part of the division's breakout.

Beckingham witnessed the second-in-command of the battalion whip out a psalm book when they were pinned down in a ditch under fire and say, "it was written for me padre".

---

59   J.C. Watts, *Surgeon At War* (London: George Allen, 1955), pp.99-100.
60   An account of the Revd Whitfield Foy, Paradata, https://www.paradata.org.uk/media/1073.

General Gale, in his post war memoirs, gave the following opinion of the work of the airborne chaplains:

> The chaplains of the division were excellent jumping with the men and earning their regard and respect. The padres did a great work but good as they were I am sure that they would be first to give praise to the men for their fine and purposeful outlook. The Revd Hales was our senior chaplain in the Normandy battle. His quiet and serene nature as well as his great personal bravery earned for him our respect and admiration. The spiritual side of a soldier's life is so important and means so much. In stress it is [their] anchor, and few who have faced up to danger will dispute this. Example means much in this life of ours and the example which good padres can set is deep in its effect. In our training hours we had included padre's hours at which men and their padres could discuss their beliefs, their fears and their religious hopes. One prays that in the days of peace we shall not lose our nearness to the creator which the conditions of war seemed to bring us.

Beckingham remembered that on Sunday, 3 September, the fifth anniversary of the outbreak of war, special services were held in memory of those of the division who had fallen in Normandy and in thanksgiving for those who had been spared. Beckingham was pleased to be presented with the Canadian parachute wings. The service for the 224th Field Ambulance was held at the chateau at St Andre, then after saying farewell to French friends Beckingham and the members of the Field Ambulance boarded HMS *Invicta* for Southampton.

The 6th Airborne Division had received a baptism of fire in Normandy, but could take some credit for the success of Operation Overlord. The padres who had accompanied them had played their part, and the evidence shows their ministry was appreciated at the heart of the Airborne Division that was in the vanguard of the invasion force.

5

The 2nd Independent Parachute Brigade in Italy, South of France and Greece, July 1943 to July 1945

When the 1st Airborne Division returned to England in December 1943, the 2nd Parachute Brigade, commanded by Brigadier C.H.V. Pritchard, remained in Italy as the 2nd Independent Parachute Brigade. This group was described by one of its padres, 'Joe' Downing, as "a mini army, with all arms except tanks",[1] and sent up the line to join the 2nd New Zealand Division. The advance to north of the River Sangro was halted and the Allies were unable to make any progress until the spring. The brigade was situated just north of the torrential river and in positions which were overlooked by the enemy, who were on the Corsagna to Guardiagrele ridge. The road leading to the positions occupied by the brigade was in full view of the enemy and became known as the 'Mad Mile'. There were four padres: two Church of England, one Church of Scotland and one Roman Catholic.

'Joe' Downing wrote: "This mile seemed particularly allergic to padres."[2] When the most forward position on 'Tank Hill' was occupied by D Company of the 5th (Scottish) Battalion, their chaplain, the Revd J.W.Robertson (Church of Scotland), went up the 'Mad Mile' to bury the dead on 11 December. His route took him through a crossroads which the Germans shelled, and he was very badly wounded and evacuated. Fr Gerard Bankes went to join the 5th Battalion the next day, and within an hour of arriving had been wounded by *nebelwerfer* fire and was not fit again until May 1946. Downing tried his luck along the road to get to the battalion, and wrote a poem entitled 'The Mad Mile' in which he expresses the futility of the effects of war on the Italian countryside and the hope that it will be not be in vain:

1   E. D. Downing, Padre *With The Paras* (privately published, undated), p.39.
2   *Ibid*, p.41.

The Mad Mile

A long road swept by the wind and the rain
Where it twisted round and round again
Till you came to the Mad Mile.

Two Thousand yards, where you looked straight down
On the valley that rose to the enemy town
This was the Mad Mile.

A mile of road where mortar and shell
Moaned through the air and fell and fell
On the length of the Mad Mile.

On to the village the mad way ran
To a little church where the homes began
At the end of the Mad Mile.

With statue and Altar, roof and bell
And window broken by mortar and shell
As they beat on the Mad Mile.

No call rings now where the bell was hung
No mass at the altar now is sung
In the wrath of the Mad Mile.

But the cars race dodging mortar and shell
By the church on the crazy piece of Hell
Which is the Mad Mile.

And the crazy world is racing past
On the crazy road to hell, to the last
Mad yard of the Mad Mile.

But the bell it will call one day at again
To the world to redeem by its unsalved pain
The curse of the Mad Mile.

The world will run on the mad sad way
Till the church is builded again one day
At the end of the Mad Mile.

While holding this position, Downing was involved in counselling a man who refused to go in the forward trenches as he had developed a phobia about being buried after this had happened to him during an air raid in London:

> It was decided to give him another chance that night and I attempted some advice which proved totally impractical and the next day I saw him being taken away under guard. He gave me a sad look and I knew I was a dismal failure. Afterwards the idea came to me that I might have volunteered to go in to the trench with him. That of course might have failed equally and in any case I would probably not have been allowed to go. But I wish I had thought of it.[3]

Downing, realising that the incident had resulted in a general lowering of morale, did in fact spend some nights in the front-line trenches with the consent of Lieutenant Colonel Coxen.[4] The 4th Battalion was in the front line at Christmas, when it was difficult to arrange services in any great numbers, as Downing recalled:

> My final decision was having one service of H.C. [Holy Communion] at Battalion Head Quarters and then go around with the Reserved Sacrament to every position. The only suitable time for the service was at midnight and I celebrated a real midnight mass in a real stable with a real manger for an altar. The whole situation, with the manger and the danger, stranger than I had ever known, made it the most real and poignant Christmas I have ever experienced.[5]

In January 1945 the Revd J.K.S. Reid arrived for the 5th (Scottish) Battalion. Brigadier Charles Pritchard was pleased to have his chaplains up to strength, was most helpful to Reid and seemed appreciative of the chaplain role. Reid's first task was to bury a victim of manslaughter and then to talk to the soldier charged with causing his death. Only a limited number of men could hold the front line at any given time, with the others housed in deserted barns and farmhouses. There was a lot of local red wine around, which was the cause of the type of incident dealt with by Reid.

The brigade held this section of the Sangro front for three months before moving on to the Cassino sector. The conditions of static warfare made it difficult for the chaplain to keep contact with the men when they were in the front line. Padre Downing found he could only see a few men in each position, because a third would be on guard and another third sleeping. His solution was to stay for three or four days with each separate group, and he always held a short service followed by Holy Communion before moving to another group. In this way it took him a month to visit his 'parish',

3   *Ibid*, p.43.
4   Museum of Army Chaplaincy Archives, Airborne Chaplains' papers deposited by the Revd P. R. C. Abram CVO, typescript, *Lower Than the Angels* (1975), p.46.
5   Downing, *Padre With The Paras*, p.42.

but it was a rewarding method, not least because it enabled him to get to know his men in depth.

After three months at Cassino the brigade was withdrawn, and by 28 May was concentrated in the Salerno sector and able to have more regular services. Padre Downing's men bought him a portable organ from the Americans to help with services, as they loved singing. Downing attended a mass in the cathedral at Salerno, but was not impressed by the service.

The sea bathing was enjoyed by all, but there were also a series of refresher jumps for the brigade and intensive training. A tragic accident when a man was killed due to a fault in his static line revealed, after investigation, that many of the lines in this batch were faulty; the cause of this was eventually traced to contamination by acid when being stored in a hanger with American aircraft. Downing was pleased that the next stop was then Rome: "As we approached the eternal city the feelings, for one with a classic education were feelings of no little awe."[6] Downing found out from the senior chaplain in Rome that there was a confirmation service planned for the following Monday, and spent a frantic few days getting his prospective confirmation candidates up to scratch and writing a letter for each of them to read while they were waiting in the church to be confirmed. He finished this task for his 12 candidates at 5:00 a.m. on the morning of the confirmation. A pleasant personal discovery came when he realised the Bishop of Lichfield's chaplain was Fred Chapman, the twin brother of Downing's fiancée.

In preparation for the invasion of southern France on 15 August, the 2nd Independent Parachute Brigade moved to Rome. Much appreciated was the occasion that several hundred of the brigade went for an audience with the Pope. The RC chaplain Fr Benedict Fenlon arranged for a Mass for the Roman Catholic men at St Peter's, so Downing arranged a brigade service at the English church of All Saints: "To use an English Church, complete with organ was a great treat."[7]

The brigade was now getting ready for Operation Dragoon, the landing in southern France, in three camps. Fr Fenlon visited them, including the glider pilots and gunners of the 64th Light Battery RA and 300th Air Landing Anti-tank Battery RA, at Tarquinia. He heard many confessions, and on the Sunday morning a record number of people made their communion at Mass. The last confessions were heard under the wing of a C47 Dakota. Fenlon had given every man of faith a chance to make his peace with God and was pleased to see that very few missed the opportunity: "Every man that wished had the fullest opportunity to make his peace with God and not many were foolish enough to harden their hearts at such a time."[8] Fenlon remembered lying down with his stick under his aircraft, No 44, stick 9 of Brigade HQ, on 14

6   *Ibid*, p.48.
7   *Ibid*, p.40.
8   Benedict Fenlon, 'Parachutist Chaplains 2' in Martin Dempsey, *The Priest Among The Soldiers* (London: Burn Oates, 1946), p.147.

August. They were given breakfast at 11:30 p.m. and then sat under the wings of the aircraft, reading the *Sunday Express* while the aircraft engines were warming up. He was astonished at this calm attitude: "This now strikes me as an amazing state of mind at such a time."[9]

On 15 August the brigade's Pathfinders landed and set up Eureka beacons, but despite the success of this operation only 73 planes placed their parachute troops in the correct area. The dispersed landings resulted in only 40 percent of the 4th Battalion reaching the RV at the correct time. The flight was uneventful, with no flak, but Fenlon described the aircraft as dark and uncomfortable. After a flask of tea they were ready to jump, and Fenlon nervously kept checking his static line and looking at his luminous watch in the very black fuselage of the Dakota. Mentally he gave a last absolution to those with him and prayed that "I would do my duty well",[10] then with a mad scramble they were moving towards the door.

Fenlon landed after a shaky drop in which his parachute oscillated violently. He wandered around looking for the RV and any of his group, feeling vulnerable: "Never will I forget the confusion of that first half hour in the gloom, challenging and being challenged and I felt rather helpless without any arms."[11] He heard gunfire nearby, eventually found his batman and followed the Pathfinders' beacon to the RV. Towards dawn they moved up to Brigade HQ and then to their objective, the village of Le Mitan, which they occupied without opposition at 6:00 a.m., an hour before the sea landings were due. Fr Fenlon made contact with the locals, who were delighted when they found out what was happening: "Their reaction was truly gratifying. Never will I forget there was no need to ask 'was our journey really necessary?' They were overcome with emotion as they came down to shake our hands."[12]

Fenlon set up his base with the 127th Parachute Field Ambulance, which had established a dressing station and operating theatre in a farmhouse. The immediate area was quiet but they could hear plenty of small-arms fire in the valley. While bringing in a casualty, Fenlon and his medical orderly narrowly escaped being involved in a nearby battle involving two German motorcycle troopers whom they came across.

The dressing station had to deal with casualties from the glider landings, but after 9:30 a.m. Fenlon wrote "things began to hum" and battle casualties started to come in. The 6th Battalion took their objective, the village of La Motte, and captured a German stores HQ. However, the battalion was only one company strong as many of its number had been dropped wide.

In the afternoon Fenlon went out on a recce with Captain Rowlands to find another site for casualties, as Le Mitan was becoming crowded. They found a farm at St Michel

9   *Ibid*, p.148.
10 *Ibid*, p.148.
11 *Ibid*, p.149.
12 *Ibid*, p.150.

which was outside the area defended by the brigade but was the only site suitable for their purposes.

The main wave of 300 gliders came in at about 6:00 p.m., resulting in more casualties, although Fenlon commented: "Considering the numbers who made the hazardous landing the German resistance was on the whole light."[13] Some Allied casualties were caused when the gliders landed, with several crashing into anti-glider obstacles. Landing areas were cloaked in mist and were hilly and steep, requiring exceptionally high glider releases. Although 2nd Brigade HQ assembled intact, the 4th, 5th and 6th Parachute Battalions were at half-strength or less. Fenlon pulled one badly injured pilot out of a crashed Horsa and heard later he had survived. All but one of Fenlon's Catholic flock survived the day, Paddy O'Flaherty, who had intoned the Mass two days earlier, being "beyond the sorrows and trials of this world". By the end of the day German resistance had petered out in Fenlon's area, and he remembered that those who could lay down under the tress and slept soundly. During the operation, only 4th Parachute Battalion was in serious contact with the enemy, killing 16 Germans and capturing 29 at a cost of seven dead and nine wounded.

Padre Reid was dropped into France with the 5th (Scottish) Battalion. During the pre-flight briefing they were told by the American commander: "We will drop you at your DZ, even of it takes you three days to walk to it." This proved prophetic, as they were dropped short of the target. Reid then met up with a dentist, and they only had one revolver between them. They discovered when they joined with more men that they had landed no less than 20 miles from their objective. On the way to the RV they were plied with wine and fruit by the local population. Padre Downing had landed in silence unopposed and met up with some Maquis, who sent them in the direction of Le Muy. Gliders began to arrive, and Downing was involved in helping casualties of one that crashed crashed.

Colonel Vic Coxen and A Company had been dropped even further off target, 25 miles from the DZ, and were annoyed on arrival at the rendezvous point. On the evening of 16 August a second glider wave came in. The brigade was pulled out on 25 August, leaving at dawn from docks at St Raphael on the troopship *Dorothy Dix*. On board they enjoyed a good breakfast, with fresh bread, butter and a plentiful supply of eggs. Reid was impressed by the waiter asking, "three or four eggs sir?" Fenlon recounted that his attempts to organise Mass on board during the voyage were thwarted by the fact that he had lost his box containing the wafer hosts during the confusion of embarking: "It was a very chastened priest who explained that there would be no mass, but I think the men understood how I felt. Please God, that unpleasant experience will never be mine again."[14] Having arrived at Naples, the brigade travelled to their Rome base in "triumphal convoy".

13   *Ibid*, p.151.
14   *Ibid*, p.152.

Fenlon was on the move again on 5 September as part of a three-day convoy to the airfields in south-east Italy. Although used to physical 'roughing it', he felt keenly the spiritual hardship of the lack of time or facilities to celebrate daily Mass, or even the daily offices, when the convoy bedded down late at night and was on the move at first light. It was on this journey that he received his only war injury, his jeep broke sharply and resulting in his face hitting the windscreen and his legs striking the dashboard. His vehicle had run into the brigadier's armoured car and was a write-off. This incident convinced him that "It's safer in the air than on the ground because there is much more room."[15]

The brigade was concentrated close to the airfields at San Pancrazio and Manduria for five weeks, and it was therefore much easier for the chaplains to be in contact with all units. As Fenlon put it: "At least I had all my eggs in one basket." Regular services were arranged, and occasional instruction and discussion. Fenlon shared the opinion of many of the padres that as well as arranging services and activities, it was important to be available to the men at all times and to keep up personal and individual contact with them. They were able to listen to the men's problems, which were often dwelt upon and became more urgent while at rest and waiting for action. He wanted men to realise that he could be approached at any time of day or night, whether it was to hear a confession or to listen to the soldier's ordinary trials and difficulties.

He also explained to the non-Catholic officers that a man who was living up to his Catholic faith, worthily going to the sacraments, would almost certainly be a man of good morals: "Such a man is at peace with God; his morale is high which means he is a good soldier."[16] It was while they were at these airfields that Reid, noticing a man acting suspiciously as if he were hiding something in his tent, discovered that three soldiers had found a deserted Italian toddler and had been looking after him in their tent. It was Reid's task to explain to the men why this could not keep him, and to find a place for the boy with the nuns in a local convent.

Operation Manna

On 13 October the brigade were briefed for a drop into Greece. The Germans were about to withdraw from the country and it was imperative that British forces occupy Athens as soon as possible to help in distribution of food to secure the city, maintain law and order, prevent opposing Greek guerrilla forces from starting a civil war and to provide necessary relief for the Greek population. John Greenacre has pointed out that the order for the operation concentrated on the requirements of the landing of airborne troops by glider and parachute, and the objectives when landed were rather more vague: "On top of the lack of clarity in the potential situation, Brigadier C.H.V.

---

15   *Ibid*, p.153.
16   *Ibid*, p.155.

Pritchard had little idea of what his tasks might be beyond seizing Megara Airfield and marching into Athens."[17]

General Anthony Farrar-Hockley, who served with 6th Battalion as a 20-year-old in Greece, recounted in a post-war interview: "Our task was to force the Germans out of Greece ... It was known that they were ready to go but they needed pushing."[18] The situation was further complicated by the strength of the Greek partisans. The most powerful of the groups were the Greek Communist Party-dominated National Liberation Front (EAM) and its military wing the Greek People's Liberation Army (ELAS). Joe Downing wrote that a rumour current at the time that disturbed many of the men was that the object of going into Greece was to restore the Greek king to the throne. Prior to jumping the brigade discovered that 4th Battalion's HQ, C Company and some mortar detachments had already taken off the day before and had been dropped 30 miles west of Athens at Megara airfield. Although they met no opposition from German patrols, they were dropped in high winds, resulting in the injury of the medical officer, who subsequently died, and 40 other ranks. Some of those injured had been taken in by local people due to the absence of the MO. Three men died after being dragged along the ground by their parachutes in the high winds.

Fenlon, Downing and Reid jumped with the main force on 14 October. Upon landing they found that many Greek citizens had come out to meet them. Downing sought out the local Greek Orthodox priests and found were very helpful, allowing him to take services for the troops in their churches:

> I noticed two orthodox priests and remembering my school classics, I went over and said "Ergo Hiereus". Of course my pronunciation was all wrong, and they stared in puzzlement until one of them tumbled on to it, and broke into a beaming smile. "Ah Yerefs! Pappas! Pappas!" and a rapturous greeting ensued. I heard later that this episode was reported in the Athens press the following day.[19]

Fenlon spoke to some in Greek and was delighted when they understood. He also met a New Zealand soldier who had been left behind during the evacuation of Greece in 1941 and had been in hiding ever since. Fenlon's batman received advice from this man not to let go of his 'Tommy gun' because some Greeks might cut his throat for it, explaining that the country was on the verge of civil war. Fenlon was able to bury the three fatalities of the drop in the churchyard at Megara. Farrar-Hockley recalled: "We had been warned that there was a schism between those who supported the old government and the Greek royal family, and a strong vigorous group of communist-led

17 John Greenacre, "'Flexible Enough to Adapt": British Airborne Forces' Experiences during Post Conflict Operations 1944-46', *British Journal for Military History*, Volume 4, Issue 1 (November 2017), p.77.
18 General A. Farrar Hockley, Paradata, https://www.paradata.org.uk/article/general-farrar-hockleys-personal-account-serving-6th-parachute-battalion-during-operation.
19 Downing, Padre *With the Paras*, p.56.

guerrillas, the EAM–ELAS". The situation was further complicated by the rivalry between the guerrilla groups.[20]

Their arrival in Athens caused scenes of much celebration among the Greek citizens. Reid described their arrival at Athens as "triumphal". Downing described "a slow and noisy entry, as the road was packed with cheering people; every so often the cheers were punctuated by guns fired in the air with true Greek abandon".[21] The CO, Brigadier Pritchard, addressed the crowds in the centre of Athens from a balcony, receiving great cheers. He was, however, worried that the situation would turn treacherous for his troops and asked repeatedly for the police chief to disperse the crowds. Luckily, as the tone of celebration changed and the situation deteriorated, rain began to fall and the brigade was able to retreat to safety.[22]

Downing attended the church service at the Greek Orthodox Cathedral with a friend, Harry Leyland. They were made very welcome and placed in chairs by the altar. He thought that the preacher, the Archimandrite, referred to them in his sermon, as every now and then everyone looked at them. He described the beautiful singing by a men's choir in eight parts and wished he could have taken them home to his church. A day or two later he donned the vestments of the Orthodox priest to celebrate for his own soldiers in the church, but he admitted to feeling "improperly dressed without the beard and the little pork pie hat".[23]

After helping with the men wounded on landing at the 127th Parachute Field Ambulance, which was based at Megara immediately after the landing, Fenlon went into Athens to visit the troops in their scattered locations. The 6th (Royal Welch) Battalion had moved north to Chalcis and Thebes, harrying the German retreat through Lamia, Larissa and Kozani. Fenlon managed to visit their posts. The humanitarian situation at Thebes was critical, as described by General Farrar-Hockley: "I took control of the town of Thebes and was in effect the military governor, where we did a great deal of relief work before the official agencies came. There were two villages where they did not seem to have a blanket between them, nor seed to put in for the following year's growth."[24] On his way back from visiting in this area, Fenlon took four Polish German soldiers prisoner; they were very grateful as they had been hiding in the mountains for two months and were afraid of being killed by any Greeks out for revenge.

On 4 November Fenlon went with the 5th Battalion to Salonika. Packed into a LCI, he observed: "No hope of mass, bad weather, sardines in tins have more comfort." For two weeks, Fenlon was the only Roman Catholic chaplain available, and set up

---

20   General A. Farrar-Hockley, Paradata, https://www.paradata.org.uk/article/general-farrar-hockleys-personal-account-serving-6th-parachute-battalion-during-operation.
21   *Ibid.*
22   Hilary St George Saunders, *The Red Beret* (London: Michel Joseph), p.273.
23   Downing, *Padre With the Paras*, p.57.
24   General A. Farrar-Hockley, Paradata, https://www.paradata.org.uk/article/general-farrar-hockleys-personal-account-serving-6th-parachute-battalion-during-operation.

Mass centres in the ruins at two chapels of the French Sisters of Mercy. However, the situation at Salonika and the whole area to the Bulgarian border was rapidly disintegrating, with the British forces unable to halt the slide to civil war. At the end of November the 5th Battalion was ordered back to Athens, where the situation was also deteriorating. Farrar-Hockley reported: "In the struggle for Athens, all three of our battalions were heavily engaged, the 5th mainly at the Acropolis area, the 6th in Omonia Square and the 4th adjoining."[25] The Parachute Brigade and the 3rd Armoured Brigade fought defensively against the attempts of ELAS to take control of the city.

Padre Reid, also with the 5th Battalion, noticed that all over the city there were signs painted on walls and buildings, of Constantine's motto 'In this sign conquer', which had been adopted by the Royal Army Chaplains Department, the difference being that the sign that accompanied it was not the cross but the hammer and sickle. He explained how the 'Jocks' had become gradually aware of the tyranny of communism, as in the villages under communist control it was necessary to be a member of the communists or your ration card was withdrawn.[26] Downing explained that in his opinion there was little doubt that the partisans had only used some of the supplies and arms given them by the Allies to fight the German troops, and now intended to use them to take over Greece for the communist cause.

On 4 December the Greek police fired at a pro-EAM rally in Athens, killing 28 and wounding 148 others. This resulted in the development of a full-scale civil war and ELAS insurgency: "Over the following six weeks the parachute brigade, along with the rest of Lt Gen Scobie's force 140, fought a full scale, brutal counter insurgency in Athens against a more numerous and determined enemy."[27] On 13 December Fenlon returned from Salonika and managed to rejoin the main body of the field ambulance at Rouf Barracks, after joining a tank-protected convoy, dashing though enemy-held streets. He described his understanding of the situation: "Everyone was slowly realising that this was to be no pretence of warfare, that we were up against a desperate enemy who would stop at no terrorism to gain his ends."[28] Farrar-Hockley recalled: "The whole of Athens was besieged by communist guerrillas ... In places we discovered they had been arresting civilians arbitrarily and killing political opponents and their families whose bodies we later discovered."[29] Amidst fears that the 9th General Hospital might be cut off, it was decided to move the field ambulance up to the city centre, so Fenlon's journey was reversed and he found himself repeating the mad dash across the enemy-occupied streets under fire: "We were all inwardly quaking as we

25   General A. Farrar-Hockley, Paradata, https://www.paradata.org.uk/article/general-farrar-hockleys-personal-account-serving-6th-parachute-battalion-during-operation.
26   Museum of Army Chaplaincy Archives, papers deposited by Revd P. R. C. Abram CVO. Typescript, *Lower Than the Angels* (1971), p.54.
27   John Greenacre, 'Flexible Enough to Adapt', p.80.
28   Fenlon, 'Parachutist Chaplains', p.162.
29   Farrar-Hockley, Paradata.

watched the bullets spitting between the wheels of the truck that followed. However we got through safely though we had a few moments while the convoy stopped in the worst spot when the leading truck became entangled in some hanging tram wires."[30]

A 200-bed field hospital was the set up in Athens university and started to receive casualties, and after the 9th Hospital was surrounded and cut off, this became the only surgical centre in the battlefield. Fenlon recorded: "In this way I became a hospital chaplain without moving from the front line." When the ceasefire happened the surgeons had completed over 500 operations. Fenlon was very aware that on the operating table "I had my first and last chance of assisting the badly wounded."[31] The 5th Battalion suffered over 100 casualties, while the 6th Battalion lost all its company commanders.

Fr L. Jones, a chaplain who was with the Corps HQ opposite the cathedral, was able to keep a Mass centre going, and as the university was close by Fenlon could help by hearing confessions. Fenlon commented on the loyalty of some Catholic soldiers who risked attending Mass by travelling through the dangerous streets to the cathedral. As the guerrillas were pushed back through the city, an alternative route to the Rouf barracks opened up, and by 23 December Fenlon was able to resume visiting the 4th Battalion. As the position of the enemy was uncertain at the time, when he was visiting different company positions he had two armed guides for his jeep. In this way he gave nearly all the Roman Catholic soldiers their Christmas communion, although he remembered: "Christmas came and went almost unnoticed. Our music was not Adeste Fideles but of Vickers, Brens and Beaufighter cannons." He was able to share a Christmas cake with a fellow chaplain, Fr Jefferies, but apart from that, "We were on hard tack because the ELAS had captured some of our food dumps and nobody felt very Christmas minded."[32] Downing recalled: "It was a terrible six weeks for Athens, and among the many causes of wretchedness was the break down in transport throughout the city and the consequent impossibility of getting food … A hungry populace was becoming desperate, and a woman would offer her body for a tin of Bully Beef."[33]

By early January 1945, when the EAM/ELAS forces had been defeated, the 5th Parachute Battalion had suffered over 130 casualties. The official history summed up the complexity of the operation:

> The scope of the brigade's activities may be illustrated by the fact that at any one period during serious rioting they were feeding 20,000 Greek civilians, and on

30   Fenlon, 'Parachutist Chaplains', p.164.
31   *Ibid*, p.164.
32   *Ibid*, p.165.
33   Downing, *Padre With the Paras*, p.57.

one day during the final battle in Athens they killed 170 rebels, wounded 70 and took 520 prisoners at considerable cost to themselves.[34]

However, the conflict in Greece had been much misunderstood by the public back home and misrepresented by the British press. Many in Britain, including some politicians, were under the impression that the British troops were fighting against freedom fighters who had defied the German Army, instead of against Germans. But Anthony Farrar-Hockley explained in his account of the operation that rather than taking on gallant freedom fighters, the British were fighting "a group who did not enjoy popular support and some of whom were murderers of their own people". The 2nd Independent Parachute Brigade went back to Italy, where it remained until VE Day.

34   Terence Otway, *Airborne Forces* (London: Imperial War Museum, 1990), p.226.

6

The 1st Airborne Division at Arnhem, September 1944

Fifteen British Army chaplains landed at Arnhem. Nine became prisoners of war, one was sheltered by the Dutch until liberation, two died of wounds and three escaped during Operation Berlin, the retreat over the River Rhine. Three Polish chaplains landed at Driel and took part in the evacuation over the Rhine. One of these was killed, Fr Misiuda. The situation of the British chaplains at Arnhem was in some ways unique, even for airborne chaplains, as there was no possibility of retreat. They were performing their spiritual and practical duties under constant fire, and all displayed physical and moral courage, mostly on the front line of battle. Any concerns about their role in conflict do not appear to have prevented the variety of tasks carried out: taking services, bringing in wounded, tending the wounded under horrendous conditions, keeping up morale by material and spiritual comfort, and in some cases directing the course of military action.

The operation did not proceed as expected and the chaplains found themselves in the thick of the battle, often ministering to the wounded and dying in aid posts which formed the front line of battle, as at Oosterbeek, and becoming prisoners of war. Very few were able to keep to their planned tasks with their units. In the fog of war, some were active in helping organise action although not bearing arms.

Padre Raymond Bowers remembered being in camp in the months leading up to Operation Market Garden. Many operations had been planned and prepared for, then abandoned. The men were often confined to camp in preparation, and Bowers, with some other chaplains of the 1st Airborne Division, managed to persuade the powers to grant social leave, which improved morale. Bowers, still a novice in the 1st Airborne, admitted that it took him a long time to settle in. He found the briefing for the proposed Arnhem operation sketchy: "We were to be flown by Americans and their briefing which I attended was a farce, as they all seemed to take the line 'follow the chap in front'."[1] Padre Selwyn Thorne had joined the 1st Airborne at Easter 1944

---

1   Museum of Army Chaplaincy Archives, an account by Raymond Bowers.

and had a similar experience of constant movement and planned operations which were cancelled.

Padre James Morrison had been with the King's Own Scottish Borderers since 1942, a unit which suddenly found itself part of the 1st Airborne Division, and had been moved from Orkney to Lincolnshire in January 1944, then "initiated into the techniques of loading gliders, dispersing from the landing zone and taking up a fighting position".

Morrison had not been surprised when it became obvious that the 1st Airborne would not play a part in D-Day: "After the glider disasters at Sicily I don't think there was much regret either. It was obvious that our turn would come later."[2] He also endured the waiting around for planned operations which were cancelled, and when news of Market Garden emerged he recalled: "It was realised that the Arnhem operation was a gamble with the odds slightly against us. But the period of inactivity had been so long that most were prepared to put aside their doubts and enter enthusiastically into the operation."

Padre Selwyn Thorne was one of the chaplains who was posted to the airborne unit rather than having volunteered: "I had a phone message saying that I had been posted to the airborne division and did I mind. I asked if that made a difference and the voice at the other end said no, it did not really. So I went!"[3] He did not receive any specific airborne training before going to Arnhem.

Preparations and landing

On Sunday, 17 September, at about 10:00 a.m., thousands of aircraft left 22 airfields. Because of the lack of aircraft for the transport of the 1st Airborne Division, over 10,000 men were carried over four days. Some troops of the first drop remained at the landing and drops zones to guard them for the drop on Monday the 18th.

On the 17th, the first drop arrived at the LZs and DZs. This first lift was very successful, with 95 percent of the troops reaching their rendezvous at the right place and the right time. Fr B.M. Egan, with the 2nd Battalion, landed on DZ X to the south-west of Wolfheze. The 2nd Battalion, under the command of Lieutenant Colonel John Frost, was the first to leave the drop zones to attempt to get to the bridge at Arnhem and capture it, following the southerly route along a road close to the Lower Rhine. They were supposed to be preceded by the Air Landing Reconnaissance Squadron, who had planned to attempt a *coup de main* on the bridge, but nearly all their jeeps failed to arrive, rendering this task impossible. Egan joined the medical unit in order to follow the advance. At dusk the battalion had reached the buildings at the north end of the bridge, and Brigade Headquarters and the Regimental Aid Post

---

2   Museum of Army Chaplaincy Archives, an account by James Morrison.
3   Museum of Army Chaplaincy Archives, letter from Selwyn Thorne to Paul Abram, 5 March 1969.

(RAP) were set up in a building of the department of public works, with first aid unit in the cellar.

Padre Robert Watkins had landed with the 1st Battalion, making a good "feather light landing". Watkins had made the decision to stay with the 1st Battalion rather than with the Field Ambulance, as the operation plans indicated that the brigade would be spread over a wide area and the Field Ambulance might be out of touch with events. He wanted to stay close to the men he knew in the 1st Battalion. His men had to wait until the 2nd Battalion, accompanied by Padre Egan, moved off towards the bridge, and the 3rd Battalion, accompanied by the Revd Phillips, set out for Arnhem. Watkins saw the first lift of gliders coming in: "To see gliders come whistling down fills one with apprehension. I suppose this lot made a good landing, but enough of them hit trees, turned over or did equally alarming things."[4] At 4:00 p.m. the 1st Battalion set out along the Ede to Arnhem road, but soon experienced heavy German resistance and became pinned down by constant fire. Between 5:00 and 8:00 p.m. half of R Company had become casualties. Watkins realised that "already we were meeting fire power to which a parachute battalion had no answer". The situation became worse thorough the night, not helped by the failure of radio communications.

Selwyn Thorne landed at Wolfheze by glider at 1:00 p.m., attached to the Light Regiment Royal Artillery. He remembered that it took several hours of flying around, waiting for the flotilla of gliders to form up, before they started on the journey. His glider had on board a jeep and trailer with medical supplies, and two motorcycles. He was accompanied by the Medical Officer and four other ranks. Travelling in a glider with vehicles was always tense, as if the landing was rough the heavy vehicles could crush the personnel on board. Thorne did not experience much flak and his glider made a good landing, after which they joined the advance of the artillery units on Arnhem. Padre B.J. Benson, who had landed by glider with the 181st Air Landing Field Ambulance, after helping tend to landing casualties, moved with the field ambulance to the crossroads at Oosterbeek, where a field hospital was being set up in the hotels and other buildings. Padre E. Phillips who had jumped in the first drop, accompanied the 3rd Battalion on its central route towards Arnhem along the Utrechtseweg road. The battalion ran into heavy opposition and at nightfall stopped at the edge of Oosterbeek.

Raymond Bowers had jumped number two in his stick, which ended up being scattered over a wide area and came under enemy fire as they landed. Bowers injured his ankle upon landing. He reached the woods at Ginkel Heath and helped bury two men killed in the jump, but then managed to get to the 133rd Para Field HQ, where he was told his ankle was broken and that he would be evacuated. However he was asked to escort two badly injured men in a jeep convoy flying a Red Cross flag in the direction of Arnhem. After a while the jeeps came under fire, returning to the house where they had set up a RAP. Bowers saw a line of German soldiers approaching and

4   Museum of Army Chaplaincy Archives, Revd R.T. Watkins, *Wartime Memoirs 1939-1945*.

indicated to them that his party were all wounded: "I had a sticky time at the end of a German Bayonet, pointing hopefully at my Red Cross armlet." A German officer then turned up and Bowers and his party were taken prisoner. Later, Bowers was told to go with four badly wounded in a German ambulance. When he got out of the ambulance he was pushed around by a German guard and consequently left behind his pouches with his Holy Communion set. "I regretted this many times later."[5]

Padre Alan Buchanan landed with his battalion, the South Staffords, near Wolfheze at DZ S. Buchanan had served with the Staffords in North Africa, Sicily and Italy, and had built up a good reputation with the men. Robert Cain of the Staffords gave the following description him: "His qualities of gentleness and humility were combined with quiet courage and a strength of character. He had a really tremendous influence on the battalion and was respected and loved by all of us. The men, always the shrewdest of judges, would do anything for him."[6] Buchanan went with B Company on the road to Arnhem, and during the march, when the company was subject to attacks and minor skirmishes, he went to gather wounded under fire several times. Cain described how the company was heavily engaged on the upper road to the bridge just above St Elisabeth's hospital: "Alan had moved up with the attack upon this road and was very much in evidence, rushing about in the open and doing what he could for the wounded."[7]

Padre G.A. Pare wrote an account of his experiences in *Arnhem Aftermath*.[8] After celebrating Holy Communion on 17 September, which he found moving as "no one knew if it would be his last", he set out as chaplain to the 1st Wing of the Glider Pilot Regiment and travelled in the glider of the commanding officer, Lieutenant Colonel Ian Murray. Also in the same glider was General Roy Urquhart, commander of the 1st Airborne Division. He was hoping that the flight and landing in the glider would be more pleasant than his experiences on D-Day, as it was in daylight. Pare commented on the way about the "great fleet of accompanying gliders". The sight was "incredibly beautiful". After a good safe landing, Pare set out to see if any of the gliders who had overshot needed help. He buried a young sapper who had been killed in the landing, and eventually found the divisional HQ. He spent the evening visiting the field ambulance and buried a pilot who had crashed his glider on landing, and eventually had three hours' sleep in a chair. He waited at the DZ for the second lift, which was due to drop on the next day at Wolfheze.

Padre Wilfrid Chignell, who had volunteered to be chaplain to the 2nd Wing Glider Pilot Regiment, was relieved that the operation had not been cancelled like so many previous ones. He wrote in his diary: "I spent the time before take-off on

5   Museum of Army Chaplaincy Archives, an account by the Revd Raymond Bowers.
6   Museum of Army Chaplaincy Archives, letter from Robert Cain VC to Paul Abram, 1 November 1971.
7   *Ibid.*
8   Ohio University, The Cornelius Ryan Collection of World War II Papers. G.A. Pare, *Arnhem Aftermath*, p.2.

the airfield before going off around as many gliders as possible, and giving the chaps a blessing."[9] Chignell felt the excitement, "not of fear but of pride",[10] as soon as they were safely up. After enduring a shaking from bursts of flak, the glider landed safely, and as Chignell put it, "We all hopped out quickly." They found an unoccupied house, where supplies were found and the party made the building their HQ for the night.

James Morrison landed at the LZ near Wolfheze at about noon on the 17th. His exit from the glider, which landed safely, was accompanied by piping from Pipe Major Laidlaw. The battalion dug in to prepare defensive positions for the second lift and had to fight off German counterattacks during the night.

The glider containing Padre John Rowell had to land in Oxfordshire, which meant that he did not arrive until the 18th, when he met up with his battalion, the 1st Battalion of the Border Regiment who were defending LZ X.

Monday, 18 September/Tuesday, 19 September

Padre Daniel McGowan, who had volunteered from the Royal Armoured Corps earlier in the year, described the tension in the weeks building up to the operation. He made 24 jumps in training, but many operations were cancelled: "This was a period of intense activity and alternating tension and relief as each operation was cancelled."[11] During this training he realised that a chaplain's role concerned all those about him, regardless of denomination. He believed that there were no religious distinctions on a plane with men preparing to jump or those on a ground exercise nearing the point of exhaustion: "During the battle and afterwards amid conditions of fear and death the uniformity of the basic needs of all men became self-evident."[12] On 18 September the waiting ended and McGowan said Mass with the deafening sound of planes roaring overhead. He was to be responsible, with the other Roman Catholic priest, Fr Bernard Egan, for the spiritual and pastoral care of the units of the Royal Army Medical Corps. On the 18th, as part of the 133rd Parachute Field Ambulance, he took off on a "sunny misty morning … to become part of the great armada forming up over East Anglia". McGowan expressed relief when the green light eventually came on, but he had a worrying time after jumping as it was the first time he had jumped with a kit bag and found himself descending too fast with the kit bag tangled in the line and himself upside down. However, he managed to disentangle himself and make a "very soft" landing on Ginkel Heath. He helped the medical orderlies search for casualties, as the heath was ablaze.[13] At dusk, having loaded the injured into a jeep, they set off for Arnhem. On the morning of the 19th they settled at Oosterbeek, where the hotels

9   Archives of the Museum of Army Flying, The Diary of the Battle of Arnhem by the Revd W.H. Chignell, p.1.
10   *Ibid*, p.2.
11   Museum of Army Chaplaincy Archives, an account by the Revd Daniel McGowan.
12   *Ibid*.
13   *Ibid*.

Shoonoord and Vreewijk were being used as hospitals. His task that day was to assist the wounded and make a careful note of the dead. During the night he assisted Dr Smith, who was using the dentist's surgery for operations.

The Revd A. Menzies, attached to the 156th Parachute Battalion, set off on 18 September and also found himself landing on Ginkel Heath. Landing under fire, he was dragged a considerable way by his parachute but managed to cut himself free. In the midst of the confusion he saw "a panic stricken white hare running around" and realised that his camera, lent to him by *Life* magazine, was with his collapsible bicycle which was nowhere to be seen on the landing ground around him. He soon met up with Captain J.S. Buck the battalion MO. The battalion set off for towards Arnhem, and after burying victims of the landing in a nearby wood, Menzies accompanied them. Finding a jeep, he went "flying around; picking up wounded and taking them to a civilian hospital at Wolfheze, after a difficult journey under fire along forest tracks".[14] He spent the night of the 18th helping the surgeon at the Wolfheze hospital. His work consisted of "holding instruments while the doctors performed some operations on the wounded".[15]

John Rowell's eventual landing was smooth and peaceful, and after stopping to talk to senior chaplain Albert Harlow, he went to the RAP which had been set up in a barn. Rowell recalled that there were some casualties from crashed gliders, and that in the evening they set out for Oosterbeek. When they arrived at the farm where they were to stay the night, Rowell buried two paratroopers in the nearby wood, narrowly avoiding fire from an enemy plane by jumping into the graves for cover. Rowell remembered watching a supply drop which was obviously going into enemy hands. In the afternoon of the 18th they moved into a house near the Hartenstein hotel, where the RAP stayed for the rest of the battle. Rowell had no doubts at that stage that the Second Army would eventually reach them.

After defending the second lift, Morrison accompanied the King's Own Scottish Borderers towards Arnhem. Encountering fierce opposition, they fell back on Oosterbeek and Morrison stayed with the RAP, which had to move around several houses as the perimeter shrank: "From this time on I was fully occupied at the RAP, helping as best I could to treat the wounded and keep up the spirits of these remarkably resilient men."[16]

On Monday the 18th Selwyn Thorne had arrived at the former home of a Dutch Calvinist minister where Mrs ter Horst had given permission for the artillery to set up an aid post in the vicarage. At this point it was not crowded, and seriously injured men could go to the larger field hospitals in Oosterbeek, but as the days went on it was to become a crucial part of caring for the wounded of the retreating paratroopers. In a post-war account, Thorne remembered feeling quite upbeat and optimistic on the

---

14   Museum of Army Chaplaincy Archives, an account by the Revd A. Menzies.
15   *Ibid.*
16   Museum of Army Chaplaincy Archives, an account by the Revd J. Morrison.

Monday and Tuesday: "We felt thrilled as we thought we were going to win the war." He felt at this stage they were coping well with the casualties.[17]

Padre Pare had been waiting for the second lift, but at 11:00 a.m. he came under fire for the first time as his trenches were strafed by a *Messerschmitt*: "It was a most nerve racking experience, for the trench was not deep enough and the spurt of bullets unpleasantly close."[18] At 2:00 p.m. the second lift landed and flak had started, along with small-arms fire from the wood. Pare attached himself to a RAP, joining a party with the regimental doctor in two ambulance jeeps sent to locate wounded. Having found a group of wounded men and arranged for them to be escorted back to the aid post, Pare decided to try to get near the dead and wounded men lying in the open around the crashed gliders. He described the action:

> I grasped a Red Cross flag, beckoned to two of the stretcher bearers to follow me with a stretcher and the others to await my signal, and then with a palpitating heart and waving my flag, set out across the open, the two bearers following me. Five of the Gliders were just heaps of ashes, and bodies could be seen at different points stretched out on the grass. I was still wearing my dog collar, and I mentally committed myself.[19]

Finding some men alive, Pare signalled to the ambulance jeeps to join him and the wounded were evacuated. The last man he attended to was beside a dead body, and was not injured but prostrate with grief at the death of his pal: "It was not the time for argument, so I spoke rather sharply to him and called a bearer to assist him to walk off." They had not been fired on while helping the wounded, but as soon as the first aid party made it back to the trees "a fusillade of shots rang out". Pare realised that they had been in the enemy's sights all the time, but fire had been deliberately withheld. He later learned that the German troops "respected the Red Cross scrupulously".[20] Later in the day the battalion started moving east towards Oosterbeek. During the stop start night-long nightmare journey, Pare and the medical officer ran behind a jeep containing badly wounded soldiers and early on the morning of the 19th arrived at the divisional HQ, which had been set up at Hartenstein hotel in Oosterbeek.

Wilfrid Chignell, as padre to the Glider Pilot Regiment, who were charged with guarding the LZs, was also waiting for the second drop on the 18th. During the morning he had buried the men killed in the drop. As they were waiting they were under fire from three sides, but the second lift arrived eventually. Chignell described the scene:

17   Museum of Army Chaplaincy Archives, an account by the Revd S. Thorne.
18   Revd A. Pare, *Arnhem Aftermath*, p.8.
19   *Ibid*, pp.11, 12.
20   *Ibid*, p.13.

At last, Thunderbolts and Spitfires [arrived] and now the grand old Dakotas and Horsas. What a marvellous sight and over there to the west are lots more Dakotas and we can see parachutists dropping. This is about the best sight I have ever seen in my life. These glider pilots are marvellous. They are doing wonderful landings despite the difficulty of finding room and the flak which has appeared today. Quite heavy too. There were one or two exciting landings – one glider crashed right through a hedge and another did a marvellous side skid to draw up mostly in a wood and out came everyone unhurt.[21]

However, fierce fighting developed over the supply drop zones and Chignell commented: "There was not much chance of getting at the supplies." Chignell's HQ retreated about three miles and found a good billet with a good host, but he recalled: "We had a perfectly foul night with a heavy machine gun and various other oddments firing all night, including one shot through the kitchen window yards from us."[22]

On the 19th he witnessed the third drop and reported on the bravery of the pilots risking heavy flak in order to drop supplies: "The gliders had a bad time of it as we had more or less lost control of the LZ." He commented on how proud he was of his glider pilots in action: "The Glider Pilot Regiment was being used as if it was crack infantry which was a great compliment to it."[23]

Brigadier Philip Hicks, who was in charge in the temporary absence of Urquhart, decided to use the troops brought in by the glider lift to reinforce the battalions that were having trouble advancing into Arnhem. The 2nd South Staffords, accompanied by Alan Buchanan, moved off. Menzies, after spending the night at the hospital in Wolfheze, was comforted by a report from the BBC on the morning of the 19th that Monty's 21st Army Group was about to break through to the airborne forces at Arnhem. However, the Germans arrived shortly after and Menzies was taken prisoner. He had taken some photos with his camera from *Life* magazine, but hid the camera before he was arrested. Unfortunately, the hospital was later destroyed and the camera was never recovered. As he was taken away by a German officer in a staff car, he passed a parachute container filled with red berets which had been dropped by the pilots who had risked their lives, intended to be used by the airborne troops in a triumphant entry into Arnhem. His predicament was not helped by the fact that it was his birthday. He joined a group of other POWs and they were marched off, put in a trailer and taken to join other prisoners. They were escorted by drunk SS men firing at houses and a garage seemingly at random. One of the captured men on the trailer was shot and Menzies gave him some morphine. The trailer stopped and they were made to get out: "We stood expecting to be murdered, but after a while we were put back on the jeep and drove on to a Nazi barracks where we were made to stand and be

21 Chignell, *The Diary of the Battle of Arnhem*, p.4.
22 *Ibid*, p.5.
23 *Ibid.*

shouted at by troops with rifles in their hands who were shouting about the actions of the RAF destroying their homes and families."[24] Menzies and the other officers said they were important and if they were killed there would be repercussions. Eventually the trailer returned and they were taken to join the main group of POWs, later to be taken to *Offlag* 79 at Braunschweig.

Padre Edward Phillips had dropped in the HQ stick of the 3rd Battalion. Their planned march was delayed and interrupted by heavy mortar fire. On the outskirts of Oosterbeek the battalion stopped for a few hours' rest, and Phillips walked back after dark to a deserted school as he knew there were a number of wounded there. The battalion resumed its advance on the morning of Monday the 18th. It was decided to approach Arnhem by a more southerly route, marching through Oosterbeek at dawn, hoping to join up with the 2nd Battalion at the bridge. They experienced stiff opposition and Phillips found himself with General Urquhart and Brigadier Gerald Lathbury, commander of the 1st Parachute Brigade, at the tail end of a long column. They had nearly reached St Elisabeth's hospital when they encountered a strong defensive enemy position blocking any hope of getting to the bridge, Urquhart and Lathbury having to take cover in a house. Phillips remembered that during the morning he had to "sprint across a gap by some factories on the river bank" and that there was firing from the other side of the river. He took cover in the same house that Urquhart and Lathbury were in. He was on the ground floor and the general was in the first floor flat. Mess tins of tea were hauled up by string by Urquhart. During the course of the day, a medic appeared over the back wall and reported to the MO. Phillips managed to break out of the house without too much difficulty and got through some woods by a back way to the hospital. As Philips was working in the hospital moving among the wounded, a medical orderly asked him "Are you in the bag too sir?", and he realised that the hospital had been taken by the Germans and he was a prisoner of war.[25]

Meanwhile, the battle continued at the bridge, where Egan was with the 2nd Battalion. The battalion was under heavy and continuous attack as the enemy tried to displace them from the northern end of the bridge. The two medical officers confided in Egan their worry about how few drugs that had left. The wounded were being cared for in the crowded RAP cellar alongside their German prisoners. On Tuesday evening Tiger tanks attacked and shelled the HQ. This attack was repulsed, but the position of the battalion was deteriorating rapidly, with no food or water, ammunition running out and a rising number of wounded.

On the morning of Tuesday the 19th, Buchanan and the MO, Captain Brian 'Basher' Brownscombe, set up a RAP at Arnhem Municipal Museum, about 400yds east of St Elisabeth's hospital. At this stage Buchanan, like some of his padre colleagues, found himself taking part in the action itself. He gave orders for 7

24   Museum of Army Chaplaincy Archives, an account by the Revd A. Menzies.
25   Museum of Army Chaplaincy Archives, an account by the Revd E. Phillips.

Platoon of A Company to occupy the house opposite the museum, and managed to warn troops who were behind the museum to withdraw when the Germans attacked the eastern side of the museum.

On the morning of the 18th the 1st Battalion was still involved in heavy fighting in the woods between Wolfheze and Oosterbeek as they attempted to break through to Arnhem. Robert Watkins tended the wounded, but in the confusion of the fighting became separated from the main medical unit and gave first aid wherever possible, helped by Dutch civilians. The 1st Battalion fought its way through the streets all day, losing men, and reached a road junction just west of St Elisabeth's hospital by about 3:00 p.m. There were by then only about 100 men left. During the day Watkins struggled to give first aid with dwindling supplies, moving casualties into the homes of the Dutch who were helping in any way they could.

The next day, at 4:00 a.m., Lieutenant Colonel Dobie planned an advance to the bridge with his battalion and what remained of the 3rd Battalion, supported on their left flank by the 2nd South Staffords, followed by the 11th Parachute Battalion. However, the attack was repulsed and the 1st Battalion was scattered. While the transport officer, Lieutenant J.L. Williams, coordinated the remaining force, Watkins went on reconnaissance. They seemed to be the only ones trying to restore order and regroup the men. It was at this point that Watkins realised he was acting as a soldier rather than a chaplain, commenting later: "I was perforce beginning to be the soldier."[26] But he continued to play a dual role, taking control and giving orders in the confusion that existed as the British forces retreated to the perimeter. He took a jeep out from St Elisabeth's hospital to pick up wounded in the gardens and houses in the vicinity: "Why I got away with it I shall never know, for I had no Red Cross markings or flag, nor did it occur to me to look for any." Later he took some wounded to the Shoonoord and visited the HQ at the Hartenstein, where he had a conversation with General Urquhart and caught up with the situation, also briefing the general on the situation at St Elisabeth's. What was left of the four battalions retreated to Oosterbeek and were sent to defend the south-eastern side of the perimeter, where Watkins and Lieutenant Williams set about organising the troops until officers from Headquarters were sent to relieve them. Major R.T.H. Lonsdale arrived at their position on the emerging perimeter, where Williams and Watkins briefed him on the situation. Lonsdale's diary recounted the meeting:

> I proceeded past the church at Oosterbeek to the area of the railway line. It was here that I was very pleased to see John Williams of the1st Battalion and Padre Watkins, and from them I was briefed as to the positions now held by the 1st, 3rd and 11th Battalion remnants.[27]

---

26   Watkins, *Wartime Memoirs 1939-1945*.
27   Diary of Major R. Lonsdale, quoted by Watkins, *Wartime Memoirs*.

At the Divisional HQ at the Hartenstein hotel, Pare was reunited with many men of his regiment who were dug in around the grounds, beginning to establish a defensive position, and he was able to consult the senior chaplain, the Revd Harlow. That morning Harlow gave him the task of burying Major General Friedrich Kussin, the German *Feld-Kommandatur* of Arnhem, who had been killed in a jeep at Wolfheze crossroads. Pare was given two young SS troopers to help him, and they buried Kussin, his driver and interpreter, and also managed to bury some British troops, a German soldier and a Dutch civilian. He decided on a common grave for the general and the three soldiers in his car. He was able to share out some chocolate and cigarettes with the SS troopers, who were young, hungry and scared. Pare recounted: "I could feel no animosity to them."[28]

That afternoon Pare witnessed the disastrous glider landing and supply drop at L zone: "Prayers must have come to all our hearts as we watched this terrible drama which resulted in many casualties."[29] For the first time he realised that the operation was facing considerable opposition, but still placed faith in the eventual appearance of the Second Army. He decided to stay at the field hospital set up at the Shoonoord hotel at the Oosterbeek crossroads. Together with the Vreewijk and Tafelberg hotel, this became the main hospital area and the place where the chaplains felt they could best meet the wounded and minister to them spiritually and practically. Pare met up with Padres Benson, Watkins and McGowan, who briefed each other on the situation in different parts of the battlefield. He also met Padre Irwin and had a conversation with him about the merits of wearing a dog collar. Pare advised him to wear one so that the men could identify him as a padre without effort.

Wednesday, 20 September

With his division seriously weakened, Urquhart decided to form a defensive perimeter around Oosterbeek and hold out until XXX Corps reached them. This meant that the 2nd Battalion at the bridge was abandoned to its fate. As the battle raged on Tuesday and Wednesday, the RAP cellar became crowded with injured British and German troops. Fr Bernard Egan left the relative safety of the cellar to visit soldiers in other hideouts around the north end of the bridge, and was hit while returning to the aid post. Wounded in the back and legs, he joined the 200 men lying wounded amidst the blood and dust of the cellar. Lieutenant Colonel Frost arranged a temporary ceasefire, and Egan was evacuated with the other wounded. He was taken first to the St Elisabeth hospital and then became a POW at Mühlhausen until the camp's liberation in 1945.

Wilfrid Chignell, still at the landing zones, went round to visit his men to see how they were getting on, dealing with the wounded and trying to raise morale: "I

28   Pare, *Arnhem Aftermath*, p.25.
29   *Ibid.*

believe in going round with my beret and stick as it seems to cheer the chaps to see 'a cheery beret'."[30]

Alan Buchanan left the wounded at the museum in the care of a medical orderly and went to help the MO, Brownscombe, at a temporary first aid post where there were heavy casualties. While there, unwilling to leave the injured men, he was taken prisoner. Between 20 and 27 September he was allowed to visit both St Elisabeth's hospital and the Municipal hospital. After the war, in 1945, he gave evidence to a war crimes tribunal about the murder of Dr Brownscombe by a drunken SS NCO, Karl Lerche. Also involved was a Danish member of the SS war propaganda unit, Knud Fleming Larsen, who had been drinking with Lerche. Buchanan and Daniel McGowan were able to give information about Larsen. Buchanan had seen Larsen talking to Brownscombe shortly before the shooting and had attempted with Brownscombe to get rid of him. Buchanan went upstairs and when he returned Brownscombe was lying outside, shot in the head: "I went outside and found his body lying in a pool of blood … I looked for the Dane but there appeared to be absolutely no one within the hospital grounds."[31] McGowan was able to testify that Brownscombe had been talking to Larsen shortly before the shooting and also found on Brownscombe's body an address for Larsen, which was later taken from McGowan among his other papers when he was recaptured after escaping, but he could remember the name and that the address was in Copenhagen.[32] Eventually it was established that Lerche had slipped away from the party a little while earlier and shot Brownscombe from some bushes before escaping. He was traced and brought to trial after the war, receiving a sentence of 10 years' hard labour.

As the defensive perimeter became established, with the Divisional HQ at the Hartenstein hotel at its centre, the hospitals at the crossroads were on the front line. Senior padre Harlow, an older man with grey hair, helped promote a calm atmosphere, and as well as providing a listening ear for his fellow chaplains, helped MO Lieutenant D.M. Randall with the wounded in the cellar of the Hartenstein HQ.

Padre Irwin had ventured our wearing his makeshift cardboard collar but was killed by an exploding mortar shell at the door to a first aid post on Wednesday, 22 September. His body was found near the Hartenstein, and there are no records of him being brought to a first aid post, so it is likely he died where he fell.[33] The Shoonoord took a direct hit and a RC chaplain, Fr B.J. Benson, lost an arm. Graeme Warrack, a MO, recalled this incident in his diary kept during the battle:

30   Chignell, *The Diary of the Battle of Arnhem*, p.5.
31   United Nations War Crimes Commission, British National Office charge No UK G/B 275. Affidavit sworn by Alan Buchanann, 26 June 1945. Facsimile of the document is on p.133. Chris van Roekel, *The Torn Horizon, The Airborne Chaplains at Arnhem* (Oosterbeek: Jan and Wendela ter Horst and Chris van Roekel, 2000), p.133.
32   *Ibid*, affidavit by Daniel McGowan.
33   Chris van Roekel, *The Torn Horizon,* p.65.

Fr Benson seemed to lose the will to live, as he felt he would not be able to perform the mass without his arm. Canon Law which was in use until 1983 stated "excluded from celebrating Holy Communion are priests who are unable to properly perform the sacrament".[34]

Benson died on 27 September and was buried by Fr McGowan at St Elisabeth's hospital. Dr M.E. Herford, who had worked closely with Benson, recounted that his death was not explained on physical grounds, but that the sacraments were the main sources of inspiration to Benson: "He was in good health and had not lost much blood. The operation was well performed soon after wounding. He believed, however, that never again would he be able properly to celebrate mass. He literally turned his face to the wall and died within 72 hours."[35]

In the course of the next few hours the Germans took control of the crossroads and started evacuating walking wounded, both British and German. Fr McGowan went to the Roman Catholic church nearby to celebrate Mass, and when he returned he was taken prisoner by the German forces that had arrived in his absence. He was put in charge of 35 wounded and they were taken to a school, where there were no supplies of food or water. McGowan managed to obtain some fruit from the cellar of a nearby house, and the next morning the group were taken to the Municipal hospital.

Meanwhile, on the evening of the 20th the hospitals at the crossroads were once again in British hands after being held by the Germans for a few hours, and Pare started visiting all the wounded and was able to hold a service on each floor of the hospital. He remembered: "In the evening when the men had been bedded down at crossroads I went around the wards holding short services: It was helpful to these helpless men and our prayer for relief was heartfelt." The situation at the crossroad hospitals was deteriorating as more and more wounded came in, and Pare found himself increasingly ministering to dying men: "I remember one unfortunate Scots boy telling me that he was dying and dictating a message to his mother ... somehow I was given the power to settle and comfort."[36]

Major Lonsdale had now taken over command of the Thompson group on the south-eastern perimeter. By now Watkins was exhausted and his morale was low:

I was desperately tired, tired to the point of lowered spirits. I suspect that there is a point in every endurance test where every step is a burden and one's second wind is yet to come. Also I and all of us had a bad feeling that we had not got to the Bridge and had had to leave those who were then unsupported. My business was to encourage at a time when I needed encouragement. But any parson knows

34 Explained in a footnote of *Torn Horizon*, p.57.
35 Museum of Army Chaplaincy Archives, an account by Dr M.E. Herford.
36 Pare, *Arnhem Aftermath*, p.25.

all about behaving more cheerfully in public than he feels. I did get to every single position in that morning.[37]

Thursday, 21 September

Lieutenant Williams's exhausted men and Watkins were assigned to a position on the south-eastern part of the perimeter. On Thursday afternoon they were withdrawn from the polder where they had been coming under heavy fire and rendezvoused in the church, where Watkins heard a part of Major Lonsdale's address. The old vicarage had become crowded in the extreme as Thursday brought increasing casualties, leaving very few available officers and causing Watkins once again to assume a leadership role. Lonsdale met up with Watkins while visiting a barn opposite the church, and together they visited the men of the 1st and 3rd Battalions in the field by the river. Lonsdale's diary recorded: "On arrival in that sector Watkins and I had words with the soldiers who were at this stage in remarkably good heart."[38]

Chignell was becoming increasingly frustrated by continued attacks:"Most of us are feeling the strain of little sleep. Shortage of water and almost continuous fighting. Mortars and shelling. It is not a very comfy feeling to be surrounded for five days as we have been." There were continued rumours of the Second Army's approach, but Chignell was doubtful: "The news of Second Army is getting to be no more than bally rumours."[39]

During the day Chignell went out to get the wounded:

> There were some wounded in the wood in front of our line which I went off to collect with Martin Culverwell, who held a Red Cross flag in front of me. We made contact with some Germans and they came out and helped us and we helped them with their wounded. They were only youngsters and one of them was a Dane. We did what we could for the wounded of both sides and brought them back to our place. While we were binding up one German some fool started off with a machine gun and for a minute or two there was some hectic firing going on around us, but fortunately it soon stopped.[40]

At the bridge, fighting continued until 9:00 a.m. when the Germans eventually overran and took possession of the structure.

37   Watkins, *Wartime Memoirs 1939-1945*.
38   Major Lonsdale's diary, quoted by R. Watkins, *Wartime Memoirs 1939-1945*.
39   Chignell, *Diary of the Battle of Arnhem*, p.5.
40   *Ibid*.

Friday, 22 September

On Friday and Saturday Watkins used his Red Cross flag to move freely around the units in his part of the perimeter, and as well as moving wounded into the vicarage, praying and helping raise morale, his freedom of movement allowed him to keep some of the pinned-down units in touch with each other. For example, he was able to pass on information that the Guard's Armoured Division would probably reach the southern Rhine on the Friday night.

Saturday, 23 September

Meanwhile, the situation at Padre Thorne's medical unit at Kate ter Horst's house was deteriorating. Kate and her young family, including a baby, took refuge in the cellar and were present throughout the battle, Kate somehow managing to care for them and help with the wounded. General Sir Frank King described the effect she had on the wounded soldiers: "She was a paragon of strength and stamina, helping the doctor and his orderlies; comforting the dying and giving new strength to the sick."[41] The old vicarage had become crowded in the extreme as Thursday brought increasing casualties. As the perimeter formed and then shrank, the post was overcrowded with serious casualties and from the Wednesday onward was under fire. It became so full that it was only possible to reach the wounded by walking on the handles of the stretchers.[42] Kate ter Horst described Thorne as "a kind little man with curly hair and spectacles who is on the go the whole day". He impressed her on two counts. Firstly, he could be seen cleaning a filthy lavatory, and secondly, his reassurance that the food in the house would not be taken from the children. Watkins, upon meeting Thorne at the aid post, initially thought that he seemed a bit bewildered, but he soon realised that Thorne had an iron determination to minster to the medical staff and wounded. In Watkins' opinion, "he grew as the days went by". In his wartime diary Watkins reflected:

> Thorne and I, in an unspoken way, complimented one another. His job was inside that place, mine was outside. He knew nothing of how things were going since his world was inside, while I brought in bits of news about happenings and about people. He practised the proper functions of a priest in there, prayer, calm - normality, if that is the right word. I was as unkempt as the men outside, involved with them and their job, trying to be myself in their shoes. I hope that

41   Frank King, Introduction to Kate ter Horst, *Angel of Arnhem*, p.13.
42   Museum of Army Chaplaincy, papers deposited by Revd P.R.C. Abram CVO. *Lower Than Angels*, p.100.

mine was a ministry, though an odd one. I know that Thorne's was an authentic ministry.[43]

By Friday the situation at the RAP had deteriorated further, with shortages of water and food. The German artillery was moving forward as the perimeter shrank, and there was much shelling around the old vicarage. Kate ter Horst remembered a conversation with the MO in which he said that he had prayed that the house would not be hit again, and then added: "If we were hit again I hope it would kill them all right off … It'd bad enough to be wounded once; don't let them be hit again and further mutilated, it's better that all of them should be killed at once."[44]

The dead were piled up outside and, despite gunfire, Thorne managed to bury 14 men at dawn on the 23rd. A footnote in Kate ter Horst's account of the battle states that in total 57 airborne troops had been buried behind the vicarage, probably mostly by Thorne.[45] He gave Kate ter Horst his Bible in English and asked he to read the 91st psalm, verses 1-7, to the groups of wounded, beginning with the words "He that dwelleth in the secret place of the Most High /shall abide under the shadow of the Almighty", ending with verse 7, "A thousand shall fall at thy side/ and ten thousand at thy right hand/ but it shall not come by thee."

Thorne was described as being "Small, neat and quiet"[46] and "a model of calm and meticulous neatness".[47] He simply got on with his job of assisting the doctor, acting as an orderly and fulfilling his priestly functions to the wounded and dying, showing God's love at all times. He was willing to any job that came along, including cleaning the lavatory. He described how General Urquhart visited the RAP: "He had the temerity to say he hoped I was being useful. As I was in my shirt sleeves mopping up blood at the time, I replied with some asperity that I hoped I was. I was told afterwards that it was the right technique!"[48]

Another side to his character was shown when a Tiger tank approached the vicarage and prepared to shell it. Bombardier Bolden and Thorne rushed out, flourishing a Red Cross flag and yelling to the tank commander to cease fire as it was an aid post. The tank commander agreed, so long as the machine gun on the roof was removed. Although Kate ter Horst and Watkins did not remember a machine gun, Thorne distinctly recalled giving the order for it to be taken down, as he reckoned that was the only military order he had ever given. In his 1968 account of his experiences at Arnhem he wrote:

43   Watkins, *Wartime Memoirs 1939-1945*.
44   Kate ter Horst, *Angel of Arnhem*, p.51.
45   *Ibid*, p.54.
46   *Ibid*, p.101.
47   Chris van Roekel, *The Torn Horizon*, p.55.
48   Museum of Army Chaplaincy, letter from Selwyn Thorne to Paul Abram, 16 September 1969.

Yes there was a machine gun on the roof of the house. I remember that very clearly as I had to tell them to move once we had the tank commander's assurance that he would leave us alone as we were a hospital. I remember yelling at them and saying that in fact I had no authority to give them orders but that they would go all the same. Somehow they did. So it was not in fact the tank that did the dislodging.[49]

On one occasion when Watkins returned to the hospital rendered unrecognisable with mud and blood, Thorne quietly sat him down, calmed him and cleaned him up. When the evacuation commenced, Thorne chose to stay with the wounded and became a prisoner of war.

James Morrison spent the last few days of the battle in a house where the RAP had ended up after moving continuously. The owners of the house and their pregnant daughter were sheltering in the cellar, and when he went down to visit them on the Saturday evening they began singing softly: "The words I could not understand but I knew the tune and we sang together, each in our own language, 'Abide With Me'." Many year later Morrison met a young woman who introduced herself to him as "the baby in the cellar".[50]

At the crossroads, conditions were also deteriorating. Chignell reported that, "Jerry certainly had the range of our spot for he has had 5 direct hits today." He held a short service in the cellar in which everyone joined in, including the Roman Catholics: " I should have liked a Eucharist but that would have meant that the RCs definitely, and Nonconformists probably, would have had no part."[51] He was stretcher-bearing for the rest of the day: "In evening lost control of the woods. In consequence I had to clear out with my wounded down to Div HQ where there is a better medical spot."

At the dressing stations at the crossroads it was a glorious evening, and at 6:00 p.m. Warrack, Padre Harlow and another officer, Graham Roberts, stood upstairs wondering and thinking what a strange war it was.[52]

Sunday saw fierce fighting and many more casualties arriving at the vicarage aid post. Watkins was particularly upset by the death of a young major at a dressing station whose body was placed in the garden through lack of space. Abram described Watkins's feelings: "Watkins, for all the carnage around him, found himself filled with helpless fury that such a man should be reduced to the status of disposable flesh."[53] However, he did not feel he could share this with others, and Abram commented:

49   Museum of Army Chaplaincy, an account by the Revd Selwyn Thorne.
50   Museum of Army Chaplaincy, an account by the Revd J. Morrison.
51   Chignell, *Diary of the Battle of Arnhem*, p.6.
52   The Wellcome Library, 'Arnhem Diary'. Transcript of the diary written by Colonel Graeme Warrack, ADMS1 Airborne Division during and immediately after Operation Market Garden. 17 September - 1 October 1944. Entry for Saturday 23 Septembe Abram, *Lower Than the Angels*, p.98.
53   *Ibid*, p.98.

"Battle is something that a chaplain can share with others, but there are certain aspects which he cannot share, which he must carry alone and which have no place in the military history."

In preparation for the evacuation on Monday, Watkins was given the task of ensuring that every unit and group received their written orders. He arranged that even though the seriously wounded were to be left behind, as the vicarage was so near the river he could take a group of less wounded men to the boats, and he escorted them across. He then returned to collect more wounded, but dawn was breaking and he was unable to. Now stuck on the wrong side of the river and separated from the troops remaining on the north side, he decided to swim across to the south side and joined those who had been evacuated.

Watkins was awarded the Military Cross. His citation read:

> During the entire operation at Arnhem 17th-25th September 1944 Padre Watkins conducted himself with considerable fortitude and dash. Operating within the divisional perimeter he made himself responsible for carrying information from commander to commander invariably through intense shell and mortar and always when the need was greatest. His endless tending of the wounded under fire, and his continued organising of their evacuation to dressing stations, often made possible by his untiring personal effort and example, afforded an unparalleled example to all ranks. His demeanour throughout, his unfailing courage and his complete disregard for his own safety guaranteed the morale of the whole force which never wavered in the least.[54]

By Saturday the water and food situation at the Oosterbeek crossroads was desperate. Pare devised a system of draining off water from the guttering to help. During Saturday the Shoonoord was retaken by the Germans, but Pare's routine of visiting and practical help continued as the Germans evacuated the walking wounded and the lines of battle moved across the hospital/hotel area. Pare was invited to go with a German jeep under a white flag and Red Cross flag to visit St Michael's hospital near Arnhem, where he was able to catch up with the Revd Harlow, who was awaiting interrogation, before returning to the Shoonoord. Pare was prevented from having a large Sunday service by renewed fighting and shelling in the area, but he recounted the poignant singing of 'Abide With Me'. The text for his sermon that day was from the Gospel of St Matthew, Chapter 6: "Therefore, take no thought for your life, what you shall eat, or what ye shall drink, nor for your body what you shall put on. Is not the life more than meat and the body more than raiment?" He recalled: "At this particular service, with men stretched out on the floor and a couple of lamps flickering, I really felt the presence of the almighty with his sheltering wings over this place."[55]

---

54   Chris van Roekel, *The Torn Horizon*, p.65.
55   *Ibid*, p.36.

Padre John Rowell had been at a RAP near the Tafelberg hotel throughout the battle, working with the wounded and assisting them to the Advanced Dressing Station (ADS) at the Tafelberg. During the week the number of wounded had increased and they came increasingly under fire. Along with other aid posts and dressing stations, they had problems with lack of supplies and water. When the post suffered a direct hit the wounded were moved to the cellar.

On Monday Rowell was given the news that there was to be an evacuation over the Rhine. The wounded were to remain with the RAMC staff, but Rowell was to take about a dozen walking wounded across the river. At about 10 p.m. they started the "slow crawl" down to the river. He seems to have been lucky and had an uneventful journey, and took his party over in two boats. Once on the other bank they walked to Driel and were then transported to a Roman Catholic college in Nijmegen, where after a "glorious shave" he stood on a kitchen table and conducted a service "of thanksgiving for our delivery and of memory for those who had died".[56]

Padre Morrison was informed that he would be helping the walking wounded in the evacuation over the Rhine, and prepared for the move, but on the evening received no orders until he went to the battalion HQ and found the commanding officer and his party just leaving. Morrison returned the RAP to break the news that they would not be leaving after all. He later discovered that it would have been very unlikely that his wounded men would have succeeded in crossing. The doctor, three medical staff and Morrison stayed to look after the wounded, and the following day the walking wounded were taken away by the Germans with the MO, leaving Morrison and a medical sergeant in charge of the more seriously wounded. Eventually the wounded were taken to Almelo in eastern Holland and Morrison was sent to a POW camp. However, during his brief stay in the German hospital a German Army chaplain[57] visited and took a letter to send to Morrison's wife giving details of the men who were with him, information which she was able to pass on to others.

Pare fell asleep exhausted on the evening of Monday, 25 September, still hoping that the sounds of battle outside heralded the eventual arrival of the Second Army. When he awoke it was to the news that the airborne forces had retreated across the Rhine, leaving the badly wounded in the care of the medics and chaplains. RSM Bryson asked Pare to break the news to the patients that the main force had been evacuated, which was greeted with dismay at the realisation that they would be taken prisoner. Before being taken to Apeldoorn later in the afternoon he went around the piles of British dead at the back of the Shoonoord, noting the names of the soldiers in his notebook. As the British waited in the hospital, one of them used the damaged piano to strike up some popular songs, and when the Germans arrived to take them away they were amazed to find the defeated wounded soldiers singing.

---

56   Museum of Army Chaplaincy Archives, an account by the Revd John Rowell.
57   Museum of Army Chaplaincy Archives, an account by the Revd J. Morrison.

Dan McGowan, after being taken prisoner, was in put in charge of a group of 35 wounded soldiers and left in an abandoned church with little food or water. He managed to negotiate supplies of preserved fruit from the cellars of neighbouring houses, but on 21 September the party was transferred to St Elisabeth's hospital and McGowan joined the medics and padres working there looking after British and German casualties. The German nursing nuns and the civilian nursing team were still there. Also present were MOs Major C.P. Longford and Captains Lippman-Kessel, Logan and Devlin, and others of their RAMC colleagues, plus depleted numbers of medical orderlies. McGowan described the scene that awaited him: "The marble floors and staircases were covered with a sticky grime of blood and dust. All were exhausted. However, the wounded were being gradually moved to Apeldoorn."[58] He also met up again with Buchanan. While at St Elisabeth's, McGowan was able to say Mass at 7:00 a.m. for the men and staff and then take Holy Communion on the wards. He visited everyone, both Allied and German, in the morning and evening, and these visiting sessions were a great help in keeping up hope and spirits. A salvaged wireless was set up in the hospital's loft and he was able to relay the BBC news to the patients.

One of the casualties was Brigadier J.W. 'Shan' Hackett of the 4th Parachute Brigade. Writing in 1971, he commented on the dilemma facing McGowan in administering Mass:

> McGowan conducted non-denominational services among the wounded in the hospital and, as many were dying, I pressed him continually to give the Eucharist to anyone who wished to take it, irrespective of denomination. This, of course for a priest of his church was in those days a virtually impossible thing to do. In the end he did this and, when he returned from his prison camp at the end of the war, he was put on severe penance.[59]

In his book *I Was a Stranger*, John Hackett elaborated further on this incident:

> It caused me no surprise to learn that in St Elizabeth's hospital he [McGowan] was bringing men together in the wards and corridors for prayer whether they were members of his own church or not. This was good, but was it, I wondered, enough? Men were dying. Some were devout Christians but were Protestants. Would he, I asked Danny, as a Christian priest deny them the sacrament of Holy Communion? He had to he said, but it was clear that he had already given much thought to what he saw as a terrible dilemma. I pressed him. He suffered a great deal from his conscience I know, but in the end it brought him to a

58 Museum of Army Chaplaincy Archives, an account by Fr Daniel McGowan.
59 Museum of Army Chaplaincy Archives, letter from Brigadier John Hackett to Abram, December 1971.

decision which in all the circumstances he was certain must be right. He began to administer the sacrament to any who sought it.[60]

On the morning of the 26th, when Operation Berlin had become known, McGowan heard news of evaders, British troops, still in the area. After a reconnoitre in the immediate vicinity of the hospital, McGowan decided to look further afield and, armed with a rucksack of supplies, stood outside the hospital and hitched a lift: "The German driver raised no objection and dropped me without question at the Schoornood hotel at Oosterbeek."[61] The Germans there were surprised to see him, but amazingly raised no objections to this smartly dressed padre with red beret, immaculate uniform, clerical collar and shiny boots, who looked as if he knew exactly what he was doing, going about his business. For the next 14 days, he spent some of each day in the deserted but chaotic battleground. He noted the names of all the dead he found, and was able to bury some of them, picking up the pay books scattered on the battlefield which were invaluable for records and scouring the crashed gliders for any useful objects.

The Germans were seemingly unaware of the primary purpose of the battlefield wanderings of McGowan. Early on his first day it was not long before he heard soft and cautious cries for help from the undergrowth, and came across a small group of haggard and wounded men hiding there. McGowan gave them food from his haversack, took their names to add to his casualty list and that evening alerted the Dutch resistance to their plight, after which they were picked up and taken to relative safety. This was repeated over the following two weeks, ensuring that some evaders got to safety right under the noses of the German Army. The records he kept of the dead, wounded and evaders were typed up each evening and passed, via the Dutch underground, to the Second Army and the Red Cross at the Hague.

Not every day went well. Sometimes he was arrested and brought back to St Elisabeth's hospital. Yet this did not deter him, as Hackett commented: "His real armour, however was the transparent honesty of his purpose and the boldness of his approach. His command of German was poor, but I knew what a determined person he was. I was almost sorry for any German who tried to obstruct him, when Danny McGowan was set on doing what he saw as his duty."[62]

Hackett had been operated on by the South African Lippman-Kessel and planned his escape as he was recovering. McGowan brought him much of the equipment he would need. McGowan had hidden away Hackett's smock, battle dress jacket, boots and other possessions that Hackett had with him when he was brought to the hospital, and also collected other useful escape items.

60   John Hackett, *I Was A Stranger* (London: Chatto and Windus, 1977), p.28.
61   Museum of Army Chaplaincy Archives, an account by the Revd D. McGowan.
62   Hackett, *I Was a Stranger*, p.29.

British weapons had accumulated at St Elisabeth's, and the senior British officer, Major G.J. Longland, heard that the SS intended to collect them at 8:00 a.m. one morning. A plan was hatched to smuggle the arms out of the hospital to the resistance. Captain Lippman-Kessel and McGowan arranged a mock funeral. Lippman-Kessel and three orderlies carried the 'corpses', in reality weapons covered with blankets, out of the hospital on two stretchers in a solemn procession, and these were duly buried in two shallow graves which had been dug near the mortuary, with McGowan pretending to say the funeral service. The next day the SS collected the British arms from the hospital, minus three Bren guns, a German light machine gun, some grenades and boxes of ammunition, which were dug up and taken away by the resistance.

In a letter to Abram in October 1969, McGowan expressed the wish that this story not be told, or at least 'toned down': "It might pass in war time, but I think it would be left put today. I would be grateful for its deletion or toning down."[63]. However, since the incident has since become part of the story of the airborne padres at Arnhem, the author has included it here.

On 24 September, after the truce, many of the casualties that had been left behind were evacuated to Apeldoorn, to the Wilhelm III barracks, where Lieutenant Colonel Martin Herford, one of the MOs accompanying them, was able to ameliorate conditions by liaising with the enemy with his fluent German. It was decided that the British should run the hospital with their own medical services, whilst remaining prisoners. There were three blocks, and senior chaplain Harlow placed the three captured chaplains - Thorne, Buchanan and Pare - in charge of each block. They were later joined by McGowan, and there followed a steady stream of patients evacuated from Arnhem. The chaplains were allowed out of the camp to visit airborne men in other Apeldoorn hospitals. They were able to collect news from Dutch doctors and civilians to give to the troops. A chapel was set up for regular services, and Padre Pare even tried his hand at being a barber. He also worked hard to enlarge his list of glider pilots who had been killed or wounded. Padre Bowers, who had broken his ankle badly upon landing, was a patient at Apeldoorn before being sent to a POW camp; he remembered being visited by Buchanan, whom he described as "one of the finest padres I ever met in the army".[64]

On 6 October a hospital train arrived to take a group of wounded to Germany. Pare and Thorne were ordered to accompany them. After a night on the train, waiting to depart, Pare and Thorne divided up their charges between them. When it eventually set off, the train was too long and heavy to go more than 20mph, so Pare considered escape. Thorne felt that his duty lay in staying with the men, but Pare thought differently. He believed the Allies would cross the Rhine within the next few weeks, and felt it unlikely that he would be allowed to stay with the men anyway. He had

63   Museum of Army Chaplaincy Archives, letter from the Revd Daniel McGowan to Paul Abram, 10 October 1969.
64   R.F. Bowers, *On the Move*, quoted in van Roekel, *Torn Horizon*.

important information regarding casualties and information to get back to Britain, and felt strongly that it was his duty to escape. Having put a compass, map, torch and some money into his parachute smock, and having told the CO of the field ambulance his intentions, he jumped from the last coach of the train. After some hair-raising adventures and near captures, he was given the identity of a deaf mute, Piet Baars, by the Dutch resistance and successfully lived in the village of Elburg until February 1945. His act as a deaf mute was so successful that many of the villagers did not know his real identity. In February he was hidden when the Germans raided Elburg. Despite two attempts to get near enough to the Rhine to cross, he was unable to do so and was still in Elburg when it was liberated by Canadian forces.

On 12 October the final party of wounded arrived from Arnhem, accompanied by Daniel McGowan. As there were now only 550 patients at Apeldoorn, looked after by about 200 medics, it became obvious that many of the medical staff would soon be sent off to POW camps. Plans for escape thus began to be hatched. MO Herford decided to escape as his duties as liaison officer were over, and Lieutenant Colonel Warrack was anxious that the list of wounded and killed should get back to Britain as soon as possible.[65] Herford persuaded McGowan to join him, and an escape was planned to take place after the evening service on 15 October. Warrack read from the Book of Acts, appropriately about Peter's escape from prison, and Harlow preached on being strong in captivity and to do what their consciences thought right. Harlow ended with the prayer, "Go forth into the world in peace, be of good courage, hold fast to that which is right."[66]

With the aid of Warrack, the pair climbed out of a small window in the operating theatre, McGowan only just managing as his portly frame became stuck. After waiting for hours in the dark and rain outside the window, they managed to avoid the sentries and escape the camp. They did not want to endanger any of the Dutch people by asking for help, so after several days, and cold, wet and hungry, they reached the drop zone where they had landed at Arnhem. Herford was glad of McGowan's company: "The experience of Dan McGowan in moving amongst the Germans was, indeed, providential, and his cheerful confidence literally heaven sent."[67] They managed to pass through German troops by putting on gas capes that they had found in one of the gliders and wearing their berets inside out, and eventually arrived at the river. However, they then became separated, and although Herford managed to escape over the Rhine, McGowan was recaptured.

With Thorne, McGowan and Pare absent, the burden of looking after the wounded airmen at Apeldoorn fell heavily on Buchanan and Harlow. Harlow left with the final large transport on 26 October, leaving Buchanan to carry on the care of the more

65   Letter from MO M. Herford, 3 March 1969.
66   Paul Abram, *Arnhem Aftermath*, RAChD Journal Vol XXI, No.112, November 1969.
67   *Ibid.*

seriously wounded left in the St Joseph's foundation, consisting of amputation cases, head wounds, open fractures and cases of sepsis.

The padres who dropped and landed at Arnhem were in the thick of battle from the beginning, taking on a variety of roles, depending on their position in the battle and their personality. Watkins, seeing the need for leadership in the chaos, took on a military role, Thorne steadfastly cared for those in the RAP at the old vicarage, and Egan supported the men in the desperate struggle at the bridge. All padres cared for the wounded and comforted the dying in rapidly deteriorating conditions, all showing courage and self-sacrifice, and two giving up their lives in the ultimate sacrifice.

The Polish Independent Parachute Brigade which parachuted into the Driel area, south of the Rhine, on 21 September had three padres on their strength. Fr Mientki was attached to brigade Headquarters dealing with the many wounded. Fr Bendorz found the local Roman Catholic parish priest, who gave him a crucifix in thankfulness for their liberation. Fr Misiuda crossed the Rhine with the 3rd Battalion to support the British troops, despite the efforts of his commander to prevent him. After digging in in support of the Border Regiment, they received orders on 25 September and Misiuda was killed while escorting a groups of walking wounded towards the river.

Fifty-nine decorations were published for the small group of men who successfully escaped Arnhem, and these were awarded in an investiture ceremony at Buckingham Palace on 6 December 1944. Watkins was present to receive his Military Cross:

> That first list [of decorations led to a call for some recognition of the division as a whole. This took the form of a Buckingham Palace parade. Four hundred men assembled at Wellington Barracks and marched to the palace and into one of its salons. In an adjoining place there was a special investiture for 1st Airborne Division. The Queen accompanied the King. He also had a word with the other four hundred.

Watkins explained the reasons which he thought had led to his being mentioned twice in Despatches and winning the Military Cross: "That all happened because I was a long time with a medal-winning outfit. It is a trite thing to say that these things just happen, for that is not true. I think an honest statement would be that I was so often put into situations where someone had to do something or sit in a hole."

Abram, in his introduction to his draft history of airborne chaplains, said that the role of the chaplain was to "serve his fellow men because as soldiers they need God … He is an essential channel for God and is in a position to remind men of their humanity by his presence, unarmed among them."[68] At Arnhem the chaplains exercised this ministry of presence all day and all night throughout the battle, and were able to be of spiritual and physical support to the men they served.

68   Abram, *Lower Than Angels* . p.iv

7

Airborne Chaplains in the Special Air Service, 1941-45

The Special Air Service was formed in July 1941 by David Stirling. It was originally devised as a commando force operating behind enemy lines in North Africa. After a disastrous first parachute drop in support of Operation Crusader in November 1941, Major Stirling's teams achieved success in attacking enemy airfields in Libya, transported by the Long Range Desert Group.

Stirling had original arrived in the Middle East as part of Lieutenant Colonel Bob Laycock's No 8 Commando, later called Layforce. Padre Ronald Lunt arrived in the Middle East in February 1941 as chaplain to No 7 Commando, which was brigaded with Stirling's commandos, and trained with them. He remembered doing "a lot of amphibious training" and embarking on several abortive missions. This force suffered heavy casualties in the battle of Crete in May 1941 and the battle of the Litani River in Lebanon in June 1941. When the commandos were posted to strengthen the Guards regiments in the Middle East, Lunt saw action with them in the Knightsbridge box in the Western Desert, winning a Military Cross in 1943. At this point Stirling asked for Lunt to be posted as chaplain to the Special Air Service unit that he had formed. Lunt remembered: "He secured for me a posting in his unit which was training near Acre." Lunt was thrilled with the turn of events "It was of course, quite wonderful being welcomed into a team as something of an old friend."[1]

In January 1943 Stirling was captured, and in April 1943 the 1st SAS was reorganised into a Special Raiding Squadron under the command of Paddy Mayne and a Special Boat Squadron. Lunt recalled that as Mayne's squadron was training to operate on land, rather than on small seaborne missions in which there was no room for a padre, he was allowed to stay with Mayne and his men. Lunt accompanied the SAS to Acre in Syria, where they completed training in assault by landing craft, parachute and ski.

Preparing for Operation Husky, the Allied invasion of Sicily in July 1943, Mayne decided that the SAS would go in by sea. They sailed in the *Ulster Monarch* and went

---

[1] Museum of Army Chaplaincy Archives, letter from Ronald Lunt to Abram, 1 November 1967.

in on assault landing craft at about 1:00 a.m. on 10 July. Their objective was to capture and destroy the searchlights and guns at Capo Murro de Porco. The cliffs overlooked the main landing grounds to be used by the British forces, and if the guns were not silenced the invasion fleet would come under heavy fire as they approached. A wind had sprung up and the sea was very rough. Lunt was glad to get ashore as he felt very sick and several soldiers had been sick into his helmet. The attack was a complete surprise and the men quickly scaled their bamboo ladders. Lunt landed clutching a Thomas splint, medical supplies and the Reserved Sacrament. The padre's role on operations was usually to move on the opposite wing to the medical officer. At 5:20 a.m. Mayne fired a green Very pistol to announce the success of the attack on the batteries. Their destruction allowed the safe passage of the invasion fleet. Over 500 prisoners were taken.

Two days later the *Ulster Monarch* took them in to clear the port of Augusta, supported by fire from two Royal Navy destroyers. Intelligence reports suggested that the town had been evacuated, but the high ground that overlooked Augusta was still occupied by the enemy. As the landing craft approached the shore, one of the men remembered: "We were singing and shouting as we came in and the padre [Ronald Lunt] was with us. He told us to shut up but we were all happy go lucky and thought 'these Italians are going to be easy'."[2] Upon landing the unit came under heavy fire from the German guns above the town, but succeeded in securing Augusta. Their success in this was celebrated, according to Ben Macintyre in his history of the SAS, by "a spontaneous spectacular and extremely boisterous looting party".[3] Although accounts of this are missing from Lunt's account, one of the men, Deakins, remembered Lunt "stockpiling bottles of wine presumably, as one wag commented, 'for communion'."[4]

Lunt, in a post-war account, explained the unique aspects of being a padre to the SAS: "The SAS were an irregular force and proud of it. The commanders throughout gave to the padre their greatest friendship and support. Where the SAS went he went too. There was never any question of having to ask special permission from Cairo to go on parachute training, or to accompany one's parish on operations." Lunt felt that as the SAS operated in small parties, it was easier to get to know individuals well. He felt sometimes that he was regarded as an odd job man, but relished the opportunities this gave him to share in the life of the unit and get closer to the men. In a post-war letter to Paul Abram he considered: "I was, I admit always a very amateur airborne soldier, a pretty amateur chaplain, prepared to fill in a small community any gap that needed filling." He immediately proved this a too-modest assessment by admitting that one of the 'odd jobs' he was asked to do was "being sent forward by the brigadier

2   Gavin Mortimer, *Stirling's Men: The Inside History of the SAS In World War Two* (London: Weidenfeld and Nicolson, 2004), p.121.
3   Ben Macintyre, *SAS: Rogue Heroes – the Authorized Wartime History* (London: Penguin Random House, 2016), p.198.
4   Mortimer, *Stirling's Men*, p.139.

to negotiate the surrender of a Sicilian Village".[5] He kept up the Padre's Hours and regular services, although very rarely was there a church parade. He found that the members of the SAS were "especially responsive to spiritual things if they were put before them in a challenging way".[6] When training in Syria, and also in Sicily after the landings, Lunt described how they became hopeful that some planned operation was going to materialise, only to be cancelled at the last moment. He deemed it fortunate that much of the time he was out of contact with any divisional organisation of chaplains: "Even the Deputy Chaplain did not know till afterward where one had been."[7]

On 4 September 243 men of the Special Raiding Squadron landed at Bagnara on the toe of Italy to secure the port, prevent its demolition and hold it until the main Allied force arrived. Lunt was then involved in the next stage of the war in Italy over the Apennines to Bari. The last action he saw in Italy consisted in the taking of Termoli on the Adriatic coast, Operation Devon, which developed into a bitter struggle with German troops to hold it after it had been taken. Attempts to retake the town by the 16th *Panzer* Division resulted in heavy casualties. Lunt was reported as slapping the face of a man who was in hysterics, telling him, "You're not going to die." The Special Raiding Squadron, with a strength of 207 all ranks, lost 21 killed, 24 wounded and 23 missing in this action. Shelling had resulted in horrendous injuries and deaths, with human remains scattered about: "Lunt wrapped each remains in a blanket." The bodies were buried in the public gardens: "A silent crowd of men emerged from the billets, with heads bared … in a quiet voice the padre read the service."[8]

On Boxing Day 1943 the 1st SAS returned to England, Lunt later serving in Norway towards the end of the war. The Special Air Service Brigade was formed in 1944, consisting of the 1st and 2nd Special Air Service, the French 3rd and 4th Special Air Service and the Belgian Special Air Service.

Fraser McLuskey was born in Scotland and educated at Aberdeen Grammar School and Edinburgh University, and became a minister of the Church of Scotland. After travelling in Germany, being chaplain of the University of Glasgow and driving an ambulance in the Glasgow blitz, he decided, at the age of 29, to enlist as an Army chaplain. After training at Tidworth, McLuskey's first posting was to the Northern Command, and he was disappointed not to be joining a Scottish regiment. He quickly discovered that in this posting he felt "a thousand times further from the war than I had done in my civilian life in Glasgow". He found it depressing to be ministering on a strictly denominational basis to upwards of 50 different units of all descriptions: "Here I learned how very exacting it was, how exhausting and depressing and at times

5   Museum of Army Chaplaincy Archives, letter from Lunt to Paul Abram, 1 November 1967.
6   Museum of Army Chaplaincy Archives, papers deposited by Revd P.R.C. Abram CVO. Typescript, *Lower Than the Angels* (1975), p.131.
7   Museum of Army Chaplaincy Archives, an account by Ronald Lunt.
8   Mortimer, *Stirling's Men*, p.156.

how rewarding … Here I learned that it is sometimes difficult for a padre to find a real welcome in a static formation as it is easy in a fighting unit in the field."[9] He described this peripatetic ministry:

> My welcome was kindly enough and I conducted services, confirmation classes and Padre's Hours but I was a stranger among strangers. There was a real job to be done and it didn't lack its encouragements, but my thoughts often turned to the very different lot of the regimental chaplain who is part of the family to which he ministers.[10]

He was just becoming reconciled to his lot when a letter arrived asking for young and fit padres to volunteer for service with parachute units, and after a few months he was posted to the Airborne Divisions, arriving at Hardwick Hall early in 1944.

He found that there were four other padres on his course: two Roman Catholics, one Church of England and one Church of Scotland. He was relieved to find that, as he put it, "parachuting, at least need be hardly done on a denominational basis".[11] On his first night he had a taste of the camaraderie and fellowship that he was to experience in the Parachute Regiment, as, lost in the snow, he wandered into the sergeants' mess and received a great welcome, being immediately presented with a pint: "I was tasting the fellowship that I shall always associate with the Parachute Regiment … I had wandered in as a stranger. A stranger feeling very cold, very apprehensive and very much the new boy, but before minutes had passed was one of them, part of the parachute family."[12]

The instructors then put them through the physical training and tests. These included road work, gym and rope work, carrying a man your own weight over a specific course and "milling" for three minutes. After two weeks he was pronounced "fit to drop". One of the padres on the course with him excelled in the boxing ring and another at cross-country running. During the course the chaplains, due to bad weather, were asked to organise a 'Brains Trust' for the men. It was a success, as McLuskey commented:

> The padres certainly learned a great deal from the session, how eager the ordinary man is to explore the territory of religion! How passionately he desires sincerity from professing Christians and a life to match their creed … One at least of the padres clambered off the platform when the hour was done feeling that the man

---

9   J. Fraser McLuskey, *Parachute Padre* (London: SCM Press, 1951), p.23.
10   J. Fraser McLuskey, *The Cloud and the Fire* (Pentland Press, 1993), p.64.
11   McLuskey, *Parachute Padre*, p.25.
12   *Ibid*, p.27.

in the street is disappointed that the church seems to ask so little of him, and that, apparently it asks so little of itself.[13]

McLuskey was full of admiration for the instructors. He described himself as a "timid soul" and recalled: "They convinced us that our parachutes were the best in the world and that of course they would open. They showed us how to fall. They showed us how to make a proper exit from a plane. They showed us how to control our parachute during descent." He was also convinced that prayer and the power of God helped.

McLuskey had been expecting to be posted to the 1st or 6th Airborne Divisions, ready for the anticipated invasion of Europe, but upon presenting himself for interview at 21st Army Group Headquarters in London he was told that the only remaining vacancy for an airborne padre was with an organisation called the Special Air Service Brigade, which his interviewer did not seem to know much about as it was apparently "frightfully hush hush". He was delighted that this mysterious unit was based in Scotland and jumped at the chance of being nearer home.

Arriving at Kilmarnock railway station early the next morning, he was intrigued to be picked up by a vehicle bearing the SAS emblem and the motto 'Who Dares Wins'. His initial appearance was obviously unexpected, but he was offered breakfast. He immediately felt at home in the mess, observing how young many of the officers were and how many of them had an Africa Star and the Special Air Service version of the parachute wings. At Brigade HQ later he was told that his job would be to act as padre to the Special Air Service Brigade, both the 1st and 2nd Regiment, and also the Brigade HQ. Shortly after, the 2nd Battalion acquired a padre of its own and McLuskey became permanently attached to the 1st Battalion. Discovering that the job of the SAS was to drop behind enemy lines, he wondered where a padre fitted into that. He decided quite quickly that, "If my congregation was going to celebrate the invasion by disappearing in small groups into the heart of France, then it must take me with it."[14]

Despite being without battlefield experience, and any battle honours, McLuskey felt he soon settled down well in the company of battle-hardened veterans of Sicily, Italy and Africa: "There was a great deal of glamour about this bunch. But the most experienced operatives were those who took themselves least seriously and provided you fitted in, you were made one of this very distinguished family."[15]

At this time the brigade was partly resting and partly training new recruits. MacLuskey recounted the various training exercises. Some of these 'schemes', as they were called, had some interesting results, such as the capture of a submarine, the disappearance of a car belonging to the Home Guard and the appearance of a stolen fire engine manned by ruffians singing 'Lili Marlene'. McLuskey, however, observed

13   *Ibid*, p.31.
14   *Ibid*, p.48.
15   *Ibid*, p.50.

that these exploits were of tremendous value to the new recruits, preparing them for the time when they would be facing this sort of treatment and worse from the hands of the Gestapo or the French Milice.

He realised that not many of the men were enthusiastic churchmen, but that they were glad to be given the opportunity of services and seemed respectful of the Church. He commented on the fact that many of them had lived much of their lives outside the orbit of the Church and the fellowship of Christian community and worship, and pondered on the way the Church should handle the interest shown in Army services: "Army services had brought them to within the orbit of the Christian church and given them and the church an opportunity. What would they make of the opportunity? What would the church make of it?"[16]

The 1st Battalion was transferred to a sealed camp at Fairford in Gloucestershire on 10 June. Reconnaissance parties from the battalion were dropped into France on 6 and 11 June, and it was now the turn of the main party. McLuskey explained in his official report on the operation the main objectives of Operation Houndsworth, in which A Squadron of the 1st Battalion was dropped into the Djion area in Burgundy.[17] They were tasked with disrupting German lines of communication and supply, helping coordinate the French resistance and preventing German reinforcements reaching the Normandy beaches, especially the 2nd SS *Panzer* Division *Das Reich*, which was based around Toulouse. In his account of Operation Houndsworth, author Roger Ford explained: "The operation instructions which defined the mission made it clear that the targets of the railway lines linking Dijon and Chalons sur Saone and the Le Creusot-Nevers line further south would be of the utmost importance in the days between D+8 and D+ 24 which gave the Houndsworth party little time to establish itself and become effective."[18]

On 21 June the main body of A Squadron was to be flown in. McLuskey had obtained permission from the squadron commander, Major Bill Fraser, to drop with the operation. He described the bewildering array of equipment and rations that he packed into his kit bag. Although he carried no arms, he had to take the equipment for his ministry to the troops he was accompanying: "I had not the least idea how I would function as a padre on the other side, but I wanted to be as well prepared as I could." He was allowed a small panier to put some equipment in, and packed a maroon silk altar cloth with the regimental emblem, a winged dagger on an oak cross. He also took a few hymn books, copies of the New Testament, some copies of a day book of prayer and a few books as a little library. His precious airborne set for Holy Communion he carried in his kit bag. At the last minute he remembered his jack knife, putting it in the pocket of his parachute smock.

---

16   *Ibid*, p.54.
17   TNA WO 218/921, Report on1st SAS Operation covering the period 21 June to 29 September 1944 by the chaplain to the 1st SAS Regiment.
18   Roger Ford, *Fire from the Forest: the SAS in France 1944* (London: Cassell, 2003), p.80.

Before take-off they were issued with maps, and McLuskey discovered they would be dropping in the department of La Nievre, about 70 miles south-west of Dijon. As the time for take-off approached, both McLuskey and the men thought about their chances of survival on this dangerous mission. One of the planes taking another group had failed to drop them and then failed to return. Another rumour concerned a plane that had landed to find the Germans waiting for them, and all on board were captured. McLuskey spent that last half an hour before take-off writing a last letter home, which he called "an essay in the impossible".[19]

Once safely airborne, McLuskey settled down for the three-and-half-hour flight. The Stirling aircraft held 16 troops, and he was to jump first in the second stick, making him no 9. He slept for much of the journey, only waking up for the cups of tea passed around. The lights from the reception committee were recognised and the two sticks prepared to jump. Ian Wellsted, who had been dropped with the reconnaissance party on 6 June, described the drop:

> The drop was not a great success … the pilot insisted on dropping the whole stick of 16 in one long line, which meant there was a mile between the first and last man. He ran up the line of lights in the wrong direction, and did not signal the first man to go until he was over the last light. The result was the stick being scattered for miles among the trees."[20]

McLuskey realised he was coming down in trees, and felt the impact as his kit bag hit the trees and then himself. He ended up hanging upside down from a tree. He got out his knife and attempted to cut himself free, but could not remember later whether he succeeded or whether the branch had broken. He woke in the morning being violently sick as a result of concussion, but still in possession of his kit bag. He was picked up by a paratrooper named Mick, who looked after him in his weakened state, and he became aware of what Special Air Service comradeship in action was. Wellsted, who saw McLuskey's parachute hanging in a high tree, later wrote: "The harness had been cut and it was obvious that the man in question who had cut himself loose in the dark had dropped a good thirty feet to the ground. Later I found the man, it was Fraser McLuskey … a minister of the Church of Scotland and the finest padre one could imagine."[21]

The squadron eventually formed up and was driven by the *Maquis* in a large red bus to the outpost in the forest of their leader, Jean, and had lunch with 200 of the *Maquis* resisters. McLuskey commented: "The camp looked like a cross between a

19   McLuskey, *Parachute Padre*, p.62.
20   Ian Wellsted, *SAS with the Maquis: In Action with the French resistance June–September 1944* (London: Greenhill Books, 1994), p.61.
21   *Ibid.*

scene from Robin Hood and a Hollywood film set."[22] McLuskey then went to the HQ camp which Major Fraser, who had dropped 10 days earlier, had established. Fraser's report on Operation Houndsworth has the following entry for 22 June: "Captain BRADFORD, The PADRE, Lt BALL, and men dropped successfully at LES VALLOTES." The day after landing, when McLuskey woke up after his first night in a sleeping bag in the forest, it was Ian Wellsted who brought him a cup of tea: "I was wakened the following morning by a gentle tap. A familiar voice announced that breakfast was being served and a mug of tea and a plate of tinned bacon was placed at my side. No minister of religion could have received a kinder or more acceptable welcome from his parishioner."[23]

The drop had been on a Thursday, and on the first Sunday McLuskey tentatively suggested a service and found to his surprise that everyone expected one. His service materials were found in the paniers that had landed and, two empty paniers created an altar: "With the cross and the altar cloth it focused worship quite effectively." All 30 or so men in the camp attended that first act of worship, which had its own organ and choir. The men gathered in an informal circle, and although obviously not regular churchgoers, stood for the prayer and sat on the ground for the lesson and the address. McLusky commented on the fact that non-churchgoers seemed happy in the service: "Few of them in different circumstances would have gone on their own accord to worship God. All that was undeniably true. It was just as true that in this forest glade they were finding the activity of worship the most natural thing in the world."[24] However, he could see no trace of 'foxhole religion': "It was not simply to curry favour with God that they stood before God." At the end of the service, "The hymn books were collected and carefully packed away, men drifted off to clean their weapons. We had waited on God. We had renewed our strength."[25] Writing 39 years later in his autobiography, McLuskey elaborated on the thoughts going through his head at that first service: "We were engaged on a task on which we believed we could ask his blessing … our aim was the liberation of our fellow men from a hideous tyranny on which any life worth the name must depend."[26]

Fraser's report for 24 June states: "Maquis Jean had a 'flap' and Bren Gun groups were sent out to cover roads." McLuskey remembered that on the evening of Sunday, 24 June, after the service, he heard gunfire nearby and was told that the Germans had attacked the *Maquis* group nearby in the wood. McLuskey was put into action at the regimental aid post. The German attack was beaten off, but Sergeant Major Seekings was wounded in the head, McLuskey helping with his treatment. The report of this action at Vermont, by Captain Wiseman, described how his group had come across

22   McLuskey, *Parachute Padre*, p.76.
23   *Ibid*, p.76.
24   *Ibid*, p.79.
25   *Ibid*, p.80.
26   McLuskey, *Cloud and Fire*, p.70.

a German patrol and Sergeant Major Seekings had been shot while shouting out a warning.[27] That night McLuskey was kept awake listening to fire between the *Maquis* and the Germans, and got the impression that although a great deal of ammunition was expended, neither force could have had much idea what it was shooting at. This was borne out by Wiseman's report: "The Maquis expended considerable ammunition but caused no casualties throughout a most disturbed night."[28]

On the morning of 27 June the squadron started to move out in appalling rain. Bill Fraser had decided to move the camp to a valley near the village of Mazignen. They had had to leave the camp in a hurry, but over the next few days managed to return to pick up some of the food and equipment left, and among the equipment rescued was McLuskey's 'church'.

McLuskey described a drop of three jeeps, fuel and more supplies, after which he reckoned that "having survived these first few weeks we could survive anything". The jeeps made it possible to disperse the squadron into smaller groups, ready for action. One jeep was given to Captain Wiseman's group, who travellded 70 or 80 miles to Dijon. McLusky stayed with HQ and Fraser's group. Another jeep was given to Alan Muirhead's group, who had already been blowing railway lines and bridges and had successfully mortared a German arms factory. McLuskey went with Fraser to visit them, stayed a fortnight and took part in some more early morning welcomes to supply parachute drops.

When McLuskey was at HQ again, an American B24 Liberator and a Halifax which were supplying the operation collided over the dropping site. The next day McLuskey went with a party to investigate the wreckage of the Liberator. The crew had all perished in their seats, but he was able to identify them by their dog tags. The villagers dug a grave and McLuskey read the burial service, his first in France. He reflected on the homes the American airmen had come from: "At that grave side the two worlds met, the old world in its chains and the New World coming to its aid. We were one family: these men were our men and in this last earthly rite I was very glad to be their minister."[29] The remains of the Halifax were nearer the road, and the mayor of Mazignen felt he had to report the crash to the German authorities at Lornes, as failure to do so could have resulted in serious repercussions for the village if the Germans found the plane.

A party of Germans arrived and took the bodies of the crew to the nearby cemetery and buried them. A few days later McLuskey went to the grave with a section of men and conducted a brief memorial service. The ceremony was packed with villagers, who were there at considerable personal risk. Deep in the forest, the grave of the Liberator

27   TNA WO 218/921, Report on1st SAS Operation covering the period 21 June to 29 September 1944 by Captain Wiseman.
28   *Ibid.*
29   McLuskey, *Parachute Padre*, p.95.

crew was covered with flowers and wreaths. Major Fraser's account mentioned that a total of 16 men from the two planes were buried.

Another RAF Halifax bomber, Y – Yoke, which was part of a group from 640 Squadron attacking a railway junction and marshalling yards, came down near Muirhead's campsite in the Bois de l'Essart, four miles west of Djion. This crew was buried by McLuskey in a small *Maquis* cemetery, and he shared the ceremony with the local Roman Catholic priest from Ouroux, Pere Benoit Legrain, who had been very supportive of the *Maquis*.

McLuskey soon took part in one of the objectives of the operation disrupting supplies and communications, joining a demolition party operating out of the town of Anost. His role was to guard the three jeeps with two other men. Later, with the German retreating from France to the German border, the task of the men was to make their withdrawal as difficult as possible with ambushes, road blocks and demolition of bridges. McLuskey often took part in reconnaissance patrols to look for likely sites to set up ambushes. He acted as the driver of a jeep which ambushed a German patrol car, and also witnessed the ambush of a large German convoy by three jeeps from the squadron. He reckoned that many of these hit-and-run raids and ambushes were effective: "Between them they accounted for a substantial amount of German equipment and personnel, and provided many a headache for the organisers of the German withdrawal. Our third role, to slow up German movement out of France, was faithfully fulfilled."[30]

McLuskey was frequently requested for a service in all three camps, being asked, "When's the service padre?" For these he used an altar of paniers, an oak cross and regimental altar cloth. Ian Wellsted gave a first-hand account of how McLuskey's services were enjoyed and raised morale:

> Church parade was another welcome reminder of home. Using a variety of vehicles, but with amazing regularity, Fraser McLuskey toured from troop to troop with his basket of library books, his packet of army hymnals, his SAS altar cloth and his collapsible wooden cross. Week after week he held his voluntary church parades, which everyone attended irrespective of nationality or denomination, and which brought spiritual comfort where it was needed.[31]

McLuskey thought liturgical purists would be aghast at the regimental badge being on the altar cloth, but commented: "I don't think God was displeased. That cloth helped to join heaven and earth for us when the altar was set up and the simple service began … We found God and God found us in the forests and fields of Morven."[32] The service would consist of hymns, prayers and a short address, and afterwards a

---

30   *Ibid*, p.117.
31   Wellsted, *SAS With the Maquis*, p.105.
32   McLuskey, *Parachute Padre*, p.78.

short service of Holy Communion for those who wanted to communicate. He pointed out that in the forest, "in circumstances that could hardly have been more different from those of Sunday worship, the simple traditional acts of Christian worship came to life." Wellsted described a typical service: "On Sunday afternoons, with the sun filtering between the leaves and dancing in patterns on the pine-matted earth, he would lay his altar cloth on a derelict pannier and set up his cross. In ones or twos his congregation would wander in dressed more like buccaneers than worshipers and carrying containers on which to sit."[33]

McLuskey put the enthusiasm for singing down to the fact that "here is an offering men can make to God, who has set music in their hearts", and always carried his hymn books to camp services, choosing the hymns carefully. He was aware that many of the men would have not attended a church service at home, but considered that "in this forest glade they were finding the activity of worship the most natural thing in the world".[34] Obviously the volume allowed in the singing varied with the location of the camp and the likelihood of German patrols in the area (Wiseman's camp in Dijon being of necessity the most silent). Wellsted remembered the men"singing the hymns louder or softer as the occasion demanded".[35] McLuskey considered that the danger they shared united the men in worship, but that "fear is not to be despised an incentive to worship as fear humbles people and strips them of their pretentions".[36]

McLuskey was able to visit the *Maquis* hospital from the base at Mazignen, and did so regularly and worked closely with the regimental MO, Michael Macready. On journeys further afield to visit troops, he travelled either in a jeep or a small Citroen car, which he and his batman Harry Wilson had difficulty fitting into. McLuskey developed a close relationship with his batman, a large, 6ft 4in, 13-stone former Scots Guardsman who had apparently not been assigned to McLuskey but seemed to take over the role of looking after the padre after landing in France. Indeed, Wilson became known as the 'the padre's bodyguard' or 'the padre's private army'. He carried a Bren gun and a stock of grenades at all times in whatever vehicle they were using. When traveling by jeep, there was a manned Vickers gun for protection. McLuskey remembered: "Harry felt his responsibilities for the care of the padre very keenly. I carried no arms in France and Harry obviously felt it necessary to be well armed enough for two."[37]

McLuskey, like many of his fellow chaplains, wondered whether the fact that he did not carry arms meant he was adding to the liabilities of the men. He felt that he had to obey the Geneva Convention as non-combatant and not carry arms. Moreover, he felt that the men liked to see him unarmed: "They wished to see him as [a] man of

33   Wellsted, *SAS With the Maquis*, p.106.
34   McLuskey, *Parachute Padre*, p.79.
35   *Ibid.*
36   *Ibid*, p.122.
37   *Ibid*, p.136.

peace – the peace which they know is the will of God for all men. For these men their unarmed padre was the symbol [that] the arms they must bear were dedicated to the cause of peace and the service of God."[38] Wellsted confirmed that McLuskey did not carry a gun, but pointed out that although the padre did not bear arms he was much of the time in places of peril, often driving one of the jeeps on ambush or sabotage missions: "The way he could handle a jeep, when he found himself inadvertently driving in an unexpected road strafe had to be seen to be believed."[39]

Despite the decision to remain unarmed, McLuskey felt that he must accompany the men on their patrols and expeditions: "From my point of view there was no other way of sharing their lot. It was clear to me that my calling could only be obeyed as I identified myself in fullest measure with the little group to whom I was appointed to minister."[40] His obituary in August 2005 mentioned that he "went with them whenever possible as driver, ambulance man or interpreter".[41] Accompanied by Wilson, McLuskey carried on visiting the camps and the hospital, visiting patients and taking services as part of his routine. At one camp he started a confirmation class: "When there were communicants in the camp, whatever their denomination I could celebrate the sacrament."[42] On 5 September 1944, A Squadron returned to Britain, and until the end of the month McLuskey was transferred to C Squadron, which after a few weeks of harrying the retreating Germans travelled to Paris and flew home for leave. In Cosne, before leaving for England, he arranged a thanksgiving service and was impressed by the turnout, which included most of the squadron.

McLuskey's time in France made a strong and deep impression on him. He commented on the relationship the airborne men of the SAS were able to develop with the French people,: remembering "the courage and loyal friendship of the country people among whom we lived and the Maquis with whom we worked".[43] In his autobiography he looked back fondly on the time he spent in France: "In all the circumstances it is not surprising that so short a period came to form such a large and abiding part of our lives."[44]

In October he returned from leave and found himself posted with the battalion to Brussels, where plans were being made for the role of the SAS in the advance through Germany. He was assigned to a group who were using armoured jeeps to reconnoitre and act as pathfinders for the armoured cars of the Second Army, but found his job as chaplain difficult as the regiment was so dispersed widely. He did not find his circumstances as challenging or rewarding as they had been in France: "The sense of close knit fellowship was inevitably lost …. It was a particularly hard winter and my

38   *Ibid*, p.137.
39   Wellsted, *SAS With the Maquis*, p.106.
40   McLuskey, *Parachute Padre*, p.137.
41   The *Daily Telegraph*, 19 August 2005.
42   McLuskey, *Parachute Padre*, p.138.
43   McLuskey, *Parachute Padre*, p.172.
44   McLuskey, *The Cloud and the Fire*, p.78.

recollections of the dreary flatness of the low countries are as uncomfortable as they are vague."[45] McLuskey was involved in the Rhine crossing, Operation Varsity, in March 1945 shortly after the main force, but arrived before clearing up operations had begun, so men and animals still lay where they had fallen: "The horror of war hit us with a new force."[46]

As he then progressed across Germany, McLuskey was appalled by the devastation wreaked by war. Nothing had prepared him for the extent of the damage: "Towns had been obliterated without one landmark left." As a chaplain and German-speaker, he acted as an unofficial public relations officer. He was worried about the looting being carried out by the men, and although he found it understandable in some ways, "it was no less saddening". He commented on "the dangers of the campaign as a guerrilla minority in France had seemed to bring out the best in almost everyone. Now, as a tiny part of a mighty force which we knew would soon have Germany at its mercy, the quality of our soldiering, the quality of our living was menaced as never before."[47]

After arriving at Lubeck, the SAS was posted with the 6th Airborne Division to Norway, as it was unclear whether the German forces there would surrender without a fight (see Chapter 9).

McLuskey was given leave before going to Norway and visited the family of his wife Irene in Wuppertal. He was reunited with various members of Irene's family, but discovered that her mother, father, sister-in-law and her children had been killed in an Allied bombing raid, although all three of her brothers had survived the war.

John Kent had joined up as an Army chaplain immediately after finishing serving his title as a curate in 1943. After a while with the Royal Tank Regiment he transferred to airborne forces and was posted to the 2nd SAS Regiment. His training at Ringway was brief, obtaining his wings after a week and travelling to Monkton, Ayr, where he was introduced to the regiment and its commanding officer, Brian Franks. The CO wanted Kent to hold church parades, but warned him that he would never get men to come along voluntarily. Kent later observed:

> In the event he turned out only to be partly right: he was absolutely right in barracks and almost absolutely wrong when I came to detachments. Whenever I tried to hold a service in barracks on a voluntary basis, I was lucky if I got a dozen, sometimes it was only 3 or 4. But if I went off with a detachment on training, whether it was a single stick or a whole squadron, I got virtually 100% attendance at anything I laid on.[48]

45   McLuskey, *The Cloud and the Fire*, p.79.
46   *Ibid.*
47   Ibid., p, 80.
48   Museum of Army Chaplaincy Archives, an account by John Kent.

After D-Day the battalion moved to a tented hut on Salisbury Plain and operations began for the 2nd Battalion SAS. The nature of the operations were small in scale, in groups of between six and 12 men, and therefore they were not accompanied by a doctor or padre. When operations on a larger scale started coming in, the padre and doctor were detailed to go on operations, but most were cancelled at the last minute and neither man actually went on an operation. Kent saw his role in such circumstances as talking to the men before they set off and taking a short service: "I believe in some way they found this valuable."[49] When the regiment moved to Wivenhoe in Sussex, Kent took the opportunity to set up some Padre's Hours, which he found "never very fruitful, but quite fun in an argumentative kind of way".[50] Brigadier Gerald Lathbury explained why Kent did not get to see any action as chaplain with the 2nd SAS: "1 SAS on the whole in France operated in much larger parties than 2 SAS and were therefore more accessible to the chaplain. It is therefore safe to say that Kent had no chance of going on operations until the crossing of the Rhine."[51]

Kent had come to this conclusion himself, and as what he knew would be the last big operation of the war, Operation Varsity, approached he realised the need to be in action with the men was very important to him.

As the SAS was no longer operating behind enemy lines, its role in the Rhine crossing was to form an advanced reconnaissance unit, using jeeps armed with Vickers machine guns. The CO explained to Kent that there was physically no room for a padre on the jeep, which had a driver, a commander gunner and another gunner who was also a radio man. Kent decided to ask if he could go as a driver with the rank of private. To his surprise, the CO agreed and Kent prepared to go into battle:

> I therefore stripped off pips, put an automatic [pistol] on to my belt and discarded my collar and the idiotic Red Cross card and went in functioning as a private soldier. This incidentally was a period I thoroughly enjoyed: there were times when it was frightening and there were times when there were burials and other grim duties but most of the time I really was functioning as a private soldier.[52]

He did not, of course, ask the permission of the Royal Army Chaplain's Department for his course of action.

Kent's unit continued its reconnaissance role, operating in northern Germany around Hamburg and along the Elbe until the local ceasefire several days before VE Day, by which time they were embarking for England and their next mission in Norway.

---

49   *Ibid.*
50   *Ibid.*
51   Museum of Army Chaplaincy Archives, an account by Gerald Lathbury.
52   Museum of Army Chaplaincy Archives, an account by John Kent.

Restored to his role as chaplain, Kent left by air to Norway almost as soon as they returned from Germany. He remembered that it was by no means certain that the German forces in Norway were going to surrender, but they did and Kent found the time there "full of fun and interesting: full of human incident, but at the same time I was very bothered about the demoralisation of the Regiment. They had been an extraordinary band of brothers, but right at the end of the war in Germany and later in Norway they began looting … and the spirit of the Regiment degenerated." Kent initially had a poor opinion of this behaviour, but later realised that the issue was not a simple one: "The release of tension and of danger was bound to release also so much that had been kept under control before and all kinds of immoral behaviour were not only natural but, in a way, very necessary."[53]

This account of the three SAS chaplains shows how a chaplain could be successfully embedded in the most active and secret units in the British Army and play an essential part in the morale and wellbeing of those units.

53   *Ibid.*

8

Victory in Europe: Airborne Forces in Europe, 1945

On his return from D-Day, the Revd George Hales was appointed as Deputy Assistant Chaplain General to the airborne corps and replaced as 6th Airborne senior chaplain by the Revd A.F. Cameron. The Allied advance had been held up by the German Army's stubborn defence of the Siegfried Line, and on 16 December Hitler launched a surprise offensive in the Ardennes. His objective was to cross the River Meuse and retake Antwerp, cutting off the largely British and Canadian forces in Holland and Belgium, splitting the Allied armies and breaking their lines of communication. By 22 December the German forces had captured St Vith and were besieging Bastogne. The 6th Airborne Division was required to return to the continent and be put into the line with the British XXX Corps as part of the Allied counterattack.

The men of the 6th Airborne Division had been preparing for Christmas, but on Christmas Day they found themselves travelling across Belgium. The Revd J.F. Vaughan-Jones bemoaned the fact the he was unable to celebrate Holy Communion as the Royal Ulster Rifles were on the move all day. Captain David Tibbs, the MO, described the journey: "It was bitterly cold with snow storms and endless fog."[1] Padre John Hall nearly missed his battalion, the Devons, as he had gone with the second-in-command to collect turkeys and carol sheets, and upon his return the unit was moving out. They took the turkeys and carol sheets with them. Unlike Vaughan-Jones with the Royal Ulsters, the Devons had turkey for Christmas.

Captain Revd Leslie Beckingham, although still attached to the 224th Field Ambulance and the Canadian Parachute Battalion on his return to Britain, had been living with the RASC (Royal Army Service Corps) at Bulford on Salisbury Plain, and it was with them that he travelled to the Ardennes on Christmas Day. He described the conditions he found there: "Soon we were in the mountains of the Ardennes and fighting not only a desperate enemy but cold and ice that made agony for the men in the forward positions … It was an unpleasant time for all but much more for those with

---

1   David Tibbs and Neil Barber, *Parachute Doctor: The Memoirs of Captain David Tibbs* (Sevenoaks, Kent: Sabrestorm Publishing, 2012), p.75.

the battalions than for myself with the RASC."[2] Padre John Gwinnett remembered a service in the snow when the assistant adjutant, Malcolm Reid, was playing a portable organ acquired for the occasion: "It seemed that as fast as he pulled out the stops the noise of the guns pushed them in again."[3]

The 6th Airborne Division had been tasked to clear territory which was being fiercely defended by German troops, spearheading the advance against the enemy salient. On 3 January their objective was the village of Bure. David Tibbs described how the 13th Parachute Battalion was painfully exposed while attacking Bure, so the commander decided to advance quickly and rush the village, fighting from house to house. The main constraint to their progress was a large tank dominating the main street. Tibbs set up a Regimental Aid Post in a house with a cellar in the village to deal with the casualties of the fierce fighting. He discovered that five men were lying in another cellar, with no access past the tank to get them out. Sergeant Scott of the medical team decided to take an ambulance to rescue them, and Padre Whitfield Foy asked if he could accompany him. Tibbs gave permission, but later commented: "If I had known precisely what was planned I might have stopped such lunacy, but off they went."[4]

The ambulance, clearly marked with the Red Cross, trundled up the road and came to a halt outside the house where the wounded men were, just yards away from the tank and its guns. In a moment of high tension and drama, the tank commander's head and shoulders appeared out the turret, presenting a perfect target. He then shouted, in good English: "This time you can do it, but do not come back." The ambulance loaded the wounded and proceeded back down the road, heading for the Field Ambulance two miles to the rear. Tibbs commented: "Two men were the heroes of the hour, Sergeant Scott with padre Foy in strong support and of course the enemy tank commander, what men."[5] Tibbs recalled that a story went around that when the tank commander put his head out of the turret to direct his men once too often and was shot, some of the British men shed tears: "Such is war and the strange bonding it can create on both sides."[6]

Lieutenant Colonel P. Gleadell, commanding the 12th Devons, in his diary for 7 January 1945, recounted another incident in which Foy was involved in the rescuing of wounded in the village:

As a result of a very gallant personal recce by Padre Foy of 13 para a wounded man was located at the convent in the Western half of Bure. A patrol, including a jeep driven by private Brand (12 Devons) and accompanied by the MO, Captain

2   Account by A.L. Beckingham, http://www.pegasusarchive.org/normandy/frames.htm.
3   Museum of Army Chaplaincy Archives, notes made by John Gwinnett given to Sir John Smyth.
4   Tibbs, *Parachute Doctor*, p.79.
5   *Ibid*, p.80.
6   *Ibid*.

Kaye, moved into Bure in daylight in the face of enemy tanks and evacuated the wounded officer. When backing out of the convent the jeep was blown up by a mine, killing the officer and badly wounding Brand.[7]

Foy was awarded a Military Cross for his continued bravery in the action at Bure. The recommendation form for his decoration read:

> During the attack on Bure on January 3 1945 A company of the 13th Parachute received very heavy casualties on the start line. When this information reached the Rev Foy he at once went forward to help. In spite of the fact that most casualties were lying in exposed positions on the forward slope of a hill and the enemy artillery fire was both accurate and intense he moved about, completely disregarding the fire and his own danger, and moved the wounded to safety, while reassuring them and keeping up their morale. On moving to the village he several times joined parties bringing in casualties under heavy shell fire, was untiring in his attention to the wounded and completely without sign of fear in his movements and actions. During the action volunteers were called for to obtain identifications of dead and to search for wounded in positions still under enemy observation and heavy fire. Rev Foy at once volunteered and taking a small party boldly went out. Then in spite of most vicious fire directed against him, he moved from place to place in his search and finishing his work returned to the Battalion with two wounded men. His example and extraordinary courage and devotion to duty were of inestimable value to the morale of all ranks throughout a most bitter engagement.[8]

When more settled conditions prevailed at the end of January, John Hall was able to present some men for confirmation at Nijmegen. The men were patrolling the ground on one side of the Maas River and the Germans were on the other side. Vaughan-Jones organised a rest centre in a barn where men could go and dry off, relax and enjoy a hot bath, with water heated by a copper in the cowshed.

At the end of February the division returned to England, except for RASC, REME and RE detachments, and the Revd Beckingham stayed with these units. He reported working harder than he had ever done before, trying to get around many units scattered over a wide are, but when Padre Hyde of the 7th Parachute Battalion dislocated his shoulder playing rugby, Beckingham was flown back quickly to take his place on Operation Varsity. He had one week to get around and make himself known to the battalion before going into action, but reported that they were a "splendid battalion", and that thanks to their CO, Colonel Pine-Coffin, he had settled down quickly.

---

7   Museum of Army Chaplaincy Archives, Airborne Chaplains papers deposited by the Revd P.R.C. Abram CVO. Typescript, *Lower Than the Angels* (1971), p.123.
8   Recommendation form dated 8 January 1945. Reproduced by Paradata.

In March 1945 the 6th Airborne Division were to take part in the one of the final major acts of the war. Operation Varsity was the airborne part of the Allied crossing of the Rhine, which was the last great barrier to the conquest of Germany. The ground troops part, Operation Plunder, involved Montgomery's 21st Army Group, consisting of over a million men.

Those troops who parachuted into and landed by glider in German territory took part in the largest single-lift airborne operation of the war, with 540 American Dakota aircraft carrying the 12 parachute battalions - five British, one Canadian and six from the US - closely followed by 1,300 gliders packed with troops.[9] The 6th Airborne Division was to land on and seize the high ground of the Diersfordt wood, which was overlooking the part of the Rhine to be crossed by the land operation. Despite determined opposition and initial heavy casualties, within five-and-a-half hours all objectives were taken and the link-up with the ground forces achieved. Out of their original 7,220 troops, the 6th Airborne Division lost 1,400 men either killed, wounded or missing in action.

During the final week before the operation, a chaplain's conference was held, George Hales wished the chaplains God speed and they were briefed by senior chaplain Peter Cameron. Vaughan-Jones, who had transferred from the Ulster Rifles to the Gunners, arranged an eve-of-battle service. The altar was the bonnet of the general's jeep and 30 men took part, with 13 staying for communion. Later, Vaughan-Jones took a service in a nearby village church for the 2nd Air Landing Tank Regiment, Royal Artillery. Vaughan-Jones took his text from 1. Peter 4 vv 12-19 and used the last verse, "So then, those who suffer according to God's will should commit themselves to their faithful Creator and continue to do good", to encourage the men to commit their souls to God before action. Vaughan-Jones took off from RAF Great Dunmow in Essex on 24 March 24 in a Horsa glider, with the Medical Officer, Captain P.D. James RAMC, four other ranks, a jeep and trailer, and 2two lightweight moto-cycles, landing successfully on Landing Zone P. He took charge of unloading the glider, which proved difficult. He then helped set up the RAP and the MDS.

Vaughan-Jones also conducted a short service of matins while waiting for his glider to be towed out. Again the readings appointed for the day were apt: "I shall not die but live and declare the works of the Lord" (Psalm 118, v 14) and "The lord is on my side; I will not fear what men do unto me" (Psalm 118, v 17).

The airborne troops were to be dropped directly onto their objectives to prevent the enemy artillery on the other side of the Rhine from causing heavy casualties to the troops crossing the river by boat. There would be no element of surprise as the drop was in daylight. Beckingham explained that the drop on Operation Varsity was completely different to his experiences in Normandy. It was timed for 10:20 a.m., some three or four hours after the land troops has started to cross the river in assault craft.

9   Website of The Parachute Regiment, https://web.archive.org/web/20060803032605/
http://www.army.mod.uk/para/history/rhine.htm.

He found the experience of dropping by parachute much more pleasant as the drop was from higher up: he estimated between 800ft and 1,000ft. However, this increased the casualty rate for the paratroopers as they came under fire from German AA guns on their descent. The 7th Battalion arrived last of the 5th Parachute Brigade. They jumped amid heavy flak at 10:08 a.m., suffering casualties in the air. MO David Tibbs described how the lives of his stick were saved by the sergeant, jumping first, refusing to jump until the plane had cleared the trees. The men in the two planes near them dropped their sticks into the trees, where many men became trapped in branches and were an easy target. When they reached the ground they came under heavy mortaring and shelling. The DZ was obscured by smoke, and some of the men actually fell into German gun pits and were firing on the enemy before landing. [10] Beckingham himself landed in a quieter spot, soon reached the RV and found Dr Wagstaff and the RAMC orderlies and his batman, who presented him, to his surprise and pleasure, with a cup of tea, having parachuted into Germany with a flask of tea: "I have yet to meet anyone else who was privileged to drink hot tea within a few minutes of landing in Germany during a fierce battle."[11] However, he was soon in the thick of it as the German shelling and mortaring produced many casualties. He calculated that there were 93 casualties in the battalion on the first day, including 17 killed.

Shortly after the parachute drop the gliders came in. They were targeted by the many 40mm German guns which caused many losses in the tightly formed glider approach. Tibbs commented: "Gliders were on fire in the air, crashing to the ground or being raked with fire as soon as they landed. It was a depressing sight and nearly one third of the glider force perished in that landing. Over 900 men died in a few minutes."[12] The tail of the glider Vaughan-Jones landed in would not open to release the jeep, and the men who disembarked huddled under the wing of the glider under fire. Vaughan-Jones took the initiative and told the men to either finish unloading the glider or move away. He led the way back into the glider and eventually it was unloaded.[13]

Among the high casualty rate of the first day of the operation were two chaplains who we killed. The Revd J.F. Kenny dropped with the 224th Parachute Field Ambulance. The war diary of the Ambulance[14] describes how they dropped very close to a German strongpoint consisting of 71 enemy troops. Kenny's body was found in the early evening when the DZ was being cleared of casualties. His parachute had become tangled up in trees and he had been shot as he hung there. The Revd Walter Ogilvy dropped with the 8th Battalion and was ambushed by two Germans

---

10 An account by the Revd Beckingham, http://www.pegasusarchive.org/normandy/frames. htm.
11 *Ibid.*
12 David Tibbs and Neil Barber, *Parachute Doctor*, p.94.
13 Museum of Army Chaplaincy Archives, Abram, *Lower Than the Angels*, p.125.
14 TNA WO 177/8310.

with *Schmeissers* at close range. The battalion war diary[15] reported that Lieutenant P.C. Roberts and the Revd Ogilvy were attending German prisoners of war. Ogilvy died soon after being taken to a dressing station at Bergefurth.The chaplain of the Canadian Battalion, the Revd D.C. Candy, buried both chaplains. John Gwinnett commented: "Unfortunately the chaplaincy services in the 3rd Parachute Brigade suffered again. This meant that Douglas Candy and I had to do our best to cover the brigade in fast moving times. Somehow we managed it and both of us came out of the experience more seasoned."[16]

Padre Maurice McGowan with the 6th Air Landing Brigade was badly wounded when his glider crashed upon landing. Padre John Hall went in by glider with the12th Devons. His glider hit an obstruction as it came down and made a 'pancake' landing. Germans in a nearby house opened fire as the glider landed, but soon came out with their hands up. The chaplain helped those wounded in the landing and then went to battalion headquarters. He spent most of the day burying men from the glider assault where they had fallen.

Padre Gwinnett dropped as part of 3rd Brigade Headquarters. He was awarded a Military Cross for his actions from 24 March to 30 April, his citation reading:

> For outstanding gallantry and devotion to duty from 24th March to 30th April, 1945, from Schneppenberg Forest to River Elbe.The Reverend Gwinnett made his second operational drop which was over the Rhine on March 24th 1945. The Brigade sustained many casualties on the Drop Zone which was for many hours covered by artillery, mortar and machine gun fire. Throughout this period the Reverend Gwinnett showed complete contempt of danger in organising the evacuation of the casualties and administering the dying. His calmness and fine example under heavy fire proved an inspiration to all who saw him. During the advance to the Elbe, in any action that the battalion fought, such as at Lutherheim - Lembeck - Greven - Dortmund-Ems Canal - Masendorf, the Reverend Gwinnett was always to be found in the forefront of the battle. His courage and inspiring example throughout this and other campaigns has long been a byword in the Brigade.[17]

The night was quiet but it was not possible for Gwinnett to hold services during the next day, Sunday, as enemy shelling was very accurate. Later, the first tanks appeared and Vaughan-Jones reported to the senior chaplain. He collected all the the bodies he could find with the senior chaplain, and they selected a field to commence burials. Among the bodies he found was the pilot of the glider he had landed in.

---

15   TNA WO 171/5135.
16   Museum of Army Chaplaincy Archives, notes sent by the Revd John Gwinnett to John Smyth VC.
17   Citation reproduced at http://www.pegasusarchive.org/normandy/frames.htm.

As the airborne troops started to advance across Germany, Beckingham reported that enemy soldiers surrendered quickly. John Hall worked closely with Kaye, the MO, and his main job was conducting burials. Two incidents which caused casualties occurred as the 7th Battalion and the 224th Ambulance advanced. During the taking of Neustadt airport, the battalion was leading the divisional advance and halfway across the airfield the troops in lorries came under fire, resulting in 17 casualties, six of which were fatal. One of the dead was one of a pair of brothers, well known to Beckingham from his earliest day with the Ambulance, who were devout Christians: "It was not easy telling the brother that survived what had happened, but such was the task of the chaplain and always grace was given for the difficult tasks."[18]

The next object of the 7th Battalion was the capture of Neustadt bridge. This attack resulted in severe casualties as the bridge was blown when one platoon had crossed and others were crossing. The platoon that had crossed set up a bridgehead and succeeded in taking the bridge, but there were 19 fatalities, 19 injured and six missing. The problem for the Ambulance was that some of the injured were now unreachable on the other side of a fast-flowing river. Beckingham pointed out that the doctor and his men were already tired after the incident at the airfield: "The night's work was one to be long remembered."[19] Whilst caring for the wounded and recovering the bodies, Beckingham realised that it was 8 April, his birthday.

By Easter, the 6th Airborne Division had reached the Dortmund-Ems canal, and Hall held a service for the 12th Devons in a cowshed which was under fire. Before starting he had to feed the cows to stop hem lowing throughout the service. Vaughan-Jones held his service in a potato field, at which there were 15 communicants. At this stage Vaughan-Jones was pleased to exchange the motorbike he had landed with for a car. This made the rapid movements he had to make to keep up with the mobile gunners less difficult. He kept up with visits to batteries as much as he could. Gwinnett remembered that all the way to Wismar on the Baltic every effort was made to hold services, "sometimes in a ditch, a slit trench or a quiet corner of a field for communion".[20]

The Revd J.O. Jenkins was taken prisoner after taking a wrong turning near Osnabruck, but managed to escape and return to the battalion. On 9 May, the day of the German surrender, a thanksgiving service was held for the 9th Battalion at Wismar, taken by Gwinnett, while Hall took a service for the 12th Devons in the village church of Hohen Viecheln. Senior chaplain Cameron called the chaplains together to organise a divisional thanksgiving service, which was held at the Nikolai Kirche at Wismar, at which over 2,000 men attended. Here the adjutant, Malcolm Reid, who had struggled with recalcitrant portable organs throughout the campaign,

18   Account by A.L. Beckingham, http://www.pegasusarchive.org/normandy/frames.htm.
19   *Ibid.*
20   Museum of Army Chaplaincy Archives, notes made by John Gwinnett given to Sir John Smyth.

had his opportunity to play a real organ. However, the organ in the Nikolai church was enormous and Reid was uncertain that he could operate all the stops efficiently. There was no electricity, so prisoners of war were pressed into pumping. To his great surprise, on the day, a German lady organist turned up at the church, sat at the organ with him and pulled out all the right stops at the right time, just as if "nothing had happened", as Gwinnett commented.

9

The 1st Airborne Division in Norway and Denmark – Operation Doomsday

On 8 May 1945 the German High Command signed an unconditional surrender on Luneburg Heath. At this time there were still 350,000 German troops occupying Norway. Once the surrender of Germany had taken place, plans for the disbanding, control and evacuation of these German troops could go ahead. The 1st Airborne Division was involved in these plans for an Allied liberation force for Norway. Their task was also to prevent the sabotage of important military and civilian facilities, re-establish local and national government, maintain law and order and to render help to the Norwegian authorities in whatever way practicable until the arrival of Force134, the main occupation force. Although no full-scale resistance was anticipated, the Allies thought it essential their troops should have a presence at this crucial time required for political purposes. The outline plans for the operation noted: "We shall certainly be faced with strong political pressure from the Norwegian Government to intervene early, while the Swedish and Soviet Governments may also be interested in the early establishment of Allied control in Norway."[1]

Three days before the 8 May surrender, the 1st Parachute Battalion of the1st Parachute Brigade landed at Copenhagen in Denmark to preserve law and order after outbreaks of fighting between Danish civilians and German troops. Padre Robert Watkins described how they went on a war footing but also packed "some more peaceable kit".[2]. Their job was to stop any attempt by the German Army to establish a final redoubt in Denmark, but also, if necessary, to protect the Germans from the Danish population. German garrisons were manned by elderly and low-category

---

1   TNA, WO 219/2485, Operation Doomsday and Apostle: Outline Plans, 1945, quoted by John Greenacre, "Flexible Enough to Adapt": British Airborne Forces' Experiences during Post Conflict Operations 1944-46, *British Journal for Military History*, Volume 4, Issue 1, November 2017, p.80.
2   Museum of Army Chaplaincy Archives, the Revd R.T. Watkins, *Wartime Memoirs 1939-1945*.

fighting men, and the last garrison in Denmark surrendered on 16 May. The battalion took over the job of organising the evacuation of all the German troops from the island of Zealand, upon which Copenhagen stands, and Watkins visited the men who were spread out all over Zealand.

He also took services in the English church in Copenhagen, which had been closed for five years during the German occupation. These services were attended by the English expatriates, who had been interned and were now free, after the church had been cleaned and restored to order by a working party of German prisoners. They were also attended by representatives of the Danish Government and the Danish royal family, as well as the Military Mission. The church was packed, with many Danes attending for the first service, which was widely reported in the Danish press. Paul Abram, in his account, considered that: "The extraordinary Danish interest reflected the country's gratitude to Great Britain, their appreciation of British troops and a desire to hear the English language spoken again."[3] Watkins had some busy Sunday mornings, with two services at the English church in between one at the Lutheran church. He had some qualms as a Methodist presiding in an Anglican church, but as he was the only padre present in the area there was no choice. This dilemma was resolved when, after five weeks, an Anglican naval chaplain arrived on the cruiser HMS *Birmingham*. This chaplain took over the services in the English church, but Watkins continued to preach there. During his dealings with the released internees, Watkins came across Father C.C. Martindale, a distinguished Jesuit preacher, writer and lecturer, who was sick and in need of urgent repatriation, which Watkins arranged.

Watkins likened the rest of his posting to Denmark to a holiday. He was billeted with a delightful Danish family, had the use of an Opel car and did much sightseeing on his visits to units of the 1st Battalion. The German troops offered little resistance, organizing themselves for evacuation under British orders. Watkins regarded himself as very much on his own as padre in this situation, as the troops were spread out all over the country, creating difficulties in visiting them.

Padre Ronald Lunt, now Senior Chaplain of the 1st Airborne Division, remembered how emphasis in training after Arnhem was placed on preparing for deployment in the Far East, but "with the surrender of the Germans it [1st Airborne Division] was immediately alerted for operational duties which as usual were kept so secret few knew of the destination until 24 hours before setting off".[4]

The 1st Airborne Division landed in Norway at Gardermoen and Sola airfields between 8 and 13 May. There was no German resistance, but several transport gliders and aircraft crashed on landing and caused 40 fatalities. One of the first duties of the divisional padres was to conduct the burial services. Thirteen Borderers were among the dead, and their padre, John Rowell, who had been posted to Norway,

---

3   Museum of Army Chaplaincy Archives, Airborne chaplains' papers deposited by the Revd P.R.C. Abram CVO. Typescript, *Lower Than the Angels* (1975), p.142.
4   Museum of Army Chaplaincy Archives, letter from Ronald Lunt to Abram, 21 Dec 1971.

found that his first task was to bury the men of his battalion. Norwegian forces and, representatives of the resistance and government were present at the funeral. Padre Lunt also witnessed the triumphant procession of the Allied troops into Oslo. Allied forces were welcomed with wholehearted enthusiasm and feted as heroes, both in Denmark and in Norway.[5] Lunt described the progress of the jeeps, each greeted by crowds and covered with spring flowers. Shots could be heard in Oslo that evening, but Lunt soon realised that it was the resistance letting off steam and celebrating their liberation.

Strategic points were quickly captured and the occupying force spread over the country, Airborne Divisional Headquarters remaining in Oslo, with the SAS stationed in Bergen. Major General Urquhart's Assistant Director of Medical Services was put in charge of both military and civilian service throughout Norway. Another important task for the 1st Airborne Division was to track down and apprehend German soldiers wanted for war crimes by investigating the POW camps, gathering evidence for war crimes trials and exhuming bodies of those who were thought to have been victims.[6]

Although Lunt's task was primarily the care of the men in the division, he inevitably became involved in the civil and religious affairs of the country. He was thrilled and honoured to attend the release of Bishop Eivind Beggrav, who had led the resistance of the Norwegian church to the Nazi occupation. Although imprisoned in solitary confinement since Easter 1942 in an isolated location in the forests north of Oslo, Beggrav had managed, with the support of his guards, to meet with the Norwegian underground. Lunt developed a friendship with this "heroic pillar of the faith".[7]

Bishop Beggrav was unable to attend the thanksgiving service held by the division on 27 May, but he sent a message:

> Our friends of the British Army, the Church Of Norway greets you, thankful as we are towards God and man. The name of God is I AM. We have experienced it in these years of darkness, when we often do not see him – HE IS, and has called upon us to be our servants and friends. Do know it, soldiers of the British Army, servants of God's great cause in the world. HE IS and we are his family if we serve him through all the battles against his and our foe, evil and sin. Our motto is this GOD IS. We are his brethren. God bless you and Great Britain, now and forever.[8]

As the division was dispersed, only four of the padres were present at the service. Major General Urquhart read the lesson and Lunt preached the sermon.

---

5   *Ibid.*
6   John Greenacre, "Flexible Enough to Adapt": British Airborne Forces' Experiences during Post Conflict Operations 1944-46, *British Journal for Military History*, Volume 4, Issue 1, November 2017, p.82.
7   Museum of Army Chaplaincy Archives, an account by Ronald Lunt.
8   *Ibid.*

During the war the Anglican church building, which Queen Maud of Norway, daughter of British king Edward VII, had liked to attend until her death in 1938, had been damaged, but the congregation had kept together as a house group and was overjoyed when the church was reopened. The church was attended by members of the 1st Airborne Division and Norwegians, and the divisional padres held weekday Holy Communion services. The padres settled into a routine and began regular padre's meetings once more. They gave a great deal of consideration to developing a common theme in their preaching, asking each other questions such as: "What must our message be in the morrow of victory and liberation? Can we find a common word which together we will deliver to our units? What is the word of God for this day?" Lunt felt that the padres of every denomination worked well together in this situation. The men of the airborne division were widely dispersed, and when the Deputy Assistant chaplain general to the airborne forces, George Hales, came to visit Lunt tried to give him an idea of the difficulties he faced by whisking him around as many units as possible, impressing upon him that the chaplains had to do much travelling if units were not to be neglected. Lunt was able to contribute to the wellbeing of the British troops in Norway for three months by participating in special programmes put out by the Norwegian Broadcasting Corporation. He had experience before the war of broadcasting with the British Expeditionary Forces.

Watkins related that no sooner had he had arrived back in England than he was told to report to Norway, where there was still a shortage of padres. When he arrived in Oslo he was critical of the way that the Airborne Divisional HQ had, he thought, settled themselves down too comfortably. He was in Norway by mid-July and was able to take part in radio programmes for the troops. Having listened to one or two of the programmes, he decided that a down-to-earth approach was needed, and involved as many people as he could in the talks and interviews he presented. His theme was very much about the transition from war to peace and the opportunities in civilian trades and training possibilities. He had moved from Oslo to Kristiansand at this point, and set about recording some more interesting material:

> There was enough variety among officers and men to make that worthwhile …
> So I got a technique of putting out a sort of magazine programme leading to an
> epilogue. It was all very interesting – to me at any rate. I eventually put together
> seven of these programmes, all recoded and assembled in Kristiansand and put
> out from Oslo, some after I had left the country.[9]

Lunt travelled on a reconnaissance tour of the southern coast of Norway to arrange a scheme of soldiers being able to spend their leave with local families, which was set up in Fevik. The British and American troops appreciated fully the shortages that the Norwegians had endured and were very willing to share their 'compo' rations

9   Watkins, *World War Two Memoirs 1939-1945.*

with their new friends. Lunt related that the success of this and of the friendships that grew up was such that "Chaplains needed to acquaint themselves with the regulations covering soldiers wanting to marry in a foreign country."[10] The chaplains were involved in counselling soldiers who wanted to marry Norwegian girls. Indeed, Lunt was personally involved in this issue as he became engaged to a Norwegian girl, Veslemoy Sopp Foss, himself, and they were married on 14 August by Bishop Beggrav. After his wedding he returned to England and Alan Buchanan replaced him as Senior Chaplain. It was possibly because of this personal happiness that Lunt described his time in Norway as, "A situation which was pleasurable rather than exciting or pastorally demanding."[11]

In Kristiansand, Watkins was given the opportunity to witness war tribunals. They were presided over by Norwegian military officers, with British legal branch assistance. He felt uneasy about some of the trails he witnessed. He felt they were "legally just but ethically wrong", in that although he had no doubts about the guilt of the accused, he felt it was not wise for the victims to be the judges. During his time in Norway, Watkins and a Methodist RAF chaplain were sent to the first post-war conference of the Scandinavian Methodists at Trondheim to convey the greetings of the British Methodist Conference.

While he was at Trondheim, Watkins met Alexander Britnev, a British officer formerly with the 1st Parachute Battalion who was acting as an interpreter and liaison officer, as he was Russian-born and there were many Russians in Norway. In Watkins' opinion the Russians were "officially there to repatriate their own nationals, and unofficially to make a nuisance of themselves".[12] Britnev explained that during the war the Germans had brought large numbers of forced labourers to Norway, the workers being mainly from Russia and the Baltic states. The conditions in these camps, he said, had been horrific. Watkins found that those who had survived the work camps were not to be repatriated to their homes in Estonia, Latvia or Lithuania, but were to be sent by the Russians to labour camps in Siberia because of their supposed contamination by Western influence. Britnev took Watkins to dinner with some Red Army officers who confirmed to him openly that this was the case. Moreover, Watkins realised that: "The allies accepted this was patent, since these people were being shipped away in British ships, not to Baltic ports but to the Russian Arctic ports. We knew and we connived."[13] He was approached for help by a Lutheran pastor from one of these camps, who said there were other pastors in the camp and also many Jews and Protestants. He begged Watkins to try to arrange for them to go to a Western country. Watkins duly wrote to

---

10   Ibid.
11   Museum of Army Chaplaincy Archives, a letter from Ronald Lunt, August 22. 1969.
12   Watkins, *World War Memoirs 1939-1945*.
13   *Ibid.*

many Members of Parliament, but received no helpful response, leaving him feeling "helpless and ashamed".[14]

Fraser McLuskey described his time in Norway with the 1st Battalion SAS as "unexpectedly carefree". He was stationed mainly in Bergen, quartered in blocks of modern flats, and as with the other padres in Norway that summer he commented on the glorious weather. As some of the SAS units were in Oslo and others in Stavanger, it gave him the chance to travel; he particularly remembered "a sail up the Sogne Fjord on a moonlit night so breathtakingly lovely that it was impossible to go to bed!".[15]

Once their task was completed, the 1st Airborne Division was no longer needed in Norway, and from the end of August it began to return to Britain, being disbanded during the autumn of 1945.

14   *Ibid.*
15   Fraser McLuskey, *The Cloud and Fire* (Edinburgh: The Pentland Press, 1993), p.82.

Analysis: The role and achievements of airborne chaplains in the Second World War

Background

At the end of the First World War, the Army Chaplains Department had proved its worth to the British Army and earned the title of the Royal Army Chaplains Department. Overcoming difficulties and criticism, the army chaplains had performed a multiplicity of roles, both behind the lines and near the front line in Regimental Aid Stations, where their actions won them decorations and resulted in fatal casualties. It can be said that to a large extent they had grappled with the problems of their role in conflict successfully and had brought material, medical and spiritual comfort to the men in the maelstrom of conflict for over four years.

In the post-war era, the number of regular chaplains was cut in line with the expectations of a period of sustained peace. By 1927 the department had 141 chaplains.[1] The role of the post-war chaplain was similar to his pre-war role, in that chaplains were mainly posted to stations rather than units and no new initiatives in chaplain training were tried. Paul Abram, in an article for the RAChD journal in 1971, described the department in the 1930s. There was a waiting list for the department, as in the Depression churches could not afford a curate. He wrote about the old-fashioned attitudes to training:

> Most junior chaplains, if they did not already have mastery of the art, were sent on an equitation course. There were no Padre's Hours and instruction was limited to confirmation classes, teaching band boys and children and the weekly parade services … this system served to separate the chaplain from the men he served. The result of this was that in 1941 most regular chaplains were unenthusiastic at the thought of chaplains jumping out of aeroplanes or going on glider courses or taking part in the many activities necessary to a new concept of war.[2]

---

1   Michael Snape, *The Royal Army Chaplains' Department: Clergy Under Fire* (Woodbridge: The Boydell Press, 2008), p.264.
2   Paul Abram, "Airborne Chaplains – The Early Years", *RAChD Journal*, Vol. 22, No. 113 (May 1970), p.7.

It was realised that in order to fulfil their task in a new war, chaplains needed a greater degree of training. A chaplains' school was set up at Chester and later more permanently at Tidworth. Military aspects of training included anti-gas procedures, map reading, military law and the structure of military units and the chain of command. One of the tutors, the Revd Ronald Sinclair, gave a series of devotional addresses which helped the chaplain formulate their ideas on how to give the Christian message to soldiers. He warned against falling into the trap that many Great War chaplains had, that of concentrating too much on the physical welfare of the men, being purveyors of a sort of 'Holy Grocery':

> It is fatally easy for a chaplain to slip into the way of being content to give men only the bread that perishes, to be a dispenser of cigarettes and chocolate, all very necessary and all part of our work … but it is not what we were commissioned for. We may use the bread that perisheth not as an end in itself, but as a means of contact, and of friendship. In order that we may satisfy the deep-seated need of the souls for Christ himself.[3]

Fraser McLuskey, who went on to become an airborne chaplain serving with the SAS behind enemy lines, professed himself satisfied with the induction course at Tidworth: "We left Tidworth very much wiser and, most of us felt, very much better men."[4] By 1944 the realisation that chaplains were often in the heat of battle resulted in more practical battle courses being provided at Church Stowe which dealt with vehicle maintenance, radio communication, mines, booby traps, camouflage and security, first aid and mapping skills. It was decided that all chaplains taking part in the D-Day landings should have attended this course. The course at Church Stowe was credited with saving many chaplains' lives. The airborne padres, however, had been going through rigorous battle training and parachute training on exactly the same terms as the men and officers since 1942. Senior chaplain J.J.A. Hodgins, proactively, went around recruiting padres for airborne service, looking for younger, fitter men who were perhaps restless in their chaplaincy roles.

Service as a padre in the airborne divisions was voluntary. However, many of the airborne padres remember being summoned, either personally or having seen a request posted to units, to consider the airborne role. Padre E.C. Phillips was a padre in the infantry wing at Sandhurst when he received a telephone call telling him to report the following day to the Airborne Division.[5]

3   Alan Robinson, *Chaplains at War, The Role of Clergymen during World War Two* (London: I.B. Tauris and Co, 2008), p.101.
4   F. McLuskey, *Parachute Padre: Behind German Lines with the SAS in France 1944* (Stevenage: SCM Press), pp.18-19.
5   *West Sussex County Times*, 31 August 1945, "Parachute padre addresses Rotarians".

Many padres commented in their post-war accounts on what they considered to be the most important aspects of their training. They welcomed the opportunity to be trained alongside all ranks and share the hardships and friendships that resulted. Padre 'Joe' Downing, who went to Hardwick and Ringway for his training in 1942, commented on how much he appreciated the groups the trainees were placed in contained a mix of ranks, who completed all their training together: "No weakening of discipline followed, but rather an intense feeling of togetherness, of belonging to each other. It needs little imagination to see how supremely this mattered to a chaplain."[6]

As had been seen, it was the first airborne padres who insisted, against much opposition, that it was vital that the padres jumped alongside the men, so that they would be qualified and prepared for the coming battles. Padre Bernard Egan expressed his views on what is now known in the chaplaincy department as the ministry of presence. He argued:

> There was no doubt that the position of the parachute chaplain made all the difference to his relations with the men. He could truly say that he was one of them, and the men, for their part, liked to feel that the chaplain was undergoing the same trials as themselves. And their mutual experience of discomfort, nervousness and exhilaration, were equally shared. Personal relations with the men mean so much to a chaplain that he feels, these having been so well established, that difficulties he is likely to encounter have been more than halved.[7]

Robert Watkins considered that the experience of jumping resulted in "a door being opened to the interest and sympathy of the men. As for the padre himself, he feels that he is no strange person set down in their midst but rather is he among them as one who knows and shares their life and risky duty."[8]

Relationships with men

The airborne padres worked hard at their relationships with men and officers. Their full role in the training and combat experiences of the airborne troops facilitated these close relationships. Padre David Nimmo commented:

> But the one thing that really mattered to me as a chaplain was this - the airborne soldier looked upon his chaplain primarily as a member of the proud brotherhood to which he himself belonged, and accepted him and respected him as such. So the airborne padres were off to a "flying start". The men did not as it were, cross the street to avoid him when they saw him coming, they hailed him as a

---

6   Museum of Army Chaplaincy Archives, account by the Revd E.N. Downing.
7   Robinson, *Chaplains at War*, p.112.
8   Museum of Army Chaplaincy Archives, account by the Revd Robert Watkins.

comrade, as one of themselves. This gave the chaplain a unique opportunity to do his job. He was much less hindered than parsons and priests usually are by common prejudices against men of the cloth.[9]

John Hall realised that padres were often useful in providing a conduit between men and officers: "I think a valuable service in Normandy was providing an ear for men to talk about home and also providing a channel by which they could be 'put in the picture' about what was going on."

'Joe' Downing described that as time went on and he got to know the men of his battalion more, there was a greater freedom of communication with them and they no longer felt the need to censor their talk in front of the padre:

> For me a few years of living with the army at war brought the satisfaction and joy of finding myself getting down to a level of kinship at which this kind of constraint came to matter less as the months went by, a level in fact where there could be such a bond of love between us that utterance could be free, as made between friends.[10]

Fraser McLuskey, behind the lines in France, had opportunities to get close to the men he served with. He tried always to think of his men as individuals and was honoured to be their friend:

> Men who had given me so quickly and so freely their trust and friendship … Pride in that gift had never lessened. I suppose there is nothing I value more. I have never lived with such a group of men before, nor do I expect to do so again. It was easy to be brave in their company and difficult to be a coward. I know that I shall never wholly lose the infection of their courage and good cheer.[11]

McLuskey appreciated the special atmosphere of a unit such as the 1st SAS Battalion, and he said of the men: "Like their padre they were not without their faults, but their faults, unlike the virtues of some were very easy to live with." He took into account the strain their dangerous battle experiences put upon them: "[While] it must be admitted that at unit celebrations too much was drunk by too few, these parties were themselves the product of friendship that was genuine and sincere."[12]

Chaplains were aware that often a too vigorous approach to evangelism was counterproductive, and in replies to a questionnaire given to Second World War chaplains about chaplain priorities in 2013, chaplains from all denominations did not

9   Museum of Army Chaplaincy Archives, an account by the Revd David Nimmo.
10   E.N. 'Joe' Downing, *Padre with the Paras* (privately printed, undated).
11   J. Fraser McLuskey, *Parachute Padre* (London: SCM Press, 1951), p.55.
12   *Ibid*, p.54.

consider evangelism to be an important factor. Of the Roman Catholic chaplains, only one gave it a priority, while other Catholic chaplains thought it was inappropriate. In the opinion of the Anglican chaplains, evangelism was also a low priority. Only one Nonconformist minister gave priority to evangelism.[13] Padre John Kent began to realise a mistake in his approach: "I was never satisfied with friendship but being blindfolded by what now seems to be the very short-sighted theology of the time I was continually trying to turn friendship into conversion with virtually no success."[14]

Relationships with officers

Chaplains in the Second World War were generally held in high esteem with their commanders. The Revd Freddie Hughes, Senior Chaplain to the Eighth Army, did much to establish good relationships between his padres and commanders. There was also a cooperative relationship between General 'Boy' Browning, in charge of the airborne divisions, and Senior Chaplain John Hodgins. Padre Geoffrey Harper, Senior Chaplain in North Africa, Sicily and Italy, considered that: "Between them they saw to it that every unit commander was shown to consider the chaplain as part of the team of leaders."[15] He believed that officers could and would invite the chaplain to help them with aspects of their leadership. His experience of this were the conversations with General Hopkinson before Operation Husky, but it was an opinion shared by padres and commanding officers alike. Padre Phillips praised the commanding officers of the 1st Airborne Division for the opportunities and support they gave the padres. In an address he gave to a group of Rotarians in August 1945 he said: "I can say that nearly every Commanding Officer I have come across has been willing to support me and give all the help needed."[16]

There is evidence from Commanding Officers that confirms that of the padres. Lieutenant Colonel James Hill, writing to Abram in 1971, remembered: "Padres played such an important part in the life of a fighting battalion. After four years of commanding either a battalion or a para brigade in the war it was abundantly clear to me that the three most important men in any battalion were always the C.O., the padre and the medical officer."[17] Brigadier H.B. Coxen commented: "It is not generally recognised that the battalion commander is ever indebted to the padre for his assistance in measuring the all-important factor of morale within his unit." He particularly praised 'Joe' Downing: "Padres of the calibre of Joe Downing were able to win the confidence of their charges and 'Joe's hour' was a great barometer of

---

13   Answers to a questionnaire devised by Alan Robinson, dealt with fully in Robinson, *Chaplains at War*, pp.103-05.

14   Museum of Army Chaplaincy Archives, an account by John Kent.

15   Museum of Army Chaplaincy Archives, an account by Geoffrey Harper.

16   *West Sussex County Times*, 31 August 1945, "Parachute padre addresses Rotarians".

17   Museum of Army Chaplaincy Archives letter from James Hill to Paul Abram, 4 June 1971.

the inner feelings of the troops."[18] The CO of the 3rd Parachute Brigade, General (then Brigadier) Gerald Lathbury, recollected: "I commanded a brigade for nearly 3 years and we never had enough chaplains."[19] One aspect of the padre/commander relationship was the ability of the padre often to act as a sounding board and release for the officer. Lieutenant Colonel Paul Gleadell of the 12th Devons considered: "When commanding officers needed a safety valve, the chaplain was the one they turned to. The chaplain is an essential part, yet being slightly apart, provided just this solace. This is one of the debts I owe to Johnnie Hall, 'Letting my hair down'."[20] Chaplains were not always in agreement with their COs and could put forward the issues that were concerning the men. Brigadier Coxen said of 'Joe' Downing: "Padre Joe was not noticeably meek and if he had an issue that he felt demanded attention, he could not easily be dissuaded from his purpose."[21]

Padres cold also be instrumental in dealing with problems of discipline and morale. We have seen in Chapter 1 how they helped suggest solutions to the problem of men suddenly refusing to jump when deployed to a battalion after training. Lathbury remembered how Watkins had helped in a situation in 1944: "Sometime in the Summer of 1944 we had a bit of trouble in 1 Para after a change of command ... Watkins was of considerable help in what was a difficult situation. This leads me to say that a good chaplain can be of the greatest help in his connections at whatever level, if he is pretty close to the men."[22]

Watkins had discovered early on at Hardwick and Ringway that young officers often needed help in dealing with the problems of the men:

> I learned that very often the padre's job is only in part to deal with the man; the other part is to counsel the officer concerned how to handle the man. I like to think that a chaplain has more to give to young subalterns than most about the difficult art of man-management. In the special circumstances of Hardwick I learned to try quietly to show young officers how to deal with men with problems.[23]

J. Lawson, a medical officer who served at Arnhem, pointed out how important it was that there was cooperation between COs and chaplains: "His ministry starts with the

18 Brigadier H.B. Coxen in foreword to E.N. 'Joe' Downing, *Padre with the Paras*.
19 Museum of Army Chaplaincy Archives, letter from General Sir Gerald Lathbury to Paul Abram, 4 November 1971.
20 Museum of Army Chaplaincy Archives, letter of 2 August 1971 from Major General Paul Gleadell to Paul Abram.
21 Coxen, foreword to *Padre with the Paras*.
22 Museum of Army Chaplaincy Archives, letter from General Sir Gerald Lathbury to Paul Abram, 4 November 1971.
23 Museum of Army Chaplaincy Archives, R.T. Watkins, *World War Two Memoirs 1939-45*.

CO and encompasses everyone within the unit. The chaplain is the Colonel's first advisor, but he in turn needs the CO's support."[24]

Watkins explained how the relationship worked both ways:

> By contrast I learned a great deal from senior regular officers, not all of the churchmen. Some of those in the 1st Parachute Brigade were of the highest calibre, as their subsequent record shows, and to them and to the CO of the 2nd Essex I owed much, not only for their friendship and support but for the way in which, unbeknown to themselves, they helped me to discover what chaplaincy ought to be.[25]

Religion and religious services

From the beginning of their training, airborne padres had the advantage when organising religious services and church parades in training that they had an equality of experience with their men which encouraged participation in services. Many chaplains found that if in camp the attendance varied, when the unit was out on training assignments there was a much fuller participation. As in the First World War, padres did their best to persuade COs to abandon church parades and to have voluntary services. Watkins found from the beginning at Hardwick Hall that services in camp were hard going:

> I have never known voluntary services in camp to be a great success. I soon gave up the idea at Hardwick. Those who wanted to go to church preferred to go to a church away from the camp, and who could blame them? I had a Sunday Holy Communion in the Chapel, and Egan had his Mass. Midweek I got into the way of having a Wednesday 9.30 pm Compline alternating with a freer form of evening prayers.

But, he added, "it was quite another matter overseas".[26]

Most, but not all, chaplains were in favour of the Padre's Hours introduced by General Browning. Padre David Nimmo was enthusiastically in favour of them:

> Our golden opportunity lay in the "padre's hour". Here, once a week and during training hours, the men were encouraged to voice their thoughts, doubts and questions – with no holds barred. They soon realised that they could say freely

---

24   Museum of Army Chaplaincy Archive, account "A medical Officer at Arnhem" by J. Lawson.

25   Museum of Army Chaplaincy Archives, Watkins, *World War Two Memoirs 1939-1945*.

26   Watkins, *World War Two Memoirs 1939--1945*.

what they were really thinking and raise the questions they wanted chewed over. It was a refreshing, deepening, enriching experiment for us and also I believe for them. We didn't always know or find out the answers that were being sought but we learned a lot from each other as we rubbed minds together.[27]

'Joe' Downing sometimes found Padre's Hours challenging. He believed at first that the questions posed to him in them were designed to catch him out, but as time went on this thought disappeared. Questions on church parades and welfare provisions provided frequent topics for discussion. He found help in a First World War chaplain's work: "A most valuable filling for a Padre's Hour I found in Studdert Kennedy's dialect poems. Woodbine Willie could make a point so strongly and poignantly that I often fell back on him. I wished and wish that I could be anything like that."[28]

Robert Watkins was at first not in favour of the Padre's Hours as he considered that the chaplains had to find out themselves how to conduct them, and as far as the airborne forces were concerned the unit commanders found their initial introduction a distraction from getting the training towards a war footing. During the North African campaign, the padres took services whenever possible in the mobile actions that were taking place as they advanced slowly on Tunis. It was during this time that Padre Watkins formulated the "family prayers" which provided a short informal non-Eucharistic and nondenominational service for use in the front line.

When the airborne forces reverted to their correct role of dropping behind enemy lines to facilitate the advancing forces - at Sicily, D-Day and Arnhem - the padres took pre-battle service with the units and often continued to take small services under the wings of aeroplanes and gliders up to take-off. As we have seen, these services were vividly remembered by the men taking part. A great variety of services were carried out on the field of battle, ranging from prayers in foxholes to the celebratory service at Wismar. Again, the evidence is that these services were appreciated by men and officers. Urquhart, CO of the airborne troops at Arnhem, wrote:

> I can remember the incident when Chignell came into the particular room of the cellar which the general staff and I were using just before the withdrawal. He was quite excellent. Without asking he said he would like to say a prayer with those present. And this he did. And I certainly appreciated this gesture. I am sure this helped everyone. After this spiritual boost I handed around the bottle of Whiskey which I had in my bag since we landed. All in the cellar had a swig.[29]

27   Museum of Army Chaplaincy Archives, an account by the Revd D. Nimmo.
28   Downing, *Padre With the Paras*, p.12.
29   Museum of Army Chaplaincy Archives, letter from Major General Roy Urqhuart to Abram, 10 June 1971.

Fraser McLuskey took many simple services in the French forests and reflected on the fact that although the services were simple, they contained the symbolism of cross and altar:

> It is the perennial temptation of the churchman to fall in love with the forms of worship and to mistake the form for the substance. It is the equally strong temptation of the 'worship God anywhere' exponent to deny the dependence of substance on the forms of expression … the human spirit demands freedom from the sway of externals and is yet dependent on those same externals in some shape or form.[30]

McLuskey perhaps encapsulated the feelings of many of the airborne padres when he described his feelings after a simple service in a forest glade: "We had waited on God, we had renewed our strength."[31] It was McLuskey who articulated most fully the sense that the engagement of man with God and prayer in battle conditions is more than foxhole religion:

> It was not simply to curry favour that they stood before God. The life we had begun to lead together tested our sense of values … The deep basic needs of men, no longer overlaid by social custom and convention, stood revealed. Because one of these needs is the need of God, there was no feeling of strangeness as we stood together and said the Lord's Prayer … as men drew closer to one another, we drew closer to him.

A striking aspect of services by the airborne padres in battle was the absence of concern over denomination or denominational differences. This was an attitude begun by Watkins and Bernard Egan, the first airborne padres, who ministered pastorally to all regardless of their flock, apart from the prohibition of non-Roman Catholics from receiving communion at Mass. They had made the decision that the original chapel at Hardwick should be used for all denominations, Watkins explained: "At this date it was usual for camp chapels to be exclusively denominational. It was important to us that in the special circumstances of Hardwick this chapel should be home for chaplains of whatever denomination. For that reason, it was not consecrated. It did say something that chaplains could with complete loyalty to their orders all use the same altar."[32] Both Lieutenant Colonel John Frost and Major General Richard Gale mentioned the non-denominational attitude of Egan. Frost remembered: "Father Egan was always known as father by Catholics and Protestants alike. It says much for his good sense and loving kindness that many Protestants hardly knew he was of

---

30   McLuskey, *Parachute Padre*, p.123.
31   *Ibid*, p.78.
32   Watkins, *World War Two Memoirs 1939-1945*.

a different denomination."[33] Gale added: " Egan, quiet, pensive but warm, made an appeal as a man as well as a padre to Roman Catholics and Protestants alike."[34] As we have seen, the decision to administer Holy Communion to all the men who wanted it, regardless of their denomination, had a disastrous effect on the future career of Daniel McGowan, Roman Catholic priest at Arnhem.

In contrast with the First World War, when Protestant padres were rarely allowed access to the Roman Catholic churches in France and Belgium, the airborne chaplains received a warm welcome in Italy and Greece. Some went out of their way to cultivate the local Roman Catholic and Greek Orthodox priests, resulting in some services in their churches which were definitely ecumenical, puzzling to the locals and strictly against RAChD regulations. Denominational issues and rivalries were few. The Revd McLuskey had commented in training: "While one denomination or another might be held most efficacious for man's upward ascent, Church and Chapel, Protestant and Roman, bow alike all to gravity and fall with equal force."[35]

Ronald Lunt, stationed in Norway in the summer of 1945, was particularly impressed with the cooperation of the chaplains in working out their role and message in the aftermath of war: "We tried to develop a common theme and in the endeavour came to know each other specially well. And [we] gained much from each other and from our variety of backgrounds, denominations and experiences."[36]

In battle

We have seen how airborne chaplains were in action at every stage of the airborne forces' operations in the war, apart from the very early operations. The Revd Freddie Hughes, later to became Chaplain General, started to define this role, dividing chaplains' duty in battle into seven stages:

> The approach to battle;
> Eve of battle services;
> Companionship at zero hour;
> Practical service during battles;
> Settling men down in the aftermath;
> Burying the dead;
> Holding memorial and thanksgiving services.

33   Museum of Army Chaplaincy Archives, letter from John Frost, 4 March (year unknown) to Paul Abram.
34   Museum of Army Chaplaincy Archives, letter from Richard Gale to Abram, 22 January (year not stated).
35   McLuskey, *Parachute Padre*, p.25.
36   Museum of Army Chaplaincy Archives, an account by the Revd Ronald Lunt.

We have seen how services, both for large units and small groups just before take-off, were appreciated by the men. The sermons delivered at the services before D-Day and Arnhem were not designed to be bellicose or merely to encourage military endeavour, even though Eighth Army Senior Chaplain Padre Freddie Hughes had encouraged his chaplains to give the troops "the knowledge that they are discharging the purpose of God by fighting the enemy". The men did appreciate that they had the blessing of God on their task, and as we have seen, John Gwinnett's sermon with the text "fear knocked at the door" was remembered and commented on by many men.

Their ministry of presence was fully felt as they sat huddled in gliders and led sticks of paratroopers in aeroplanes. In a newspaper report on airborne padres in October 1944, "a padre" was quoted as saying:

> The padres find that they can do a great deal of good in the tense moments before the drop begins by talking to one man or another "About trivialities, mostly, we do not have to hurl our religion at the men. It's enough that they look at us and say to themselves 'Well at least here is a bloke who does not have to do it." That feeling makes a great difference to the man in a period of considerable mental stress and it makes a great deal of difference to him afterwards in his attitude to the chaplain.[37]

When at the beginning of the campaign in North Africa padres were left off the loading tables, the first padre in action, Roy Price, made sure they were included, determined that the efforts of chaplains such as Watkins and Egan, who had won the right of chaplains to jump, would not have been in vain.

Upon landing, the airborne padres, in all the theatres of war that they operated in, often took the initiative in gathering groups of men who had landed or dropped wide and finding the rendezvous point. In Sicily and at Arnhem, they took on a leadership role in the chaos of landing and rendezvousing. Often their first task was to bury those killed on landing, before finding the medical unit that they were usually attached to. In the heat of battle after arriving, the chaplains did not usually have the opportunity for many official services, but were able to give spiritual care individually and in small groups. When troops were further back from the line, or withdrawn for rest periods, as in the long North African campaign, more formal services could be arranged.

The bravery of the airborne padres can be seen in accounts of their calmness under fire and their heroic bringing in of wounded and care for them in dangerous situations. The uniqueness of their position as padres accompanying airborne troops was that they were in positions where they could not retreat to bases or hospitals behind the line, and spent their time in forward aid posts and with the men in battle situations.

As we have seen, there were times when airborne chaplains took military initiatives which were not strictly their remit. We have seen evidence that particularly in

37   *The Cornishman*, 15 October 1944, p.7.

the1st Airborne Division in North Africa, Sicily and at Arnhem, chaplains took on leadership roles in the chaos of landing and battle to the extent of Price attempting to deliver arms to his unit and Murdo Macdonald setting a plane on fire. David Coulter, in his examination of padres of the Church of Scotland, has claimed that Macdonald went further: "He found himself not only bearing arms but actually commanding a platoon when his battalion was decimated in action in North Africa."[38]

The chaplains' ability to move around more freely under a Red Cross flag allowed them to deliver information and orders, for example McMurdo in North Africa and Watkins at Arnhem. Chaplains were not allowed to carry arms, but there is evidence that some were armed on D-Day. Padre McVeigh was captured with his shillelagh, Padre Briscoe narrowly escaped capture in possession of a pistol and according to Lieutenant Colonel Pine-Coffin, CO of 7th Battalion of the 6th Airborne Division, George Parry was armed: "I often wonder what other padres did about carrying weapons. George, I believe, did carry something as I had advised him and others to do." Pine-Coffin described how he left spare Sten guns available for medical staff and padres upon boarding on the grounds that "everyone coming down by parachute would be legitimate prey to the Germans who could not be expected to know who was who".[39] The actions of Macdonald burning the enemy plane and Daniel McGowan smuggling arms out of the hospital at Arnhem could certainly not be described a non-combatant. The diary of Watkins at Arnhem, when as one of the only officers left in the battalion he had to take on a military leadership role, shows him agonising over this turn of events:

> Thus it will be seen how from Tuesday morning onwards, or rather from Monday night onwards, the chaplain was being forced into becoming someone else as well. As the senior officer left of a battalion which rallied about 150 men on Tuesday morning and brought out of Arnhem about 100 I was responsible for them. I have hitherto been reluctant to write about this because this is not what a chaplain is supposed to do and it is open to misconstruction. The reader must judge for himself.[40]

Medical Officer John Binning commented on his perception of the role of the chaplains in combat:

> I recall seeing padres departing at all hours of the day and night to go and hold a service or simply to "see the boys" in their huts or in a bivouac in the field. Certainly in the field they proved their worth and won the everlasting praise of

38 David Coulter, University of Edinburgh PhD, *The Church of Scotland and Army Chaplains in the Second World War* (1997), p.180.
39 Museum of Army Chaplaincy Archives, an account by Geoffrey Pine-Coffin.
40 Watkins, *World War Two Memoirs 1939-45*.

all and sundry. In battle they suffered casualties and were maimed and injured but they never complained. Always they were ready to help, to listen to a tale of tragedy or woe … of course in the field they committed to their fellow soldiers in arms, often at great risk to themselves.[41]

Lieutenant Colonel John Frost commented on chaplains in battle: "Church and padres rather got in the way as far as we sinners were concerned, but as soon as we saw what they could do for us before, during and after the action, they at once became well beloved and trusted members whom we did not want to be without ever again."[42] Frost was particularly impressed with Murdo Macdonald, who served with him in the 2nd Battalion during the action at Depienne. Watkins remembered that Frost repeatedly told him what a loss to the battalion it was when Macdonald was captured. Senior Chaplain Geoffrey Harper stated: "While not wishing to over glorify the work of the chaplains in airborne forces, it does need to be stressed that they really did share in the terrors as well as all the glory the men went through."[43]

Working with the medical services

During action, padres were most often situated with the medical services. Much of the narrative we have of their activities in action comes from the diaries and accounts of the MOs, who worked closely with them and obviously welcomed their presence at RAPs, MDSs and hospitals further down the line. In battle, the chaplain continued the actions of their counterparts in the First World War, risking their lives to bring in wounded men. The Second World War chaplains all had reasonably extensive medical training and were able to be of practical help at dressing stations, particularly in situations such as the first few days of D-Day and the whole of the Arnhem operation, where the casualties could not be evacuated.

However, it was not for this role that the presence of chaplains was primarily appreciated. J. Lawson, an MO at Arnhem, reflected of the chaplain:

His main role is simply one of empathy, a listening ear to the frustrated and the hurts and angers of others. The receiver of the requests of a dying soldier regarding his wife and children. As and when possible the chaplain can often serve in the realms of first aid, but as expressed by a senior medical officer at Arnhem "the Jocks need someone to hold their hands".[44]

41   Museum of Army Chaplaincy Archives, an account by John Binning.
42   Museum of Army Chaplaincy Archives, letter from John Frost to Paul Abram, 4 March, year unknown.
43   Museum of Army Chaplaincy Archives, an account by the Revd Geoffrey Harper.
44   Museum of Army Chaplaincy Archives, an account by Medical Officer J. Lawson.

Lawson added: "The experienced MO knows that the doctors patch up their bodies but they cannot do it all on their own. Healing has another dimension outside their control." He also commented on the way that padres helped the morale of the staff of the medical units: "They need the padre with his spiritual support. The padre is not only for the patients. His ministry starts with the CO and encompasses everyone within the unit."[45]

Another medical officer, John Binning, commented on the friendship and strong bond between the Army chaplain and the RAMC, whose common stock in trade was man: "Both parties dealt in bodies and souls and my lasting impression of the chaplains to the forces is one of profound admiration for their devotion to duty and humanity."

Graeme Warrack, a MO at Arnhem, commented on the work of the chaplains with the medical services: "The padres were by necessity work right alongside the wounded and the dying. It was our great privilege and inspiration to have the trust and friendship of these great men in battle and in captivity. Without their inspired help our task would have been impossible and the morale of our patients would have wasted away. Thank you!"[46]

Burials and Remembrance

Even in battle conditions, it was very important for morale that chaplains, as far as possible even, buried the dead and marked their grave with a rough cross or peg with details on, although shell cases, tins or bottles often sufficed. They were responsible for recording a grave's position and collecting the identification discs. Often in battle even a very brief funeral ceremony was impossible, so padres would go out at night, or in a lull, to say a short service or prayer over where the bodies lay.

Padre John Hall remembered: "One thing I shall never forget about Normandy is the sweet, sickly smell of corpses. Many casualties from D-Day lay in ditches or thickets until the buzz of flies or the smell attracted attention to them. The chaplain then had to identify the body, arrange for burial and notify next of kin."[47]

Padre Watkins was very concerned that the battlefields in North Africa were made tidy and decent when troops still stationed in the area wanted to visit them. Airborne chaplains in all their campaigns made strenuous efforts to see that men were buried, and were also involved in later exhumations and reburials in concentration cemeteries. Padres were diligent in writing home to families, and often engaged in longer correspondence. Watkins always tried to place in the letter a sprig of local flower or bush.

---

45   *Ibid.*
46   Museum of Army Chaplaincy Archives, letter from Graeme Warrack to Paul Abram, March 1969.
47   Museum of Army Chaplaincy Archives, an account by the Revd John Hall.

Padres were also involved in services of remembrance. John Rowell took part in one almost as soon as the Rhine was crossed, and he and Watkins participated in a service of remembrance and thanksgiving at St Wolfram's church, Grantham, on 10 December 1944 for those who died at Arnhem. The Chaplain General preached the sermon. Many of the airborne chaplains maintained contact with the airborne troops in the years after the war, taking part in memorial services and annual get-togethers. Most notable were the ceremonies at Arnhem in which padres Harlow, McGowan, Rowell, Chignell, Pare, Egan, Buchanan, Phillips, Bowers, Menzies, Downing, Fenlon and Morrison took part between 1945 and 2000.

Morale

The attempts of the chaplains in the First World War to establish a useful and authentic role for themselves had been aided by the gradual realisation by Army commanders that they were good for morale and the determination of chaplains to establish the principle that their place was near the front line with their troops. General Douglas Haig was particularly insistent that chaplains were important for morale. The reasons given by the chaplains for proximity to the front line differed. Geoffrey Studdert Kennedy gave this advice to a fellow Great War chaplain, Theodore Bayley Hardy, who went on to win a Victoria Cross: "Your place is at the front ... work in the front and they will listen to you when they come out to rest, but if you only preach and teach behind, you are wasting your time, the men won't pay the slightest attention to you. The men will forgive you anything but lack of courage and devotion."[48]

The Revd E.C. Crosse wrote much in his First World War diary about morale. He realised that chaplains were considered important for "improving general morale" by their pastoral and material care, and sometimes their sermons and talks, and considered that religion was important in encouraging "inner discipline", but did not equate this to instilling bellicosity or glorifying war under a religious banner. He considered that there were two very different types of morale: the "fighting spirit" needed for battles and the "spirit of endurance" needed to survive life in the trenches. He stressed that their religious and pastoral duties were uppermost in the minds of the chaplains.[49] The early twentieth century historiography of chaplaincy literature, particularly that of Anglican chaplains, has been one of criticism by such well-known contemporary observers as Robert Graves and Siegfried Sassoon, but also later from

---

48   A letter from Studdert Kennedy to Mary Hardy quoted in D. Raw, *It's Only Me – A life of the Revd Theodore Bayley Hardy VC, DSO, MC 1863-1918* (Gatebeck: Frank Peters Publishing, 1998), p.21.
49   E.C. Crosse Papers, Imperial War Museum (80/22/1).

historians such as Stephen Louden[50] and Albert Marrin,[51] who have disparaged the "Holy Grocery" and morale-boosting aspects of military chaplains.

The position of chaplains in the Second World War was not an issue that was debated. All Army chaplains after June 1940 had battleground training and their presence at all places of battle in all theatres of war was taken for granted. As we have seen, the airborne padres were trained in exactly the same way as their men, and the nature of the airborne role meant that they were continually with their units, often in advanced positions with no possibility of retreat.

The Senior Chaplain to the Eighth Army, Freddie Hughes, worked with Montgomery to instil into the padres the importance of their task in enhancing morale in a military context. Alan Robinson described this as encouraging chaplains to "inculcate a dynamic mixture of Christian values and patriotism into soldiers".[52] In the letters and memoirs of the airborne padres, however, there is little overt evidence taking this position. Rather, they seem concerned with the whole personality of the soldier and the encouragement of moral and spiritual qualities which produce the courage and stamina to endure battle. The chaplains felt that, by virtue of their calling and the claims they made for God and religion, their calm participation in the preparation for battle and the action itself would help their men in the task before them. An example of this religious and non-military morale-boosting can be seen in Padre Gwinnett's "fear knocked at the door" sermon before D-Day which was so well remembered by his men as they went into battle. In his discussion of chaplains and morale in the RAChD Journal, the Revd T.H. Lovegrove, MC, wrote: "In some cases it may be the only thing a chaplain can do to be there, stand by and strengthen. For if the chaplain is truly a man of God, he not only gives men the influence and encouragement of his presence but is a medium by which the men can be aware of the divine presence."[53]

Alan Buchannan preached a sermon at the 25th commemoration of Arnhem which spoke of Christin sacrifice and valour. It was entitled "Die to Live" and took the example of new life through death given by the death of a seed potato resulting in many new potatoes. He spoke of the sacrifices of great men and women through history who had sacrificed their lives for the greater good, and looking around the cemetery e remarked: "The world can never forget what they did here."[54] Buchanan was surely a chaplain who inspired morale in its purest sense.

There is no doubt that their presence improved morale by nature of their spiritual, medical and material ministries. Graeme Warrack said of Alan Buchanan: "He was

50   Stephen Louden, *Chaplains in Conflict* (London: Avon Books, 1996).
51   Albert Marrin, *The Last Crusade: The Church of England in the First World War* (Durham, NC: Duke University Press, 1974).
52   Robinson, *Chaplains at War*, p.149.
53   T.H. Lovegrove, "The chaplain and morale", *RAChD Journal*, Vol 28, No 1.
54   The Most Revd Alan Buchanan, Archbishop, preaching at the 25th commemoration service in Arnhem.

a tower of strength wherever he happened to be." A comment from General Roy Urquhart about Padre Wilfrid Chignell at Arnhem, that he was "quite excellent" in saying a prayer which "helped everyone", could equally be applied to his chaplain colleagues.[55]

It was not only in battle that chaplains made a contribution to morale. At camps in Britain they were very much concerned with the welfare and happiness of their men, particularly in sorting out difficulties with wives and families. The chaplains had a particular responsibility helping with personal problems so that the men went into battle with a peaceful mind and free of distractions, and also to reassure them that their families would be informed of death or casualty and given pastoral support. An early example of this function was the care taken by Robert Watkins in the aftermath of the Bruneval raid in 1942, in which the casualties, though low, were 30 percent:

> With the backing of General Browning and the SCF I wrote to every home and visited the home of every prisoner of war. This was a matter not only of pastoral sympathy but of the morale of every other man. Men had to know that when the time came for them to go into action there would be care and concern beyond written regulations.[56]

He added that in the middle of a campaign such as in North Africa:

Most officers did not shirk dropping a line to next of kin, but in the midst of a campaign a combatant officer has to think of the next battle and he cannot be forever clearing up after the last one. This was a burden for the chaplain to shoulder. I have since been shown a few of the letters I wrote, poor things in my eyes, but valued by their recipients.[57]

The RAChD made strenuous efforts in the Second World War to minimise the amount of time the chaplains spent in organising social activities and providing material comforts to the detriment of their spiritual duties. However, the airborne chaplains found that behind the lines and in rest periods discussion groups, debates and organising newspapers were appreciated by the men and ameliorated the boredom of waiting for operations which might be cancelled, a situation in which airborne troops often found themselves.

The airborne padres in the context of 20th and 21st-century Army Chaplaincy

We have seen how the chaplains of the First World War laid the groundwork for the work carried out by chaplains in the Second World War.

---

55   RAChD Archives, letter from Roy Urquart to Paul Abram, 10 June 1972.
56   Watkins, *World War Two Memoirs 1939-1945*.
57   *Ibid.*

In some ways there is a remarkable continuity between the attitude of chaplains in all conflicts of the 20th and 21st century. The ministry of a chaplain advocated by Geoffrey Studdert Kennedy in his famous advice to Theodore Bayley Hardy - "Live with men, go everywhere they go … the best place for a padre is where there is danger of death"[58] - was echoed in the words of the airborne padres when they expressed the necessity of jumping with their men into battle. In his work on contemporary chaplains, Andrew Todd explained the continuity of this approach by emphasising the ministry of presence: "Because the chaplain's key role is first of all to be present, he has the capacity to respond to the human needs of the military personnel - to see their need for sleep, a listening ear or physical contact and respond accordingly."

While emphasising the continuity, however, it must be stressed that chaplains in the late 20th and 21st centuries were and are working in very differing operational and institutional contexts, and the discontinuities reflect this.

We have seen that the Second World War saw the realisation that for padres to be effective and survive, more training was essential. This was particularly so with the intensive training undergone by the airborne padres, which established their credentials with their men but also helped ensure their survival and utility to the operations. Today's Army chaplains complete their initial training at the armed forces chaplaincy centre at Amport House in Hampshire, then spend a few months with their first unit before completing the qualified officers course at Sandhurst, designed to give a military training with core military skills such as drill, field training, officership and command. Chaplains are not required to complete the weapons-handling module. During hostilities in Afghanistan, the four-week Sandhurst course was extended to 12 weeks.

In the conflicts in Afghanistan, however, Michael Snape has pointed out that although 21st-century chaplains are professionally trained and not volunteers as in the two world wars, that does not necessarily guarantee a plentiful supply of experienced chaplains available for protected battles such as the Herrick operations, where relatively inexperienced chaplains were facing difficult pastoral challenges in the same manner as temporary chaplains thrown into the conflict of the two world wars.[59]

A major difference in the attitude to the role of chaplains in battle had taken place by the beginning of the Second World War. At the time of Dunkirk, Archbishop Lang quoted a Naval Commander at Dunkirk who said the reputation of the the chaplains there was that of "last off the beach".[60] In the Second World War, their full participation in battle situations was completely accepted, and they were expected and encouraged to be with their men at every stage of their combat experience. The Revd Freddie Hughes, chaplain to the Eighth Army, had managed to achieve a

58   Letter from Studdert Kennedy to Mary Hardy, quoted in D. Raw, *It's Only Me*, p.21.
59   M. Snape and V. Henshaw, "Flanders and Helmand: chaplaincy Faith and religious change in the British Army 1914-2014", *Journal of Beliefs and Values*, 38(2), p.12.
60   Lambeth Palace Archives, The papers of Archbishop Lang LXXIX, Memorandum, ff.190.

high profile for Army chaplaincy in General Montgomery's opinion, hence Monty's famous words: "I would as soon think of going into battle without my artillery as without my chaplains."[61]

The airborne padres in battle were a powerful source of spiritual and moral support to their men, and also proved their practical utility in helping at medical posts and in some cases taking over command and leadership when required.

The situation in Helmand Province in the Herrick operations this century saw chaplains once again in the front line of conflict. The chaplains in Helmand operated in all aspects of the conflict, at bases such as Camp Bastion and on patrols with their units, at forward operating bases and with bomb disposal officers of the Counter Improvised Explosive Device task force. Padre Andy Earl explained that their job involved necessarily "going to the place where there is the most fearfulness and the most spiritual need. That means going to forward positions. It was extremely challenging and the patrols were exhilarating in a positive sense." He went everywhere with a shepherd's crook to symbolise his calling. Another chaplain, Padre Anthony Feltham White, carried a cricket bat. Chaplains were at most risk when moving around the theatre of battle and often found difficulty in obtaining transport. Padre Robin Richardson (C of E) of the 3rd Parachute Battalion, in an interview in 2016, described how the best option was to travel in the cab of an oil tanker. This position was often vacant for obvious reasons of its vulnerability in an IED attack or ambush.[62]

The circumstances of the conflict sometimes required decisions made where chaplains could not accompany their troops. An unarmed man accompanying a foot patrol, for instance, was an obvious target for snipers, and sometimes decisions had to be made which precluded the presence of the chaplain in the interests of the safety of the group. However, despite these considerations, the COs wanted their chaplains as far forward as possible.[63] Decisions about the position of the chaplain in these combat conditions had to be worked out between those who wanted the chaplains to be involved in all operations and those who preferred a modicum of safety for the chaplains.

In modern conflict padres continue the care of the injured, and although not so involved in actual treatment, are valued for their presence and prayer during surgical operations, and of course in the comfort of the dying. Another aspect of this work is the ongoing support of many severely injured survivors who would not have survived in previous conflicts.

The airborne padre in theatre in the Second World War had increasingly been used by officers as a sounding board and givers of advice. This aspect of a padre's role has

61   Nigel Hamilton, *Monty the Field Marshal, 1944-1976* (London: Sceptre, 1987), p.44.
62   Robin Richardson, 2016, interviewed at Armed Forces Chaplaincy Centre and quoted by M. Snape and V. Henshaw, "Flanders and Helmand: chaplaincy Faith and religious change in the British Army 1914-2014", *Journal of Beliefs and Values*, 38(2), p.7.
63   Padre Phillip McCormack, in an interview in 2016, quoted by Snape and Henshaw, p.11.

continued and been developed. Padre Mike Peterson has observed: "Today's training of chaplains focuses in large part on their role as ethical advisors. The chaplain has a special role in helping the chain of command know right from wrong in the morally ambiguous kinds of conflicts that now seem integral to the 21st century experience of warfare."[64]

Contemporary commentators of Army chaplaincy have revised the critical opinions of the early and mid-20th-century historians of the effect of padres on morale. Padre Andrew Totten has explained a change of emphasis in the role of modern-day chaplains as force multipliers and defines the difference between morale – the psychosocial state – and moral – the ethical state. He believes soldiers require an easing of conscience and moral sensibility: "The challenge ethically is to generate morale that is grounded on civilised behaviour."[65] The airborne padres have endeavoured in their work to provide men with the courage to continue their task by assuring them of God's presence with them without indulging in the type of explicit "fighting spirit" type of force multiplyer for which some First World War chaplains were criticised.

The taking of services has been an important part of the padre's job in all conflicts of the 20th and 21st centuries. The services in the war in Afghanistan consisted of informal services at patrols and Forward Operating Bases (FOB), larger services at bases and services preceding or at the ending of a particular action. This is not far removed from the way in which the airborne padres delivered the liturgy, from large services at base before the battle, through the intimate services which took place in hedges, dugouts, barns and fields, often under fire, all over Europe, to their participation in the thanksgiving services at Wismar at the end of the war. The way that airborne forces were glad of services in the front line can be compared with the eagerness of the troops experienced by a chaplain visiting a FOB: "Good to see you padre, can you do the thing with the bread and wine for us?"[66]

We have seen how in both world wars the role of the padre in identifying, recording and burying the dead was a vital and necessary one. Due to the decision in 1982, after the Falklands War, to repatriate the bodies of dead soldiers, there is no longer the need for burial services in theatre. This function had how been replaced by several ceremonies and rituals which have developed to mark the stages of repatriation. A vigil service is held so that the fallen man's friends can mark the occasion if they are prevented from going to the airhead service for operational reasons. There is the more formal airhead service, for example at Camp Bastion, conducted at sunset with all

64 Email conversation with Major (Padre) Mike Peterson, Course Resource and Development Officer CAF Chaplain School and Centre (all views his own).

65 Andrew Totten, "Moral Soldiering and Soldiers Morale", in Andrew Todd (ed.), *Military Chaplaincy in Contention, Explorations in Practical, Pastoral and Empirical Theology* (London: Routledge, 2013), p.31; *Ibid.*

66 Interview with the Revd James Francis, conducted in 2015 by Sally May and quoted in *The Value and Role of Military Chaplains in Contemporary British Society,* a Master of Philosophy dissertation, University of Cambridge, p.17.

personnel attending. Back in Britain there is a military service at the airfield, which marks the transfer of the body to the family's care. The coffin is then often honoured by the community, as in the repatriation occasions that became a regular occasion at Royal Wootton Bassett. One thing that has not changed is the duty the chaplain feels on the field of battle to be responsible as much as possible for the identification of bodies and to deal with their effects, to spare the trauma of their fellow soldiers, often their friends.

Contemporary chaplains, in common with the airborne padres, have found that proselytism is counterproductive, but Sally May, in her discussion of modern military chaplains, quoted an Army chaplain who summed up his ethos of evangelism: "I found God to be good, and as such I'll recommend him to the lads."[67] This was a sincere and realistic attitude to his role in evangelism with which many of the First and Second World War chaplains would have agreed.

67 "Commando Chaplains" – Channel 4, *Revelations*, quoted by Sally May in *The Value and Role of Military Chaplains in Contemporary British Society*, a Master of Philosophy dissertation, University of Cambridge, p.17.

Conclusion: Second World War chaplains in the context of 20th and 21st century military chaplaincy

The Victory Parade took place in London in June 1946. Every arm of the services was represented, including the Dominions, colonies and Allied contingents. The RAChD was represented by 12 chaplains, chosen to represent both the denominations and the varieties of service. Robert Watkins was chosen to represent the RAChD airborne chaplains and wear the Red Beret in the parade. He commented that the parade was "a celebration of years of costly human endeavour ... The day of the Parade, a Saturday, need not be described. It was an occasion for the annals of the RAChD, and it was right that a representation of the airborne chaplains should be included."[1]

I would like to put the case that the actions of airborne chaplains in the Second World War acted as a bridge between the role of chaplains at the beginning of the 20th century and the beginning of the 21st century. It was in this war that it was accepted as imperative that chaplains should be in the front line of battle and accompany their troops at all times, offering their "ministry of presence" before, during and after the battle. Airborne padres operating in a completely new operational context had these opportunities throughout the conflict. They developed closer relationships with both men and officers and established the way in which chaplains could be the moral conscience of Commanding Officers. They broke convention in their cooperation between denominations and willingness to be flexible in battlefield situations.

The Revd Paul Abram, an airborne chaplain, in his introduction to his draft history of airborne chaplains, said that one of their main jobs was to pray: "Soldiers expect their chaplain to pray, they know instinctively that he is an intermediary between themselves and God ... Sometimes the prayer [is] through the liturgy, at other times informally with a small group. Most often the prayer is offered in the quiet of the chaplain's heart." The second main role was to care: "This is most obvious in times of tragedy. At such time men look to him for hope and encouragement ... it is Christ who can speak through him." In Abrams' opinion, "The only way he can do this is by giving himself without reserve."[2]

These sentiments can be applied to airborne padres from the Second World War, but equally from all conflicts of the 20th and 21st centuries.

1   Watkins, *World War Two Memoirs 1939-1945.*
2   Museum of Army Chaplaincy Archives, papers deposited by Revd P R C Abram CVO. Type script, *Lower Than the Angels* 1971. introduction, p. 1.

Bibliography

Archival Material

Museum of Army Chaplaincy:
Papers deposited by the Revd P.R.C. Abram CVO:

Abram, Paul, Typescript, *Lower Than the Angels* (1975)
Letters to the Revd Paul Abram, 1968-75:
Bob Boyce
Robert Cain
K.A. Darling
Ricahrd Duneman
Bernard Egan
A. Farrah Hockley
E.W.C. Favell
Benedict Fenlon
John Frost
Richard Gale
James Hill
Geoffrey Harper
John Hodgins
D.R. Hunter
Murdo Macdonald
Ronald Lunt
R.G. Pine-Coffin
G.R. Stevens
Accounts sent to the Revd Paul Abram 1968-75:
John Binning
Raymond Bowers
Joe Downing
John Gwinnett
George Hales

John Hall
Geoffrey Harper
Martin Herford
John Hodgins
J.O. Jenkins
John Kent
Gerald Lathbury
Daniel McGowan
Alistair Menzies
James Morrison
David Nimmo
Roy Price
John Rowell
Richard Sweetland
Robert Watkins

John Binning, unpublished typescript 'Airborne No More'
An article from the *Methodist Recorder* based on an interview with Watkins

Museum of Army Flying Archives:
E.N. 'Joe' Downing, *Padre with the Paras* (privately printed)
The Diary of The Battle of Arnhem by the Revd W.H.C. Hignell

The National Archives:
TNA CAB120/262
TNA CAB 106/687
TNA WO177/701
TNA WO 171/1239
TNA WO 219/2485
TNA WO 218/921
TNA WO 177/8310
TNA WO 171/5135

Lambeth Palace Archives:
The papers of Archbishop Lang LXXIX

Ohio University:
The Cornelius Ryan Collection of World War II Papers. G.A. Pare, *Arnhem Aftermath*
Warfare of history Network, posted 25 December 2018, https://warfarehistorynetwork.com/tag/operation-fustian/

Paradata - A Living History of the Parachute and Airborne Forces:

Diary of Rev A.C.V. Menzies, North Africa 1943, https://www.paradata.org.uk/media/155

Letter from General Montgomery to Eighth Army, dated July 1943, facsimile produced by Paradata, https://paradata.org.uk

Biographical information on George Parry, https://www.paradata.org.uk/people/george-e-m-parry

An account of the Revd Whitfield Foy, https://www.paradata.org.uk/media/1073

General A. Farrah Hockley, https://www.paradata.org.uk/article/general-farrar-hockleys-personal-account-serving-6th-parachute-battalion-during-operation

The Pegasus Archive:
Account by A.L. Beckingham, courtesy of Hugo Mitchell, http://www.pegasusarchive.org/normandy/frames.htm

Account by Lt Richard Todd, http://www.pegasusarchive.org/normandy/frames.htm

The Wellcome Library:
'Arnhem Diary'-Transcript of the diary written by Colonel Graeme Warrack, ADMS1 Airborne Division during and immediately after Operation MARKET GARDEN. 17 September -1 October 1944.

Newspapers
Birmingham Mail
Church Times
Daily Telegraph
Gloucester Journal
Hartlepool Daily Mail
The Daily Record
West Sussex County News
Yorkshire Post and Leeds Intelligencer

Published Primary Sources

Chatterton, George, *The Wings of Pegasus* (London: Macdonald, 1962).
Fenlon, Benedict, 'Parachutist Chaplains' in Dempsey, Martin, *The Priest Among The Soldiers* (London: Burn Oates, 1946).
Gale, Richard, *With the 6th Airborne in Germany* (London: 1948).
Hackett, John, *I Was A Stranger* (London: Chatto and Windus, 1977).

Macdonald, Murdo, *The Man From Harris* (Stornaway: The *Stornaway Gazette*, undated).

McLuskey, Fraser, *Parachute Padre* (London: SCM Press, 1985).

McLuskey, Fraser, *The Cloud and Fire* (Edinburgh: The Pentland Press, 1994)

Miller, Victor, *Nothing is Impossible: A Glider Pilot's Story of Sicily, Arnhem and the Rhine Crossing* (Barnsley: Pen & Sword, 2015).

ter Horst, Kate, *Angel of Arnhem: Memories of September '44* (Kontrast: Uitgeverij, 2018).

Thompson, Julian, *Ready for Anything: The Parachute Regiment at War* (London: Fontana, 1990).

Tibbs, David and Barber, Neil, *Parachute Doctor: The Memoirs of Captain David Tibbs* (Seven Oaks: Sabrestorm, 2012).

Watts, J.C., *Surgeon At War* (London: George Allen, 1955).

Wellsted, Ian, *SAS with the Maquis: In Action with the French Resistance June–September 1944* (London: Greenhill Books, 1994).

Published Secondary Sources

Abram, 'Arnhem Aftermath', *RAChD Journal*

Barber, Neil, *The Day the Devils Dropped in: The 9th Parachute Battalion in Normandy D-Day to D+6: Merville Battery to the Chateau St Come* (Barnsley: Leo Cooper, 2003).

By Air to Battle, The *Official Account of the British Airborne Divisions* (London: His Majesty's Stationary Office, 1945).

Cherry, N, *Red Berets and Red Crosses: The Story of the Medical Services in the 1st Airborne Division in World War Two* (Renkum: R.N. Sigmond, 1999).

Ford, R., *Fire from the Forest: the SAS in France 1944* (London: Cassell, 2003).

Greenacre, John, *Churchill's Spearhead: The Development of Britain's Airborne Forces During the Second World War* (Barnsley: Pen & Sword, 2010), p.94.

Greenacre, John, '"Flexible Enough to Adapt": British Airborne Forces' Experiences during Post Conflict Operations 1944-46', *British Journal for Military History*, Volume 4, Issue 1 (November 2017), p.77.

Hamilton, Nigel, *Monty the Field Marshal, 1944-1976* (London: Sceptre, 1987).

Johnstone, Tom and Hagerty, James, *The Cross on the Sword*: *Catholic Chaplains in the Forces* (London: Geoffrey Chapman, 1996).

Mortimer, Gavin, *Stirling's Men: The Inside History of the SAS In World War Two* (London: Weidenfeld and Nicolson, 2004).

Macintyre, Ben, *SAS: Rogue Heroes – the Authorized Wartime History* (London: Penguin Random House, 2016).

Norton, G.G., *The Red Devils (Famous regiments)* (London: Leo Cooper, 1984).

Otway, Terence, *Airborne Forces* (London: Imperial War Museum, 1990).

Payne, Roger, *PARA: Voices of the British Airborne Forces in the Second World War* (Stroud: Amberley Publishing, 2014).

Peating, Robert, *Without Tradtion: 2 Para 1941-1945* (Barnsley: Pen and Sword, 1994).

Peters, Mike, *Glider Pilots in Sicily* (Barnsley: Pen and Sword, 2012).

Raw, David, *It's Only Me – A Life of the Revd Theodore Bayley Hardy VC, DSO, MC 1863-1918* (Gateback: Frank Peters Publishing, 1998).

Robinson, Alan, *Chaplains at War, The Role of Clergymen during World War Two* (London: I.B. Tauris and Co, 2008).

St George Saunders, Hilary, *The Red Beret* (London: Michel Joseph, 1950).

Tootal, Stuart, The *Manner of Men: 9 PARA's Heroic D-Day Mission* (London: John Murray, 2013).

Totten, Andrew, 'Moral Soldiering and Soldiers' Morale', in Andrew Todd (ed.), *Military Chaplaincy in Contention, Explorations in Practical, Pastoral and Empirical Theology* (London: Routledge, 2013).

Van Roekel, Chris, *The Torn Horizon, The Airborne Chaplains at Arnhem* (Oosterbeek: Jan and Wendela ter Horst and Chris Van Roekel, 2000).

Vockins, Mike, *Chig: Sky Pilot to the Glider Pilots of Arnhem* (Warwick: Helion, 2017).

Index